FAITH AN
NEGOT

FAITH AND LIFE NEGOTIATE

A Christian Story-Study

KENNETH CRAGG

The Canterbury Press
Norwich

First published 1994 by The Canterbury Press Norwich
(a publishing imprint of Hymns Ancient & Modern Limited,
a registered charity)
St Mary's Works, St Mary's Plain,
Norwich, Norfolk, NR3 3BH

British Library Cataloguing in Publication Data

A catalogue record for this book is available
from the British Library

ISBN 1–85311–088–4

Typeset by Datix International Limited
Bungay, Suffolk and
Printed and bound in Great Britain by
St Edmundsbury Press Limited
Bury St Edmunds, Suffolk

For
MELITA
With such love as 'twas then

Contents

'As is your sort of mind
So is your sort of search: you'll find
What you desire and that's to be
A Christian.'

ROBERT BROWNING

'Too bright for our infirm Delight
The Truth's superb surprise.'

EMILY DICKINSON

'Nothing justifies the writing of prefaces except that they are in fact epilogues.'

AUSTIN FARRER

'Before the feet of the wayfarer opens out the way of the Lord.'

MIGUEL DE UNAMUNO

Introduction

'Faith and Life Negotiate.' How right they should, if life is to be faithful and faith is to be alive. 'Negotiate,' too, is a fitting word if we retrieve it from the mandarins of diplomacy and the business of the counting house. It has to do with more than cheques and treaties. From its Latin source in *neg otium* it means laying aside sloth, saying No! to ease, in order to 'hold intercourse by way of transacting business.' (O.E.D.)

The poet John Donne, in *The Extasie*, says of lovers' eyes: 'Our souls negotiate there,' perhaps echoing Shakespeare's:

> 'Let every eye negotiate for itself
> And trust no agent.'

But that was in *Much Ado about Nothing* and 'faith and life' are about everything. So much more vital then their mutuality.

Any response of faith to life, any relating of life to faith, must needs be autobiographical. It is bound to be a converse inside a self for that is where life is consciously happening and faith is inwardly reached and trusted. Both are doubtless in total debt to what transcends the individual equation, but only there can they transact what is between them. Taking life as a testing ground of faith is one way of escaping a mere exercise in egoism such as, otherwise, 'life-writing' is liable to be. The hope is that the sub-title 'A Christian Story-Study' shows a will to avoid self-concern unrelated to faith-quest.

It is not always clear with compound nouns which partner is senior. With 'school-bag' there is no doubt, but what of 'school-boy.'? 'School' matters more than the boy, but not to him. In this case let the accent fall on 'story' as in 'horse-box,' 'Study' is meant to be why the 'story' is taken in hand and the will doing so. What matters is what is being conveyed – which is the only reason for the vehicle.

The chapters, therefore, are not rigorously chronological and there is little point in beginning: 'I was born . . .' The sequence moves, rather, in themes. The first has to do with how faith and boyhood somehow coincided but, of course, it could not stay that way. Under Oxford I have tried to comprise what may broadly be described as faith's maturing and amending. This means anticipating what needs chapters 3 and 4 to be fully in focus. Chapter 4, in turn, includes reflection on what pertains also to chapter 8. Chapter 5 alone – as far as anything can be – is wholly self-contained. Chapters 6 and 7 inter-depend, while chapters 9 and 10 aim to bring everything together in the faith-life negotiation against the background of all that preceded. Chapter 11 makes space for rumination and retrospect, pondering parts of the story which have no place elsewhere, and wondering about any logic in the whole – which is another way of asking about the shadowing love of God.

To have been caught in the demise of three institutions of the Church with which one was intimately involved, to have known three experiences of failure in cherished commitments, and to have had no viable reprieve from them, may be some qualification for setting them down as they occurred. They form, as it were, the negative assets of the story. That at Canterbury in 1967 was the most grievous. One may well wonder whether there is point in personal telling, since it may be wisdom to see all such things as inconsequential against the dire background of world events and the long toll of human tragedy. Even so, what was only personally pointed and precious has its bearing on inclusive matters of doctrine, order and ministry within the Church and so makes for open study of a private story.

Having these limits absolves me of the need to bring in friends and associates except insofar as their rich companionship bears upon the vital theme. There is much affection in the silences. Similarly about teaching sojourns I was privileged to have at the University of Sussex, the University of Ibadan, Union Seminary, New York, the Bangalore

Theological Seminary, the Virginia Theological Seminary or the time spent in semi-retirement in the Pennine village of Helme and among clergy and teachers in the Diocese of Wakefield, as well as briefer and more numerous occasions in different travels between Peshawar and Cape Comorin, and from Kabul to San Francisco. All had present point in the issues I have tried to concentrate at the several hinges of the story which the chapters represent.

In some twenty or so publications between *The Call of the Minaret* in 1956 and *Troubled by Truth: Life-Studies in Inter-Faith Concern* in 1992, my instinct was that authorship should avoid the personal pronoun. What belongs with scholarship is not well served by seeming, or sounding, personally pontifical. I realize, however, that one cannot affirm Christian faith without the personal pronoun, and so in *Faith and Life Negotiate* it has to be frequent. 'Has it *your* vote to be so, if it can?' was always Robert Browning's question.[1] As it is a verdict with which we are here concerned – how it began and grew and stayed – 'mine' it has to be. However, as the reader will understand, the instinct to write 'ours' is never far away. Religion is only partly 'what we do with our solitude,'[2] for without heritage it cannot exist nor abide without fellowship. Anonymity and authorship are – almost – a contradiction in terms. Even the archaeologist leaves a personal mark on what he tells, historians still more so and diarists most of all. A writer has to acknowledge: 'The pen that I am using is the pen that is using me.'

Of the many air flights – some 342 in all – during forty years of my duties and travels there was one in particular that brought home this personal equation. On a sultry afternoon in Tripoli, Libya, I was waiting for Tunis-Air bound for that city. A DC Three stood away on the tarmac. I had been through routine formalities, solo-style. There was no one else around. Two figures emerged – pilot and co-pilot, I assumed – and walked towards the plane. Unsure, I decided to follow them. I was right: it was the plane, despite the absence of a steward or stewardess. We took off, the three of us, myself the only passenger. I sat on several different seats and reflected that in the event of a crash the list of casualties would be (almost) negligible. Happily we came down en route at Sfax and Sousse and the plane was wellnigh filled.

I had begun my air experience in 1954 in a B.O.A.C. Argonaut Speedbird. Heathrow was then a motley collection of Nissen Huts. I graduated later to Viscounts and Britannias, graceful turbo-prop planes, and on later to the ill-fated Comet and then the later jets, arriving at the several Boeings 727, 737 and 747. It was sad to see splendid aircraft so soon relegated to obsolescence, though the propellered Vulcan which I remember from Iraqi Airways had a beam across the gangway over which one had to stride like some country stile in the sky. No catering trolleys there. I loved the old Elizabethan with its fuselage below the wing so that coming down to earth seemed very close indeed.

The DC Three, however, a great work-horse of the skies, was my favourite. Its twin engines pointing upward, it seemed always ready for the air and eager to be up and on. At Kalandia one day, the bumpy airstrip that served Jordanian Jerusalem until 1967, it taxied, crowded, to the runway only to return after someone on board or in the control tower discovered that it was perilously over-loaded. The tasks I had to fly to helped to diminish apprehension every time but the thought of my Melita and the boys sharpened it, caring across distances which lively correspondence could not always promptly bridge. Some flights would have a disconcerting nonchalance about them as when, in the Arab Democratic Republic of Yemen, we passengers reported on schedule at 5 a.m. to have tickets and passports examined in the beam of parked taxi headlights, not, however, to take off till after dawn at 9 a.m. At times those planes seemed to be barely skimming the peaks of the rocky terrain between Taiz and Sana or were liable to change destinations en route.

A cherished theological lesson on a DC Three was on a flight from Addis Ababa to Aden. Descending from the heights of the Ethiopian capital, we crossed the island of Socotra and the mouth of the Red Sea and began the level eastward flight along the southern littoral of the Aden

Territory. I was on the left of the plane. The sun was away overhead to the right. I detected a moving shadow on the sands below. It stayed with us. It grew larger. It was in the shape of a cross and as we came to earth we fitted exactly into it. I recalled the words of St Augustine about 'the bread and wine:' 'It is the mystery of yourselves that you receive.'

Planes were great places for musing on things that might be written. For the duration of the flight there was a suspension of the kind of action that would await arrival. There was also a suspense anticipating it, with everything depending on arrival happening. Those who live professionally in the air must have ways of coping with this and, anyway, they are occupied with their skills and duties. Mere passengers have time to ruminate on their purposes. When I was flying in the fifties, out of Jerusalem or Beirut, as the Study Secretary of the (then) Near East Council of Churches, or in the seventies as Assistant Bishop, out of Cairo, in the entire Archbishopric in the jurisdiction of George Appleton, the revered Paul to my Timothy, what, I pondered, might be awaiting my descent into the fray?

In either capacity there was a dual role. The task was at once ecclesiastical and academic. I was carrying credentials – such as they were – out of Oxford and the American University of Beirut. From the latter, there would be ex-students in wellnigh every place and, as the years passed, there were books with which I had to live for good or ill. But, as either Canon or Bishop, I had 'Holy Orders.' The entire compatibility of both fields was part of my brief. The academic would, no doubt, have been easier without the sacramental, the ecclesiastical diminished without the studious. They had to co-exist. The care of the churches had to include the business of the academies. A churchwarden in Benghazi could find access to the University in his capacity as a professor. A fascinating session ensued in its Department of Philosophy around the theme of the human and the divine in two monotheisms. Sometimes visas themselves depended on such arrangements where, otherwise, the chaplaincies would have remained isolated.

Their members anyway were living cheek by jowl with the perennial issues of faith and shared society.

When a strictly theological/ecclesiastical occasion brought me to Addis Ababa, a local Muslim lawyer, an ex-student from Beirut, invited me to an Arabic session in the Hall of the Great Mosque. They told me that never before had any ecclesiastic set foot there, still less met with them in mutual discourse. Later in that visit, I called on the Acting Patriarch of the Ethiopian Church. For such ecumenical concern was central to the task. When I told him eagerly of my visit to the Mosque, he responded rather loftily: 'Muslims? they have no theology.'

Themes and problems accumulated from every point of call. Planes, imposing their hiatus on business, perhaps their veto on everything, were proper place for taking anxious stock. Sometimes I carried perspectives on to them from correspondence waiting en route. In Cairo, for example, I sometimes arranged flights so as to obviate going out of the airport and incurring the laborious business of securing return visas. The Cathedral, via the travel agent, would have letters for me in transit. Perhaps the most thrilling was the suggestion from Dutch publishers to undertake a translation of Muhammad Kamil Husain's *Qaryah Zalimah*, his Arabic study of the crucifixion of Jesus.[3] I read the invitation in onward flight. Though I had digested its remarkable significance and written two long review-articles on it in my capacity as Editor of *The Muslim World*, Hartford's quarterly,[4] it was another thing to render the entire book into decent English prose. The idea had been the author's own suggestion to the publishers: it could hardly be refused. It was how I got involved as a would-be translator and without that coincidence it would never have happened. The venture brought me into close personal friendship with the author, to be noted later. There was lots to ponder as I headed down the Nile Valley.

Sometimes, in older propeller aircraft, reveries might also be aroused from the ground below. I recall one such flight from Beirut to Khartoum. We passed exactly over the Nile delta and stayed faithfully above the river almost all the way. There it lay like a ribbon of silver attended on either side by a wider strip of green. Beyond, to east and west, a vast hazy stretch of dull grey and brown, the dun weariness of the desert. I realized why Egyptians are gregarious people. They cluster by their vital river. It was clear from that height how daunting the proposal of exodus would be to a rabble of slaves invited to venture out of Egypt. One could understand old Moses demanding some kind of guarantee from the voice in the bush that it was not all folly, as he relayed to Yahweh what he knew to be their question: 'What is His Name?' i.e. Who is He? only to receive the only feasible answer: 'He will have to be the God of exodus if ever to be known as such.' 'He will be there and as whom there He will be.' (Exodus 3.1–14). Their only option would be trust.[5]

A peripatetic ministry which these many flights transported across the jurisdiction centred in Jerusalem had essentially to do with the Christian shape of comparable belief in 'the God of event,' only 'the event' had become the whole drama of 'the Word made flesh,' and 'Christ our Passover.' In the words and wounds of Jesus as the Christ there had been a divine disclosure of God, a biography, as it were, 'a writing-in-life' where the divine had been defined, denoted, described and dramatized. This had given the Church being: by this the faith lived: for this its ministry was meant. That ministry, clerical, but lay even more, had to be informed, refreshed, heartened and equipped. Council and Cathedral, in partnership, had wanted to concert response. My venture in their Study Programme was to be a gesture on the way, by a faith alive to place and time as they had need to be.

It had an (almost) monthly Study Paper, called 'Operation Reach,' at first, then later 'Emmaus Furlongs' and 'Grace Cup.' These reviewed themes between the three faiths of the Middle East, aiming to feed into the thinking of Christians their spiritual and intellectual liabilities in common life and personal witness. This printed effort of the Study Programme was implemented locally by seminars and discussions wherever these could be organized by enlisting existing resources and personnel. Further, a sequence of summer residential schools were arranged both in Jerusalem and in Lebanon, where as many as sixty participants could be brought together from across the lands concerned.

If there was great happiness in these ventures, there was also much inner searching and, at times, a deep unease. Could the unquiet world really be served by discursive study however realist its content? The priority of things political was urgent on every hand. Was it even fastidious to think that Islam and Judaic Zionism had any leisure from their passions and their dogmatisms to take any account of a minority Christianity, itself burdened with anxieties and no less liable to an imprisoned mind? History informs us in retrospect that we were living in interludes within conflict. The times were so informing us already. In such a setting was theology a luxury? Many Jews thought that the Holocaust had made it a malign irrelevance, while Muslims, by and large – some scholars and Sufis apart – had little place for thinking inter-communally about God and His human world. That *Allah* was *akbar* sufficed without exploring how He might be in the given turmoil. As for some 'Word made flesh,' some divine incurring of the human tragedy out of a love that could even suffer precisely in being 'a faithful Creator' – these intimations of mystery and extravagance could merit no more than routinely controversial dismissal of their possibility.

One day recalling *Hamlet* in a wandering frame of mind, it had struck me how fitting his final plea might have been for the Christ of Gethsemane:

> 'Absent thee from felicity awhile
> And in this harsh world draw thy breath in pain
> To tell my story.'

Or the plea of the sentry guard at the beginning of the play:

> 'Sit down awhile and let us once again assail your ears,
> That are so fortified against our story.'[6]

Would that be to romanticize in respect of the Church in the Middle East? Yet if we disallow the romance do we not discount the faith? Wanting to be articulate with faith in a world liable to be raucous in its politico-religious self-assurance suggested a forlorn hope. 'Fortified against' were apt words for the would-be currency of the Gospel of divine love in an arena of bitter human quarrel. Yet Christian responsibility had, in part, made it so. Incomprehension had long abetted bigotry. Could we even begin to abate the one and disentangle the other? Or would the exercise be only an inter-Christian pursuit, comforting, enlivening, but finally elusive and unreal? Were we taking ourselves too seriously or not seriously enough – with a seriousness that was still naive?

The same question might apply to a series of books which emerged from the Study Programme venture, as it was tempered and schooled by other experiences around it. My concern with the Qur'an took shape later in *The Event of the Qur'an* (1971) and *The Mind of the Qur'an* (1973), followed by *Readings in the Qur'an* (1988). What is at issue for Christians about Muhammad and for Muslims about Jesus was tackled in *Muhammad and the Christian* (1984) and *Jesus and the Muslim* (1985). *The Privilege of Man* (1967) and *The Christ and the Faiths* (1986) aimed to bring out the positive kinships of belief through which we could duly come to things we did not share. In *The Arab Christian: A History in the Middle East* an effort was made to explore the dual identity, since Arabness is so often thought to be synonymous with Islam.

In all these ways it might be said that my faith as a Christian was in negotiation with a formidable life-setting into which I believed that a sense of vocation had taken it. How did that sense come about and how has it survived? How has faith reckoned with itself in the given time and place? What follows attempts to find the answers. If they are to be honest they cannot be complacent or facile. 'God does not send his rivers like arrows to the sea.'[7] Or, changing the metaphor about faith-in-life, 'the wick has to run through the whole length of the candle.'

Chapter 1

Seaside and Season

i.

Number 21 Bright Street, South Shore, Blackpool – not my birthplace, which was a mile or so away – was the only address I knew in my first seventeen years of life. The street could hardly have been named for any particular glamour about its solid, stone-built terrace houses, nor for the quality of its inhabitants. They gave no evidence of special brilliance, being ordinary, normal, unpretentious folk. Nor could the naming have to do with enjoying more than the average ration of fitful Lancashire sunshine, as dubious in the twenties as it has ever been in northern parts.

Could it have been named for the great Rochdale radical, John Bright, whose death in 1889 coincided, I would guess, with its arrival on the scene in the parish of Holy Trinity, a bare quarter mile from the Irish sea and behind the artery first known as 'Church Street,' until a more ambitious run of shop-keepers aspired to have it re-named 'Bond Street.' It was there the cinema stood, to which we were only allowed to go by favour of Charlie Chaplin. In saluting John Bright did the locals have a canny interest in keeping Rochdale among the retinue of east Lancashire towns that made their annual pilgrimage to Blackpool in the seasonal calendar of 'wakes' by which we knew 'Bolton Week,' 'Todmorden Week,' 'Oswaldtwistle Week,' in mingling with the serenaders on the promenade? Not for them in their generation the vistas of Majorca or the Costa Brava. Blackpool made Lancashire entirely self-sufficient for the hope of fun and leisure. Grey the seas might be and the sands in season peopled beyond all seclusion but the air had tonic quality and the landladies were without peer.

In contrast to the cliffs of the North Shore, there was

only a low-level promenade at South Shore, bordered by a stretch of sand the tide never covered. Southward again was the Victoria Pier whose Floral Hall featured an orchestra offering sedate music through the summer months. It was there the word 'excerpts' made its odd way into my vocabulary. Whether they were from Strauss or Handel or Holst, I do not now remember nor, alas! did any musical capacity kindle in me, though I was fascinated by the movement of the hands and instruments, the facial features of the 'winds,' and what seemed to me the pompous self-importance of the conductor, growing more so with every season of his re-appearance. My mother liked the relaxation and the walk along the pier. There was something exciting, sitting with the tide whispering below with a music of its own.

These modest concerts were in studied contrast to the gaudier offerings of the 'Pleasure Beach' which occupied a coastal site at what was then the end of the Promenade and the beginnings of the 'sand-hills' which, for a time, were almost haunted for me by reason of a murder story and a corpse mysteriously found there. Our unaccompanied sorties – my elder brother, Herbert, and I – were often to the Pleasure Beach, though it was only occasionally we had money to spend. Indeed, we indulged a certain possessiveness about Blackpool's amenities and, though Blackpool was only itself by virtue of its visitors, we looked with a wry disdain upon their naive appreciation of it.

How odd to come so far just to slide down a circular toboggan contrived around a sort of windmill without sails, to shriek on the 'Big Dipper,' with its flexible long cars plunging down and up its peaks and round its vertiginous curves, or sit entranced in a sort of punt which wandered in the dark through 'magic caves.' For our part, we meandered between the side-shows and took our boyish satisfaction vicariously in the antics and gestures of the foreign victims. We would watch them emerge from caverns and halls of mirrors, cash-happy, indulgent, half-bemused, half-incredulous, satisfied with the inanities distancing the coal-mines, the cotton mills and the weaving sheds they had briefly left behind. These distractions were not for us – unless on rare occasions some visiting relative or friend generously enticed us into them. Otherwise, we took a proxy satisfaction in sheer familiarity. Or we lingered where the toffee-makers swung long skeins of candy, like tresses of hair, around silver-plated hooks, shouting: 'As pure as the air you breathe and whiter than a sheet of snow!' Cut deftly with large scissors as the toffee hardened, it would be offered to the assembled watchers to sample. Lads with no cash were useless loiterers to be placated now and then but mostly sent on their way, listless, with watering mouths.

An intimate at a distance as I frequented the Pleasure Beach, sometimes escaping the chaperoning of my brother – the twenty-eight months between us were always a matter of significance – I had, in my boyish diffidence, little register of the human aches and anxieties, the trivialities and tensions, that belonged with those milling crowds. Nor could I then appreciate the pathos of the excitement they sought and found. The anodynes of television were still four decades away and foreign travel a luxury for the few. To the ordinary mill-hand, spinner, or twister (as the term innocently was) of east Lancashire, Blackpool in the season – as it was always called – was the high-point of the year, the Mecca of the wistful, the vulgar and the down-to-earth.

The 'Central Beach,' not to be confused with the Beach to the south, and later called 'the golden mile,' was an even more coarsely contrived haven of the bizarre, the seductive, the esoteric. There the strange exhibit, Harold Davidson, the unfrocked Rector of Stiffkey in the Diocese of Norwich, sat in a barrel, the gaze of the passing throng whose verdicts were, no doubt, as competing as their numbers. He was later to be fatally mauled by lions in a den on the other side of England. Blackpool devoured only his dignity for its own publicity and would have been too astute to will his demise. For both of them it was a sorry livelihood. Alongside him in that lucrative mile of tawdriness and whimsicality were palmists, cabarets, dance-halls, pubs, trocaderoes and stalls of the inevitable Blackpool Rock, sticks of minted toffee with the legend running through them that this was 'Blackpool' right in your saliva.

ii.

It was all a strange nursery for our evangelical loyalty. We belonged to Christ Church, a Victorian Gothic edifice at the north end of town. From its origins in the eighteen-seventies, it had been a stronghold of a warm and simple Anglican faith, devoted alike to 'the Gospel' and 'the Book of Common Prayer.' How many times did we walk on Sundays the three miles along the promenade in all weathers, passing that 'golden mile' between the two piers, like Bunyan's wayfarers through 'Vanity Fair,' turning in beside the Cenotaph to Queen Street and the welcoming embrace of the true faith. The contrast was complete – and painful – between our earnest will to worship and the casual indifference, the secular nonchalance, through which we made our way. To our left as we went northward lay the shore-line where

> '. . . the inhasting tide doth roll
> Home from the deep, along the whole
> Wide shining strand . . .
> The open sea-shore of my soul.'[1]

It was perhaps, unknown to me in my immaturity, a parable of what invaded me there never to recede. Nor was it, in my Blackpool terms, the 'long, withdrawing roar,' of Arnold's beach at Dover and his vision of an ebbing faith and 'naked shingles of the world.'[2] Christ Church was at once more robust, more confident.

Somewhere Virginia Woolf once wrote:

> 'Why is there not a discovery in life, something one can lay hands on and say: "This is it." I have a great and astonishing sense of something there.'[3]

The something always eluded her. For me the answer to her question and her protest was: 'There is!' I found my 'discovery' in my early teens. It is with me still. Perhaps I should rather call it 'a discovering,' for I did not find it all at once and it was somehow laid before me by factors for which I had no credit but with which I could only be a grateful partner.

It belonged with what transpired within the church: it happened in those to-ings and fro-ings along the promenade, under a commonly grey sky or, in the autumn, under the myriad lights of what we locals called 'the Bluminations,' a mercantile device to 'lengthen the season,' and reputedly the most adventurous in the world. For Blackpool was good at self-reputing. At all times the clanging 'dreadnought' trams plied up and down the sea-walk and, in the summer, boatmen would be commending their barks for an hour's sail. I do not recall any strong emotions of censure or reproach over those unchurched crowds. My father, after all, was a local merchant, and they were our livelihood, but there was – freshly out of church – a half-conscious yearning about a world 'passing by on the other side' and ignoring the true benediction. I had no cause at that time to interrogate their indifference or find it as oppressive as it would be now.

My father's establishment was in Chapel Street which ran through the hinterland from the Central Pier to Central Drive under the railway which then proceeded northward behind 'the golden mile' to the Central Station with its spacious sidings – now all defunct. Off Chapel Street just by the shop was Cragg Street, so named, mysteriously, long before my time and, indeed, my father's. He was very early orphaned and had struggled hard. Indeed, as I might truly say: 'I only had one grand-parent,' for my maternal grandmother was no more than a portrait in our home, which brings me to ante-natal mystery – that haunting puzzle of all birthing, and what Edward Gibbon called 'the silent vacancy that precedes our birth.'[4] It is no less mysterious than the whither of all mortal demise. How aptly Thomas Traherne could ask of his members as – in poetic self-awareness – he surveyed them as all babes are sure to do, though adulthood takes them in an un-enquiring stride:

'These eyes and hands which here I find . . .
Where have ye been? behind
What curtain were ye hid from me . . .
I that so long was nothing from eternity?'[5]

We all arrive as 'strangers,' he went on, seeing, sensing, hearing, seeking, finding, 'strange things . . . lodged in this fair world,' 'strange all, and new,' to us – but that they should be ours, who nothing were, 'that strangest is of all, yet brought to pass.'

Brought to pass, for me, over my father's shop in Chapel Street. My mother, Emily Hides, ever sweet and patient, was the elder daughter of a commercial traveller who was said to have voyaged to and from the East Indies on a tea-clipper and who died when I was nine. Their family had left Manchester for Blackpool to implement his income by running a boarding house on the south promenade. Grandfather was a staunch church-wardenly figure who presided over a Sunday School. My father was Captain of a troop of its Church Lads' Brigade. The rest followed. They were married at Blackpool Parish Church opposite the famous Winter Gardens. My sister, Marion, seven years older, and my brother, had preceded me to make a 'pentagon' of Craggs.

The shop which was my birthplace represented the crown of long effort on my father's part from his earliest efforts as a barber, happily in the days before the coming of the safety razor. He had wrestled with adversity and slowly built up a wider trade in fancy goods, handbags and the kind of things that visitors would buy. Soon after my arrival, he moved across the street to wider premises and we ceased to live above the shop – heading, at one remove, for Bright Street. As a boy I was recruited to 'man' a stall which he enterprisingly set in the porch of the shop the better to attract the customers. From my pitch there I could contemplate the upper windows behind which I had opened eyes upon the world. My brother and I were also recruited for lathering the stubbly chins of a procession of clients, seated on a row of chairs along which my father passed with great dexterity despatching at commendable speed the harvest of their chins. This was the part of being filial I least enjoyed.

Chapel Street, with its dip beneath the railway, was a busy thoroughfare linking the beach with the hinterland of apartments and their landladies. There would be rush hours after breakfast, to and fro at lunch, and again in the evening, unless the frequent rain drove bedraggled groups at other times away from the shore to the circus or the ballrooms with – as the cynic said – their vertical expression of horizontal intent. Of the sordid side of Blackpool I was blissfully innocent. I saw my father as an admirable and awesome figure – the more so as I came to understand his struggles with poverty and privation in youth.

Born in 1878, he was doubtless named Albert in honour of the Prince Consort, so I acquired the name to correspond with my brother as Herbert after our maternal grandfather. But my parents never used my first name and Kenneth I always was. Grandpa Herbert's Sunday School convened in 'the Drill Shed,' a cavernous place not far from the shop. There I had my first nurture in that amateur tutelage to which so much is owed since Robert Raikes. By fourteen I would be engaged in it myself. The Drill Shed, unused on Sundays, was a vast armoury where we climbed to upper rooms and our steps echoed to the girdered roof in place of the strident tones of a sergeant-major.

It slowly dawned on me that I was the last hope of the family. Years later I would reflect on the coincidence of my beginnings, pre-natally, in the aftermath of the sinking of the *Titanic*, though how and why I could not tell. My father was reprieved from war service by a defect in the ear but his own brother, Fred, and members of my mother's family were victims of the horrors of 1914–18 which I passed in the helpless ignorance of infancy. My mother was the gentlest of souls. There were times when she had to check the urgent commercial instinct of my father which, on one occasion, but for her, might have led us into disaster when my father meant to buy half finished houses, intending to complete them. The market suddenly collapsed.

She brought me through a nearly fatal illness when I

was thirteen and my relation with her came to be hallowed for me by her deteriorating condition with arthritis – an affliction which, rightly or wrongly, was attributed to her bearing me. Discount it as she might, it became increasingly apparent in gnarled hands and swollen knuckles. Years before her death in 1952 she was in a wheel-chair. I never knew how to measure and interpret the entail of my nativity in my mother's biography. It only intensified a wistfulness I could never explain or satisfy. When at my first school I was given some commendatory pence it used to be mandatory to spend half of it for her – usually the aniseed balls it could secure from a shop en route home. That pathetic ritual somehow did a childish justice to the situation as I understood it. Only later were the opportunities more substantial.

These occasions were usually on Fridays when school reckonings were done and it was blissful to come home to the freshly spruced and garnished house, ready for the Sunday climax and the Yorkshire pudding – served invariably first and by itself, to take the edge off appetite.

Milk was brought – always to the back door, as convention required of tradespeople – in great cans and poured out at the door step into the household jugs with the gratuitous 'extra' to ensure 'good measure.' Brass bands came round at Christmas and the carollers. On New Year's Eve, my brother, having the darkest complexion, was therefore chosen to 'let in the New Year,' opening the door as midnight passed. Nightly came the lamp-lighter, a ladder across his shoulder and a long cane hooked to pull the chain that brought on the gas, or otherwise lean the ladder on the post and climb to it. Daylight brought him round again to put out the lights. Blackpool had been an early pioneer in street lighting by gas. To be a 'lighter' seemed a fascinating role to a child's fancy.

There was one annual horror which made me adamant I would never be 'Mayor' of Blackpool. For that dignitary had to welcome every October the walkers of the 'Manchester to Blackpool Walk,' a gruelling contest of some 52 miles. It was the haggard laggards who most distressed me as they came, gaunt and hobbling, along the promenade to the Town Hall. Once I had seen them I tried to stay at home that day for they troubled my dreams. Bitter wind and driving rain only added to the horror they aroused in me.

While Christ Church played the main part in the 'seed-time of my soul,' I must assume that the local Primary School, where I spent my years from five to eleven, was also shaping me, though I have few recollections before the major occasion when I won a scholarship to what was to become Blackpool Grammar School. We had two Primary Headmasters, the first kindly and benign with whose grand-children we had common hobbies and excursions, the second a heavy tyrant whose canings of miscreants in the Hall could be heard cautionarily in all the classrooms that surrounded it. He was a great intimidator and there were times when a very rough justice was inflicted. How could I know from what horrors some of the younger teachers had returned in the early twenties of the century, opaque to us innocents, as they struggled to come to terms with their memories and their prospects.

I was five when the 'Great War' ended and remember how the great white obelisk was erected and dedicated in an awesome ceremony on the north Promenade. Only years later, via the poetry of Wilfred Owen, did I learn through what lunacy and carnage my childhood had emerged. I was regaled with such stories as were fit for my ears by an aunt whose V.A.D. uniform stays vividly in my memory. Suitably her name was Martha. In what tedium we boys must have involved our teachers so recently reprieved from desperate experiences. I recall floundering with an essay on 'the defeat of the Spanish Armada,' and receiving a 'merit sticker' in the margin of some effusions on 'the dahlia,' but for the most part that early schooling left no mark on my memory. At least I was numerate and literate and ready for the wider world of 'secondary' education. The way to school would now no longer be on foot across the railway bridge on the Lytham Road, but by the tramcar – those intriguing vehicles which the local Corporation had adopted for the first time in the world and to which it remains firmly devoted.

iii.

School and Church in contrasting ways presided over the middle years of my second decade, the crucial teens, finding me a fledgling and grooming me to be Oxonian, each instalment, like a Dickens novel, not known until the next. Blackpool Grammar School, to give it its current title, was then housed in a two-storey red-brick building with glass-framed classrooms and spacious hall. The Headmaster, Joseph Turral, was a somewhat eccentric figure, great on 'ésprit de coeur dans l'école.' He loved stylish French and always called the annual school Party 'Une Soirée'. I felt somehow cheated by the anaemic fare we had in School Assembly, when the Head read from Paul to the Romans about 'being members of one body,' leaving the verse emasculated. We were, of course, years before Butler's Education Act, and I had still much to learn about the art of the secular.

The Head, moreover, had a strong aversion to Blackpool. It was as if he was not reconciled to the location of his headship. For he was always tilting against 'this philistine town,' with its vulgar trippers and phlegmatic landladies. True culture could only survive in youngsters schooled against the grain of their parents' environment. 'Cinema' was to be pronounced 'kineema,' in deference to the Greek. Was it a personal quirk we should tolerate, or a kind of intellectual snobbery fit to puzzle and dismay? He was, however, no tyrant and ruled benevolently. There was a fatherly strain in his affection for his 'old boys' whom he held out to us as paragons of academic virtue we must emulate, whether in the Indian Civil Service – as was then often the case – or somewhere in Whitehall.

One most celebrated among them was Albert Cooke – some three years my senior, who via Jesus College, Cambridge and a Fulbright Fellowship, became the luminary of 'Letter from America,' by then Alastair Cooke. His skill in interpretative journalism was matched for me by his performance as the robber in a One-Act play in School about

'The Bishop's Candlesticks,' which were stolen, traced and penitently returned.

The years were happy in a serious way. The General Strike of 1926 came and went, with the curiosity of improvised transport and a vague sense of something historical happening around one's ears. We were not a highly political family and my father had mellowed from his early radicalism. I had scant inkling in 1926 of what was at stake between Stanley Baldwin and A.J. Cook, the miners' leader. Miscellaneous 'charabancs' were just a novel way of reaching school in the absence of the trams.

It was in the Sixth Form that the traumas came, partly from faith-stresses still to gauge, and the anxieties of attaining Oxford. Prior to these, my chief recollection is of corridors – not of power, but of nurture, a realm of doors and glass partitions, where the mysteries of learning belonged. Sometimes one paced them en route to the masters' common room as a monitor with a pile of papers for correction – an occasion to steal a furtive glance around the array of tables, to note stubs in ash-trays and breathe the laden air and to wonder about the stories they could tell or might exchange. *In absentia* they somehow became more human, more prosaic. I wondered how they really saw their charges or coped with the tedium of our routine progress through the wiles of algebra or the conjugations of Latin verbs. The French master, R.G. Dixon, had a special place in my affections. 'Voilà la plafond,' he began in his inaugural lesson, giving us vocabulary from our immediate surroundings and letting us know we were sitting each in his *pupitre*. I resolved that my siege of Oxford would turn on his old College.

There would, however, be traumas in between. The word is not excessive. Truly there was plenty to fascinate and delight. Was not the School Song *Tarantara* from *The Pirates of Penzance* with its mock heroic:

> 'When your heart is in your boots,
> There is nothing brings it round
> Like the trumpet's martial sound . . .'

We sang it lustily on Speech Days in the Opera House

where notables gave away prizes and wangled a day's holiday out of assembled Governors. The major prizes tended to go to an élite few, among them my ever successful rival, who went on to be President of the Cambridge Union. There were consolations. Some kind donor had financed a prize in Irish history, no doubt out of a desire to encourage English youth to reach a sober honesty about that tragic scene. I gained it on two occasions but it was not *the* history prize of maximum standing.

There were eight of us in the Modern Studies Sixth of my years. There was camaradie enough, left as we were too often on our own to fend as we would with G.M. Trevelyan's *England under the Stuarts*, and J.R. Tanner's *English Constitutional Conflicts of 17th Century*, together with Chaucer's *The Prologue*, Milton's *Comus* and *Samson* and the rest. Part of my unease around these delights had to do with my faith and with the propriety of being a sixth-former anyway.

After matriculation at fifteen, my father thought it was time for me to quit school. His own hard experience and vigorous self-help against heavy odds had given him a suspicion of 'higher' education. He thought I, too, should be 'at the world,' not cossetted with books. My sister and brother were already at work in builders' offices as junior clerks. He had arranged for me to be apprenticed at a corner chemist shop to learn the trade. He was finally dissuaded by a master at the School whom he trusted as a friend, to whose pleas and prognosis he yielded. Being so reprieved from what might have been a *cul de sac* meant that I had to justify his change of mind. This only came precariously to pass when my parents came to stay in Oxford in my first summer term.

Vindication of my family's investment in my *academia*, uneasy incentive though it was, served to underline a deeper negotiation within my immaturity. Looking back I find myself intrigued by the things I never questioned yet ardently loved and I am tempted to wonder now whether fervour always means a certain imperception. Evangelical faith was the breath of our being, deep but not demonstrative, assured but not boisterous. It took me, as it were, in a familial communal stride leaving me neither room nor inclination to review its mastery. Confirmation came and went, serious and significant for me, but not itself a landmark. Its point was taken up for all five of us, in a climate of conviction and allegiance which, by consensus and yet differently, embraced us all.

At its heart was the sense of the need for a personal Saviour and of Jesus the Christ being invited into the heart. Right believing was an important part of that understanding of being 'truly Christian' but the liability to witness and serve was central too. One had to be solicitous about others coming to the same vital formula of salvation and truly concerned that they should know the truth, find the way and have the life.

There was one immediate aspect of this social-personal concern which besieged my mind. It had to do with children under age at the doors of crowded pubs. We passed by them on our way. The law did not allow their admission so their parents boozed within and left them lounging – to me forlorn looking – outside. My pity undertook them but what was I to do? I imagined all kinds of dire concomitants of this – to me – betrayal, so different from the home I knew. Doubtless I conjured up visions of neglect and deprivation of which the tippling parents were in no way guilty. But perhaps they were. Sometimes I stopped and talked to the children eliciting perhaps sighs, or giggles, or sullen silence, or tears. If, however, as oftentimes, I walked by 'the priest and the levite on the other side' would come to mind reprovingly. I might turn back, even after reaching home, half hoping they would be gone before I reached them. Or uneasily, until it was too late, I would tell myself that, anyway, the Lord could do about them what He wanted without me.

It was hardly a healthy 'freedom in the Spirit,' yet it was a 'growing pain' of that calling 'to-be-on-behalf-of' which had come to be for me so crucial to the Christian understanding of how it is with God and so must also be with us. Another street scene that always halted me was the sight of a night watchman sitting in a man-size hut often – as the vogue then was – with a charcoal fire before him in a brazier, where he would be all night on the watch against marauders of some road mending equipment near by, shovels, tar pans, brooms and the rest. One I remember quite flooring me when we got on to 'what the Bible said,' by telling me that the story about David and Bathsheba was too 'blue' to be 'sacred.' I did not understand him and turned to something more evangelical. I often handed out tracts and had a scheme to plant 'please-take-one' boxes in friendly cafés and bars. Visits to refill them often revealed their disappearance.

The warmth and authenticity of the fellowship, however, compensated for what may have been inept or even unhappy in these pressures which, if they toughened my fibre also disturbed by studies. I suppose my concerns for the pub-children was the only way I knew of holding together the inward things of our own domesticity and the actualities of a raw and all too human world. Discoveries of contrasts and debts must always be a part of growing and there are psychic costs to pay. Exacting as these may be they are surely truer to faith than the sort of mind-set D.H. Lawrence attributed in *The Man who Died* to Jesus himself, namely, learning the futility of ever wanting to put right the wrongs of human life.[6]

iv.

My father normally only went to evening Service on Sundays. He considered the morning a time to relax from his arduous week. Though a keen merchant, he would never open the shop on Sunday which he considered truly a day of rest and soul-renewal. The rest of us were up betimes and the day of services and Sunday Schools would only end with something after Evensong, when we made our paces in review of the day, overcoming shyness and, rather differently from how 'Professor Higgins' had it, learning to speak. For these were 'the things of God.' The Keswick Convention every July came into our awareness. In those days of limited horizons regionally the Lake District was the usual mecca for Lancastrians who, since they lived there, could not 'go' to Blackpool. There was also a local 'branch' of the Convention in the town every year. It cared about deepened discipleship and had a lively sense of the wide world where we prayed much and often for the 'spread of the Word.'

These, however, were only make-weights in the central significance of Christ Church, whose Vicar, from 1923 to 1932, was Frank Argyle, greatly loved by all his people. There was a thrill about the evening congregation, often numbering five hundred and devoted to the Book of Common Prayer. I did not wonder then about the chanting of all the Psalms of David according to their monthly cycle, irrespective of all the changing moods they registered when sung in that mathematical fashion, nor yet about the congruity, at many points, of their sentiments with the open grace of the New Testament. My youthful mind certainly sensed the worth and reach of ministry as that congregation knew it. At Sunday School 'Anniversary,' in the Lancashire tradition, we sang innumerable hymns about 'summer suns glowing,' and 'the best Book to read.' My brother was for some years a star choir-boy – a distinction to which I had no talent to aspire. For me the pew was the place and – until the grim demolition of the building soon after I had spoken at its Centenary Celebration – bore my teeth marks on its pine moulding conveniently adjacent at times of prayer. Though I outgrew such vagaries I long continued to wonder over asking, or rather chanting, about 'departing in peace,' when the service continued with the Creed and no one took the plea seriously or rose to leave.

I sense, in retrospect, that my parents were more placid than we youngsters. The Prayer Book crisis of 1927/28 raised great fervour in the parish and the double rejection of the so-called 'Deposited Book' was greeted with great acclaim. There was a campaign called 'the Protestant Parsons' Pilgrimage' which visited town. We lauded the four Bishops who had – as we saw it – the courage to vote against 'The Book.' The P.P.P. held a rally in the local Opera House – a rare occasion to see the inside of it. A Scottish orator, Rosslyn Mitchell, whose speech in the

House of Commons was thought to have played a part in the Book's defeat, was the evangelicals' hero. When the vote was announced, the youth group gathered in the dark to sing the doxology outside the Vicarage. I was not present.

We – or, at least, I – had no register at all of what the revision was seeking to do, not how preferable, for example, its 'Invitation' was in the Daily Office: ('Beloved we are come together in the presence of Almighty God and of the whole company of heaven . . .') to the repetitious and wordy: 'Dearly beloved brethren . . .' (men only) and its needless synonyms ('pray and beseech,' 'dissemble and cloke,' 'acknowledge and confess,') ending – as if all were still illiterate – 'saying *after* me'! More importantly, I had no awareness of what the entire issue was meaning for Archbishop Randall Davidson presiding over a Church to which our loyalty was owed. Nor was I then alive to what did, ought, or should, obtain between State and Church, in the ordering of 'Divine Worship.'

Perhaps that whole story was a symbol of what I would need to pay later in integrity for what I owed already to nurture. I have only thankfulness for the faith I learned and loved. It possessed me of 'the unsearchable riches of Christ.' Through all its risks and chances it conveyed me to the point where I could duly subdue it to the scrutiny it needed. The meanings it implanted it also postponed. Paradoxically it gave me the very clues by which, refined and chastened, I could hope to resolve its contradictions. While still a schoolboy, I ventured my first sermon outside the local sphere, in a Chapel in Fishergate, Preston, to be followed by more unpredictable occasions on Blackpool sands or in Regent Square behind the promenade. They were times at once of assurance and timidity, of ardour and reservation. My sense of obligation to doctrine and loyalty was more firmly in place than my sense of liability for their proper honesty. I had decisive criteria about what was 'right' and 'sound,' less lively ones for what was 'gentle' and 'considerate' (see Chapter 10), though I think that throughout I wanted to mingle all four descriptives could they be compatible.

One memory that tempered the partisanship of our allegiance had to do with William Temple. We still lived in Bright Street at the time. Christ Church was not alone in 'caring for the lost,' or for 'interpreting the faith.' There was annually 'the Bishop of Manchester's Mission.' After 1926–27, '. . . of Blackburn.' Clergy, housed up the coast at Rossall School, descended for some two weeks on the resort and preached to crowds on the foreshore perched on wooden stands, with an awning overhead to keep discourses dry, and space for a harmonium. Crowds were normally very attentive and the event was a great feature of 'the season.' There was a special 'stand' at South Shore for boys and girls. William Temple was due to come and address us and we contrived a special sand-pulpit on which he was expected to stand. Finding his footing a little insecure, he decided to sit upon it. I have no recollection of what he said to us but he made a profound impression simply with his ample person. Years later his writings became something of a beacon to me in my questing but, alas, I never again saw him in the flesh.

Dimly 'the Bishop's Mission' made me realize that we were part of something larger than we often knew and that the Gospel entrusted itself more widely than we might approve its doing.

Rome, of course, was very far gone. A mere stone's throw from our sanctuary of true faith was the Church of the Sacred Heart – a title that puzzled me. We often went by it but it was years before I ever stepped inside, returning one time to the town as an adult. I remember my vivid sense of something sinister and menacing. In retrospect it seems to me that the deep alienation that made Lancashire such a haunt of Protestant-Catholic contention was owing, not merely to the Irish presence, but to the seeming subterfuge simple minds identified in the subtleties and devious workings of minds like Newman's and the Tractarians who could argue from the very necessary concept of 'development,' to a sophistry that sowed distrust and insecurity in the minds of 'plain-dealers.' Perceptions of patience come hardly to those who feel themselves alerted to suspicion.

A recollection I have of Christ Church, Blackpool, prior to 1923 is of a cherubic, red-complexioned, bald-headed Vicar whose ordinary sounding name he spelled so oddly, the Revd. Samuel Schor. The reason was his Jewish extraction. He had something of the aura of a rabbi and was much in demand to explain and illustrate from models the furniture of the Tabernacle in the wilderness and the Temple in Jerusalem. He was my first initiation into themes that became central to my wistfulness. It was too early to wonder about the meaning of his change of faith and how Judaic/Christian themes could go today beyond the minutiae of a worship abandoned for the supremacy of Torah and the synagogue and Talmud. Over the heads, and the words too, of himself and his successors was the verse: 'I have a message from God unto thee,' from Judges 3.20. I took it seriously to mean what it said about the preacher. I was shattered one day to discover what it meant in context. The 'message' was a dagger plunged by an assassin into the guts of Eglon, King of Moab, plunged so far that it could not be withdrawn. The assassin had used the words as a ploy to gain entry and trust.

The text had been there for decades. What was one seriously to make of the citation as a headline for the Gospel of peace? What was one to think of the theology which could so mishandle the Scripture? What, indeed, was one to do about a Scripture which could afford, and tolerate, such crooked usage? I would have many burdens later about stories like Jephthah's daughter and Samuel assassinating Agag or the savagery of vengeance against Achan. How could we really be honest about the liabilities of the Bible or its standing as 'the Word of God'? It was when I got, years later, to the East and to Zion that the puzzles of my youth intensified at times into near despair over Christian integrity. 'The best Book to read' was too facile a rubric.

V.

It will be clear why these urgent inward questions about the loyalty that, at the same time, was everything to me, should complicate my school studies, the more so as the School had so little to contribute to them. It was not that the Church presided exclusively over my spiritual nurture, it was that the secular sphere of education renounced all part in it. The convictions of my evangelical betters continued to set my agenda and only slowly did Oxford avail to widen it. I came into a good deal of banter at School – 'Mr Evangelist Cragg on his Pilgrim's Progress,' and the like. The Jewish boys in School with whom I had close relations seemed to hold very loosely by their Synagogue to which I was never invited, though it stood next door to School. Satire did not trouble me: it quite bye-passed my inner misgivings and only served to quicken my allegiance.

As I continued my uneasy studies, distracted at times by thoughts of evangelical obligation I was failing to fulfill, my church nurture dominated my heart while, in certain areas outside the School curriculum, it possessed my mind on its own terms. The situation no doubt reflected my own slow-wittedness but I think also the deep deference I had for those I loved at home and revered at church. It may have been no bad thing to weather the normal stresses of adolescence in what was emotionally a harbour concealing what lay beyond my native coast. I do not recall any master in the Grammar School, even in the apt context of reading Pascal, assessing Cromwell, interpreting Ireland, or getting the measure of Gladstone, who ever took me in hand religiously or ventured perspectives that might have affected my convictions. The Gospel, as Christ Church loved it, had the field of my heart to itself, except insofar as I savoured for myself, tentatively, surreptitiously, the ideas that might disconcert its ministries of love. Thankfully the stresses that might have put my goal at risk were mastered when the vital scholarship came my way and a door to Oxford opened.

How do I take stock of the way in which faith and life had coincided thus far? Real negotiation still lay ahead. In a way for which I could only be enduringly grateful 'the pearl of great price' had fallen to me, as it were, in 'a field' for which I did not have to sell all that I had to be its purchaser. All that I had from home and church had bought it for me and I would be in life-long debt. In what did it consist? The answer, as I would give it now, I must attempt in Chapters 9 and 10. In the twenties and my teens I would have phrased it very traditionally – 'God *so* loved the world . . .' 'The Son of God loved me and gave Himself for me . . .' 'In Him we have forgiveness through His blood . . .' 'Believe on the Lord Jesus Christ and you will be saved . . .' The faith was about a 'personal Saviour,' to whom one turned, invited in, and vowed to serve and love and commend in a life of 'trust and obey.'

All this was 'the simplicity that is in Christ,' as Paul described it in 2 Corinthians 11.3, by which he meant a moral quality of 'singlemindedness' made such by an unfailing grace. Only the future would require of me a sense of how that quality would have to learn its continuity in perplexities of mind and spirit such as to deny 'simplicity' any other meaning. The custom of 'The Young Life Campaign,' to which Christ Church youth belonged, in meetings, indoor and outdoor, was to invite recital of texts by the rows, or the ring, of participants. I think my favourite, when I ventured any, was: 'You know the grace of our Lord Jesus, that though He was rich yet for your sakes He became poor that you, through His poverty, might be rich.' (2 Corinthians 8.9)

My New Testament perceptions were good enough to have me appreciate that the context there had to do with a tender relief operation, an offering concerted by Paul from the Gentile churches of the dispersion to be brought – as it proved by him in person – to the 'poor saints,' i.e. the Jewish Christians, in Jerusalem. It would demonstrate to any, reluctant among them about 'Gentile' fellows at all, that even these 'outsiders' were capable of a compassion grounded in a common faith and fellowship. Here was 'sacrament' in truth, physical 'conveyance' of spiritual unity. Paul risked his very liberty to 'convey' it. It spelled to me the very heart of my faith about a great 'caring,' an outgoing of inter-human-ness, a state of being-on-behalf-of-others in the world.

Paul, however, was careful to associate this quality firmly with its paradigm, its counterpart, its original, in God

Himself. Hence the verse I loved, or in John's terms: 'We love, because He first loved us.' 'He first . . .' (1 John 4.19). One could only read the world as for, and in, community, if one could read the world as altogether an intention of love. Any such conviction would underlie a credible faith in 'creation.' Whether or not we could understand the when and how of a world's origins, we could comprehend a why, namely, a divine intentionality such as the psalmist sang: 'It is He that has made us and not we ourselves.' (Psalm 100.3).

Could such assurance survive, though, in the absence of something more than intention to create? How should allegedly inclusive love match with the tragic as history told it on the very stage of creation – tragedy inseparable from the wayward creaturehood in which that intentionality had been staked and vested? It was perhaps, then, only dimly that I realized the place and role of something like what we had in Jesus, born and crucified and risen – as the Creed affirmed – if God and grace were not to be a pious fiction or a cruel enigma. Believing in God, one would need to be believing in His Christ. But we could only be believing in a Christ of those necessary dimensions of costly on-behalf-of-us-ness if belonging with, and eventuating from, the reality of God.

I have doubtless run ahead of my youthful competence to understand but these were the embryonic realities of my nurture and my heart. They were fit to assume, in due course, the obligations they would face as experience cross-examined them with doubts and fears and falterings. These are precisely the story-study on which – in suitably seaside metaphor – I am embarked.

vi.

'Season' – *seson, seison, saison* – derives from the word for 'sowing' *'serere'* and comes to mean the time when growth happens and so, in turn, a period of significance – reaping, mating, celebrating, or (for those lovely landladies) the time for trippers. 'Seasonable' is then what fits such times, like snow in winter or 'seasons of mist and mellow fruitfulness' at autumn time. If there can be such a thing as seasonable faith I am for ever grateful of the time in which it was bestowed. Not that it was ever, for me, 'out of season,' but that its seasonableness had to accommodate to all the times through which it passed.

Seasons belong with contrasts. Maybe I can suggest one to underwrite the implicit theology I have summarized. It was when I went to Tipasa, while visiting the chaplaincy in Algiers, that I became really aware of Albert Camus who celebrated that shore-line so lyrically in his *Rétour à Tipasa*. I discovered that we shared a name and a birth-year – sea and sand, as with me, and, in his case, much more sun. The three – sea, sand and sun – figured constantly in his writings and stories. I, too, loved to feel the sand in my toes. On Tipasa's beach there lay fragments of Roman ruins and pillars of ancient temples, all unknown to 'the golden mile.' My boyhood coasts were never lapped by warm blue waters like the Mediterranean, waters of the famed voyages told in the pages of Homer and Virgil. There were, to be sure, deep sympathies for me with Camus, when I became acquainted with the canals of Amsterdam and his parable from them of the labyrinthine ways of evil, of the pride latent in penitence and our human capacity for self-delusion.[7] For these were part of my Christian faith – a faith that offered, not some blind optimism in the face of wrongs within and around, but the costly reckonings of the Cross.

It was, nevertheless, the contrasts that most aroused me. I suppose he would have said that the issue staked in our so different seasides and seasons was between credulity and absurdity. One could delude oneself with the illusions of 'God in Christ,' or one could both accept and defy an irreducible meaninglessness. For me it was 'trusting' to believe that 'God is love': for him it was 'cheating.' One should have 'a smile of complicity with the brilliant smile' of the sun but never pretend that these sensuous delights corresponded to any real beneficence beyond them.[8] One would always be 'a stranger to oneself,' and 'living was keeping the absurd alive.'[9]

If, later, when Camus' writings came my way with powerful impact, I had to conclude that his ironic defiance of despair was the fruit of his life-experience, did I have also to conclude that my Christian faith stemmed likewise from how home and season had found me? Faith could only negotiate with life as life unfolded, but had its beginnings established a happy prejudice which would merely persist, just as a first draft by some junior civil servant may determine the top-level conclusions at some 'summit.'?

I think not, and there was something about Camus' mind that helps me to that verdict. But first, life as he knew it. His father, a French Algerian, had been killed on the Marne in 1914 when his son was barely one year old. His mother, a Spanish woman, was scarcely literate, 'a silent figure, asking nothing, moving without complaint through the tedious tasks of a difficult existence.'[10] Yet, the pain of the near incommunicado of mother and son as his perceptions flowered, was – in his own words – 'as if she were the immense pity in his heart which had moved outside him, had become endowed with a body and was conscientiously . . . playing the part of a poor old woman with a moving destiny.'[11] His studies in Paris alerted him bitterly to the politics of empire and the tensions of the *colonisés*. His adult years were filled with the trauma of the Algerian revolution in which he modified his early participation in the Resistance and abstained from taking sides in the war.

Fused as it was in deep irony, his philosophy of affirming the human, though only by an act of defiance of all that conspired against it, had nevertheless a yearning for transcendence sustained by the realization that 'to *argue* the absurd' was a contradiction in terms.[12] For how could any sense of the inclusively absurd ever arise to become a *necessary* negation of meaning? 'Meaning' might be elusive but any sense of its 'absence' proceeded only on the assumption of its existence. 'There is,' he wrote

> '. . . perhaps a living transcendancy of which beauty is a promise which may make us love, and prefer to any other, the limited and mortal world.'[13]

He knew, politically and morally, that reverence for some

ultimate authority is vital even in rebellion. Revolt cannot absolutize itself if it is not to end in a logic of destruction.[14] A nemesis overtakes whatever flouts the due 'measure of freedom and justice.' If, on the one hand, he thought of life as a kind of suicide one had not (yet) committed, the reason why one had not done so was the will to affirm, to assert human-ness, to engage in pity, to create in art, and to yield one's limbs in swimming to the embrace of sun and wave. These were affirmations, for which one could resist the deeply felt temptation to renounce all effort at understanding and sink into an inclusive hatred of oneself and all the human futility.[15]

> 'In our darkest nihilism I have sought only reasons to go beyond it . . . by an instinctive fidelity to a light in which I was born and in which for thousands of years men have learned to welcome life even in suffering.'[16]

Was this truly coming at the Christian truth of my first nurture but doing so, as it were, from the other side? One can start with the nihilism and find the reasons or one can welcome the reasons and with them welcome the nihilists also. How different my youth-time had been – prosaic, gentle, stable, modest, opportune for the faith I had undertaken; his – perplexed, tense, fraught with inner anger, if also blessed with literary genius. Yet 'instinctive fidelity to a light in which I was born . . .' a learning about suffering 'for thousands of years,' so well described my faith and the Church which 'learned' it. As with Fyodor Dostoevsky whom Albert Camus admired, his register of the human was 'not far from the Kingdom,' his delights close to a Christian sacramentalism in the acceptance of the ministry of the senses, his capacity for honesty and pity near to the heart of the Gospel whose very custodians he saw as 'cheating' by their taking for substantial what was only their illusion.

I have anticipated much that only came into negotiation with the lapse of years. It was perhaps foolish to dwell on a mere coincidence, if nothing more, of name and birth-year. What faithful Christian, however, could trifle with Camus' verdict that 'the Church has chosen just what it wants from its Master's suffering.'[17] Perhaps he was referring to self-satisfied dogma, self-centred priesthood, self-commending loyalty, self-exonerating partisanship.[18] Were any of these 'chosen' from Christ's 'suffering.'? Are they not rather the perversion of what that suffering meant about both humanity and God?

Clearly I would have to negotiate radically with the realism that found the Church wanting by the criterion of its own Gospel, and no less radically with how the most honest criticism would need that Gospel if it were ever to press it home. Christ Church, Blackpool, had not taught me to think this way but it had sweetly and irreversibly made me one who would need and strive to do so. Meanwhile, by the academic 'good offices' of the Grammar School, Oxford lay ahead. We had removed from 'Bright Street,' but had I?

Chapter 2

A Window in the Turl

i.

To be sure, only briefly but then all undergraduate existence is fleeting. Nowhere else are the generations so foreshortened. I had arrived for Michaelmas Term, 1931, who had hardly been south from Lancashire before. The Turl in Oxford was where I knew to find Jesus College, neighbour to Exeter and Lincoln in the narrow street joining the High to the Broad – a feat the Church of England had been achieving for centuries, for the major part with Oxford's help. The crisis which was to lead to the formation of the National Government and the parliamentary eclipse of the Labour Party was impending. Intimations of what would be coming out of Germany could already be discerned.

For me it was a propitious time. Not mine the emotions of William Wordsworth in another place:

> 'And more than all, a strangeness in my mind,
> A feeling that I was not . . . for that place.'[1]

On the contrary, Oxford had charmed me in a sunny early spring the previous March. Delighted to be housed in College, I had taken the entrance examination in the Great Hall at Christ Church. I had chosen Jesus College because our French Master at School had been there, though he had recommended Worcester College on account of its splendid gardens. I did not think gardens a prior point for academic attraction. Not long afterwards I received the following from the Principal of Jesus, A.E.W. Hazel:

> 'Your work was well thought of and I am writing to offer you admission as a Commoner to read for Honours in Modern History. If you accept this offer please ask your

> father, as you are under age, to write to me as soon as possible, stating that the offer is accepted. It is important that I should know your decision, as if you cannot accept I wish to offer the vacancy to another gentleman.'

The language reads quaintly now and my father's signature to the letter I gleefully drafted was not lightly secured. I had only the Blackpool Borough Scholarship (there were merely three for the whole education area) amounting to £105 a year, i.e. £35 a term. It would be a struggle to survive – itself no reason not to venture. The reply was sent. I began a love relation lasting these six decades spanning all the interludes of absence.

The History School it was to be. I would have read English had I been able to get to Shakespeare, Keats, George Eliot and Dickens at once without what seemed to me the pointless initial tedium of Skeat and other archaisms. Theology had not yet proposed itself and might well have been suspect. Nor was I then an ordinand. My tenancy of the bay-window room over the College porch was yet to come. Freshmen were housed in 'approved' lodgings. Mine were first in Richmond Road, off Walton Street, where that winter the water froze in the bedroom bowl. Later I had quarters off the Botley Road. From both haunts it was mandatory to report forty weekdays of the eight-week term (i.e. almost all of it) between 7.40 and 8 a.m. in the College Hall, merely to have one's name ticked on the list. The alternative was to attend Chapel at 8 a.m. which took twenty minutes and where L.B. Cross, the Fellow and Chaplain, invariably prayed: 'And make this College as a field which the Lord hath blessed that true knowledge may here for ever flourish and abound . . .' One was happy with those sentiments but not with the tedium of an otherwise pointless bicycle ride back and forth to no end except a discipline for discipline's sake such as the contemporary student would never tolerate. It was a device to obviate the temptations of the lay-abeds.

Great Tom at Christ Church still rang his long toll of bells, commemorating the original members of the Foundation at around 9.05 p.m. – signal for the closure of College doors. Gowns were worn outdoors and in classes at all times and Proctors might be encountered with the 'bull-dogs,' patrolling the University at night. For my part I was immersed in two dimensions of what Oxford could afford me – study and the Christian Union. I was too poor to join the other Union and was thus excluded from political debate. My digs cost 25 shillings a week – sitting room, bedroom and breakfast. Hall dinner, when I took it, 2 shillings and sixpence. Lunch would be had in the shape of bread, cheese and a banana, conveniently to hand at the Oxford Market next-door.

A freshman in the initial year is still very much a sixth-former on a wider stage. Under the guidance of the history tutor, J. Goronwy Edwards, we were soon into *Gesta Francorum*, a Latin chronicle of the Crusades, and the inevitable Stubbs' *Charters*. Mods. was the first target after two terms, before the long, seven-term haul to Finals. The English Literature segment of Mods. was handled by a tutor from Exeter College, to whom we went in an upstairs room along Holywell. He wore pince-nez spectacles, bore the name of L. Stampa and had a nonchalant approach to our efforts on the likes of Ben Jonson and the eternal Bard. I suppose he was often bored and he usually agreed in avuncular fashion with our offerings. On one occasion a contemporary of mine was reading his masterpiece as Stampa indited a personal letter. While the reading continued he sealed the letter, affixed a stamp and rose to go down the stair well to the Post, enjoining the victim of this discourtesy to go on reading. When the latter feared he was out of earshot he ceased, only to hear a voice from below bidding him continue. Bellowing: 'Go on man!' Stampa was out in the Street. On his return from the letter-box he commented drily on a 'satisfactory' essay, leaving behind a weird memory of tutorial delinquency. He should, of course, have been reported to Exeter College, but freshmen are too timid, in their first term, to do more than acquiesce in how the venerable prove to be the unpredictable. Stampa continued to enjoy the trust of Jesus College. Dreaming spires were capable enough of housing dreaming dons.

Matthew Arnold had known as much when he wrote his *Scholar Gypsy*. In his day he saw the eternal undergraduate captive to a venerated shrine of learning satisfying the emotions with the mystique of its culture but disillusioning the mind for want of intellectual seriousness. He saw his 'gypsy' as a disenchanted youth charmed, yet betrayed, by a home of forsaken beliefs and implausible loyalties, a place that found him still desiring in the heart what must be rejected by the head. That sense of things had only been confirmed by Newman's decision to leave Oxford and foreclose his search for finality.

It was otherwise a whole century later. Oxford was growing out of 'mystery' into greater secularity. To my regret, Divers, the compulsory 'Prelim,' in Holy Scripture, had been abolished the previous year. It might still be a place of dreams, of actual or potential piety, and still commanded a *pietas* of its own, but the religiously neutral disciplines were beginning to gain the dominance which was calculated to reduce 'Divinity – that Queen of sciences' – to declining status in her counsels. It had moved far from the *Lux Mundi* ethos and the original founding of Keble College, farther still from the aura of Oriel and the first Tractarians.

The History School, as an appropriate field of University attention, had painfully established its credentials and was graced in my day by luminaries like F.M. Powicke, Sir Charles Oman, Keith Feiling and David Ogg. I became a diligent purveyor of lectures and the Radcliffe Camera, which then housed the history library, was my frequent haunt. Uncounted times I scaled the spiral stairway to the working level or the upper deck around it where one could spy upon the comings and goings of one's comrades in moments of distraction. We were encouraged to believe in lectures, though essay topics had to rely more directly on the 'authorities' on the shelves, where perhaps some of the oratorical ones should have been. Our Principal Hazel lectured eruditely in All Souls and it was a work of loyalty to attend. C.T. Atkinson at Exeter regaled us with the art of war and practised it against any female undergraduates who defied his well-aired rubric banning them. Drawing numbers in the Schools there was Godfrey Elton, of Queen's, and also G.D.H. Cole of Univ., on the 19th century and the mysteries of economics. There was naval history oddly available at St Peter's Hall (now College) then itself scarcely launched.

I had little comprehension of those who seemed to me disinterested in the work in hand. We Grammar School boys, for the most part, lacked the habits and perspectives of the Public schoolboys. There were fewer of us and we had more at stake. However, as my own admission proved, Jesus College had a growing and generous awareness of the lowlier stream of youth. I do not imply that good intentions were not equally distributed between the progenies of differing schools.

I became canny enough much later to regret that the History School was so exclusively historical and had no philosophy in its make-up to create a more questing interrogation of time and its significance. Much energy was spent on 'Constitutions' and politics. Political Science was the only chance to be acquainted with Hobbes, Locke and Rousseau, whereby to encounter the whence and whither of social institutions. The needs I was to have ten years later in Beirut were then below the horizon but my philosophical assignment there would have been less pretentious, more presentable, had Oxford anticipated it.

However, I did make one inspired choice without knowing it. There were options in the Special Subject. Instead of the popular Cromwellian topic, the remote St Augustine, or Medieval Italy, I chose the American Revolution and the Making of the U.S. Constitution. Not only was I introduced to 'the Federalist,' Hamilton, Jefferson and the throes of the Constitutional Congress in Philadelphia but I had the benign care of the Harmsworth Professor, then a gracious Robert L. McElroy, whose fine Kentucky accent added to the pleasure and profit of his classes in Rhodes House. His was the most re-assuring, caring personality I met in Oxford letters, outside my own College. His kindliness must have pre-disposed me to those American connections which – likewise uncontrived – played so large a part in my story.

My finances left little occasion outside the business in hand. Having an acute sense of the frugality expected of me by virtue of my parents' situation and my elder brother being now again a student I had little time for idleness. As for sport, College soccer sufficed. Things international had become very sombre – when we allowed them to do so – by 1933, the year of Hitler's fatal stranglehold on the German people. I did not attend, but duly noted, the famous Union Debate with the Motion that 'This house will no longer fight for King and Country.' Its passing was later supposed – surely wrongly – to have persuaded Hitler that the youth of the western democracies would prove a craven target. There was a (Communist) October Club in College toiling with that socialist sense of betrayal that dogged the prime-minister-ship of Ramsey MacDonald in his uneasy concert with the Tories. In retrospect I should have been with them had I not been schooled to thinking that the primary business of students is their studies.

ii.

All else that had schooled me made me an apt recruit for the Christian Union and in due course I became its College Representative. The O.I.C.C.U. as it was known then, and still, met for devotion on Saturday evenings and for witness on Sunday evenings, the one in the Rectory Room of old St Ebbe's, the other in St Columba's, just off the High. There were also Daily Prayer Meetings at lunch time in a Hall opposite the Union building. It was all, in part, an extension of my parish church at home. There was, however, a certain distinction, real but intangible, between those of us who came from grammar schools and those from elsewhere who were 'Crusaders' and accustomed to the class consciousness of bodies like the C.S.S.M.[2] We were, to be sure, a different vintage. Nevertheless, I remember gratefully the Union's President on my very first Saturday, speaking from 2 Corinthians 6.9: 'as unknown and yet well-known,' and going on to underline (v.6) 'by the Holy Spirit, by love unfeigned.' And so, for the most part, it was. However, I formed few close bonds with those with whom I prayed and like whom I believed. I discovered that even God's elect have foibles. In my slow-witted way their sometime aloofness did not worry me nor alienate me. The grace of God was common bond enough even without the grace of man.

Or, indeed, of woman. The four Ladies Colleges, Somerville, Lady Margaret Hall, St Hugh's and St Hilda's, brought their complement to the O.I.C.C.U., but none do I remember in retrospect even dimly. I suppose they were part of the furniture of things. Colleges were all-male or all-female and escapades were only for the wild and for the few. Porters at closed lodges had retentive memories for late-comers who had to gain admittance on the knock after Great Tom had fallen still at 9.15 p.m. My concentrations left no occasion for the amorous and no inclination. What remained unawakened did not even have to be deferred.

In summer the Christian 'unionists' preached, or at least lifted up their voices, from a bench there used to be northward of the Martyrs' Memorial as we faced St Giles, hoping to reach with 'the Word' beyond the walls of Balliol and St John's. On Sunday afternoons, we could replenish soul and body alike, either at the Bible Readings (cum tea and cakes) by W.R. Moore, who lived retired at 6, Charlbury Road in North Oxford, or at the Greek Testament readings (likewise garnished) of Dr C.M. Chavasse, Master of St Peter's Hall. These were my Sunday fare after a.m. either at St Aldate's or in Chapel.

Sunday early afternoon was the time for writing home. Not then the easy, lazy phone call. There never was a phone in my parents' home. There was perhaps a sense in which my home-loyalty, holding my heart-affection, held back my intellectual adventuring, thus postponing yet also anchoring the reckonings I would have to make. Only slowly, on and into my curacy, did I realize that loyalty has to be refined if it is to be duly fulfilled. I had opted for an academic field in which issues of faith were only latent, not vitally aroused.

The immediate form in which I had to wrestle with what we might call 'the truth-question' and 'the self-question' was shaped for me by the prospect of ordination. I did not know whether I meant it or was meant for it, whether I had either sanctioned it or believed it sanctioned. It grew on me in the very shrinking from it. I did not join the Lancelot Andrewes Society (for ordinands) in Jesus College, thus keeping my options open, but I did accept small grants-in-aid in my third year from a Clerical Education Trust, telling myself I could repay them if I did not, in the end, proceed. What a tantalus vocation proves to be! futurizing what can be presently inconclusive. I was sure and I was dubious by turns. Did others too come by decisions so indecisively? I asked myself. Was there somehow an inevitability, at once to be suspected and not to be resisted.? Even the line of retreat was complicated by others' expectations – if retreat there had to be.

Was I letting things happen by default when the supreme fault would have been not to let them happen? I have often wondered since why an alternative vocation in politics, or medicine, or education, never seriously occurred to me. Commerce like my father's would, I fear, never have availed for me or my timidity. There was, with my antecedents, only one way in which timidity might be enlisted against itself. It was what we called then 'the overseas ministry.' My elder brother somehow always knew that he was meant for English parishes. It was therefore assumed at home that I should be the one to have 'uttermost parts' in view.

I belonged to that segment of the O.I.C.C.U. which fostered such anticipation. I had inserted in my Bible a cutting from those annual Reports of the Church Overseas which appeared in the thirties[3] in which Archbishop Cosmo Lang had written: 'With whatever authority may belong to the office which I hold I lay this charge upon the honour of the Church of England.' That seemed warrant enough. Still more importantly there was the sense of the will of Christ. A sense of the world was inseparable for me from what I understood to be the heart of the Gospel. Was it not 'the whole world' which 'God so loved' by the measure of His act in Christ? I read the world in the simplest terms as a 'vacancy' for Christ, indeed more than a 'vacancy,' a territory, in part, of usurpation by alien gods, pre-occupied and needing liberation. I had no clear idea then of 'other faiths.' It was simply that humanity was 'the parish' of the Church and that a 'great commission' had been issued at the start.[4] What Paul called 'the simplicity that is in Christ' (2. Corinthians 11.3) was enough for me.[5] At home in the parish I had been familiar with the annual 'Valedictory Meetings' of those days when recruits were farewelled to the Arctic, or Africa, or Asia, not to return within five years. I had then no knowledge of the irony of a new society, formed agonizingly and unnecessarily from its parent body, and yet finding its panacea by breaking into new fields of the broken world of paganism. I knew by name all the provinces of China, through a weekly prayer calendar about them. All lands I understood were in the divine intention equidistant from the Cross yet some were effectively so far away. They had to be 'brought near.'

Even so, the same hesitations daunted me here as those that bore on ministry in general. In my final year, Joe Fison appeared on the Oxford scene, fresh from his lay service in Cairo, to be ordained to a Tutorship in Wycliffe Hall. He left his zealous mark on many undergraduates and I found his counsel re-assuring, for he had been triumphantly through the misgivings about faith and ministry with which I was struggling. There was an infectious quality about his spirit. His lively mind encouraged me to know that hesitancy could well be the mark of the authentic and that there was a courage only the fearful knew.[6]

Finals loomed ominously in the summer of 1934, eleven Papers pressed into fewer days. Warned about the danger of excessive revision I took the train to Evesham to pay a courtesy call on our eccentric Joseph Turral, lately retired from being HeadMaster in Blackpool. He lived strangely in 'Owlet's End,' and treated me with a fatherly serenity. En route, I passed unwittingly through Ascott-under-Wychwood, the village we chose in retirement long after Dr Beeching had half destroyed the railway line. Finals came and went. Dazed by the feel of vacancy that follows such climactic things, I bought a paper-back copy of Constance

Padwick's *Temple Gairdner of Cairo* and wandered into the Christ Church Meadows to peruse it, little knowing what part its author and her hero would play in my own future.

iii.

Theology and my own immediate path waited on the outcome and I cycled home to Blackpool to await it. If I took a First my College would finance me to stay in Oxford and read Theology at Wycliffe Hall. Otherwise, it would be the Theological, Missionary College which the Bible Churchmen's Missionary Society had established in Clifton, Bristol, some years before. As my tutor informed me, I was viva-ed for a First but failed to make it after forty minutes of cross-examination. Bristol, therefore, it was. At the end of the summer I came to my new academy ready for all that it could offer but with a lingering affection for what I knew I had forfeited – which explains how, as it were, I would be surveying the downs at Clifton through the window in the Turl. It seems right, therefore, to explore my pre-Ordination studies as an interlude in the Oxford connection I was later to resume and which, in a curious way, was to affect my intellectual fortunes in Beirut.

At least there was some satisfaction during the months in Bristol by the fact that I was fulfilling family expectations. My brother had studied there before completing in Durham. The College, however, had been through a trauma (in which he had participated) in the year before I arrived. Students had divided into two camps over the 'soundness' of the Principal's theology. The unhappy episode was part of that ugly pre-occupation with a Biblical literalism which had beset the Anglican missionary mind in the twenties and had led to the formation of the new society. The College had been steadied for continuity by the appointment of Principal W. Dodgson Sykes. It was perhaps natural that, with his impeccable scholarly credentials, he should take an over-cautious line.

Wholly committed to the evangelical zeal which

hallowed us all and responding warmly to new friendships, I was nevertheless increasingly uneasy about the way we were being tutored for the General Ordination Exam, (familiarly known as G.O.E. – 'God's Own Exam'). It meant that my growingly enquiring frame of mind was obliged to defer into my curacy the issues that cried out for scrutiny until Oxford came to my rescue with its Ellerton Theological Essay Prize in 1937, by the time I was in the toils of Tranmere. Our tuition was highly protective. Biblical criticism must be noted for exam purposes and otherwise dismissed. Principal Sykes had a habit, when questions were raised, of saying: 'I will give you a sheet.' Hand-outs duly appeared – in different colours for ready identification – on what it would be well to know about the Bible, the Reformation, Liturgy and Morals. There was all too little discourse between the leadership and the led, small occasion to delve together. Only two of us were graduates and many excellent recruits perhaps needed help over stiles but we were hardly fair either to the 'unsearchable riches of Christ' nor yet to the comprehensiveness of the Church of England. Dr Sykes, for better reassurance of the founders, instituted a Bible Diploma which required Papers of 'Comment on the following' type on every book in the Bible. I advanced to about twenty of the thirty-odd Papers. But the viable role of Leviticus in the Biblical scheme or the significance of Jeremiah in prophetic suffering were matters outside our brief. I cannot be sure now of my inward conflicts in those days, steeped as retrospect is in the long overlay of other times and scenes. Looking back, however, it seems right to apply to their limitations the words from *Twelfth Night*: 'I can say little more than I have studied and that question's out of my part.'[7]

It may be germane here briefly to note the sticking point in the break-away of B.C.M.S. from its parent C.M.S. It had to do with 'the truth of all Christ's utterances,' including points of historical 'fact.' At issue, too, was the question the *Lux Mundi* essayists, and Charles Gore in particular, had faced, namely whether faith in the Incarnation had to exempt Jesus from real 'belonging' in the 1st century and have us understand divinity in terms of an 'omniscience' that could free him from all contemporary norms. Gore and his colleagues believed that there was a real *kenosis* whereby the humanity of Jesus, being thus no less divine, was truly authentic in time and place.[8] The protagonists of B.C.M.S. took the contrary view. If Jesus had uttered the words: 'David called him Lord,' then Jesus had affirmed the Davidic authorship of the psalm in question – indeed of all the Psalms. At the climax of the controversy in late 1922 Bishops Knox and Chavasse laboured long and hard to find a way to reconcile the parties in unbroken communion. They failed. The rigorists did not stay to wonder whether 'David' anyway was not a name under which to denote a whole range of psaltery by a wide diversity of singers and sufferers suitably comprehended under his aura. Nor did they pause to enquire into the perplexities of the citation with its midrashic style of Hebraic discourse.[9]

Sadly the rupture came. My reluctance about Bristol would have deepened had I really known the nature of these antecedents. The perception I could only later find would have told me that they were spiritually deplorable and intellectually obtuse. In shape unknown to me then in 1934–35, the Oxford connection would serve me by another way in bringing me wisdom via Longworth, with its aura of *Lux Mundi* and the significance, in its making, of T.H. Green, the Balliol philosopher, of whom more anon.

I passed both parts of G.O.E. in four terms with several *Benes*, as grades then were, and spent the fifth term mainly doing first-aid and simple chores in the outpatients at Bristol General Hospital, supposedly equipping me for 'foreign parts.' It was all unforgivably brief and sent me forward to my curacy with lots still to be negotiated between faith and ministry, between self and the world.

The College by the downs of Clifton later became Tyndale Hall and then, by another metamorphosis, Trinity College. I am sure it is a different institution now. It had been my family's 'safe quarters' for my mind and future. I paid it warm affection for its student comradeship and the kindliness which lay behind the scruples of its teaching. We played soccer on the downs and shouted our faith on Saturday evenings at the foot of Park Street hill where one road lay several feet below another – a place where we could preach, as it were, from the pit to the gallery. We would return to college for a warm drink and to pray our message home. I had my outside duty at the Homeopathic Hospital. If there was little 'homeopathic' about the doctrine, no small dosing with the disease itself, there was sheer grateful community in Christ. In Bristol we heard that town-crier announce the death of George V and the accession of Edward VIII.

If Bristol had delayed my faith-negotiation it had, in its own way, served it. Not temperamentally belligerent, I found bearings by which to identify where the wider theological scene must lie. I found reading outside the grain of College pre-possessions, being particularly impressed with *Essays: Catholic and Critical*, perhaps because the title was intriguing.[10] Thence to William Temple's *Christus Veritas* and *Mens Creatrix*. How sane, masterly, exciting, his prose seemed to me as I recalled that one and only fleeting encounter on the Blackpool sands. I began to indulge in bolder liberties of thought, indecisively but urgently, and carried them into my curacy. I was accepted by Geoffrey Fisher, Bishop of Chester, for ordination in March, 1936, to be curate at St Catherine's, Higher Tranmere, Birkenhead. The story belongs to Chapter 3.

iv.

Here we stay with that window in the Turl and the Oxford sequels that belonged both with Tranmere and Lebanon. For, absorbing what both curacy and chaplaincy entailed, they turned on my nexus with Jesus College. It seems right, therefore, to discount mere chronology and let what happened to my faith cohere around the Oxford role – for me at least – of Ellerton and T.H. Green. What follows pre-supposes what belongs in narrative to the two chapters following.

On one of my return visits to Oxford from Tranmere I

met an O.I.C.C.U. friend who told me, in 1936, that he had been awarded the Ellerton Theological Essay Prize. I had no notion what it was. He informed that it was available for recent B.A.s of the University and that it was offered annually. 'Have a go for '37,' he suggested. I enquired what the set topic was to be and was informed: 'The Place of Authority in Matters of Religious Belief.' It was exactly what I was wrestling with anyway, so why not let the pretension of being 'the Ellerton Essayist' be the spur and the stimulus? Consistently with the constant claims of my curacy, I set to work, reading all I could, good or bad, from Newman to W.E. Orchard,[11] on this crucial theme. I did not tell my Vicar till the thing was done. I was thinking it would be a nice tribute I could pay to my University and – perhaps – hopefully it might pay to me. The parish would not suffer. Its pastoral disciplines would greatly serve.

I was innocent, almost, at that time of philosophy, but this venture was to be 'theological.' I realized that theology, like the Bible, must begin with God and with a need of faith. The individual could not start *de novo*. Who was he or she anyway to decide what should decide him or her? Necessarily we stood in a tradition, a heritage – one, certainly, to acknowledge, to esteem, to scrutinize, but *not* to ignore. Faith could not rightly be self-generating, but it needed to be self-responsible. Hence – my essay's first section – there was a *necessary* place of authority in matters of religious belief.

But where did it lie? By what could it be authentic? The answers were multiple and bewildering. The essay – second and third sections – would have to show the *improper* place and, that disowned, the *proper* place. The headings were neat enough but how to distinguish? I came to see increasingly that Christian belief (for that was what in context 'religious' meant) must be finally a matter of trust, not of guarantee. I ventured to assert that neither soul nor mind were made for infallibility. Nor, I thought, was the humanity of God. This would be true wherever the alleged infallible was thought to be – the Bible, the Pope or the sect or the inner light. Certainly the very fabric of the

Bible, the New Testament more than all, pre-supposed human partnership with divine inspiration which the latter enabled and harnessed but did not over-ride. Moreover, God had entrusted His Word to its interpreters. The text too always needed 'some one to guide' (Acts 8.31) A Scripture so far given into our discerning care could never be rightly read as a literalist blue-print, or as a telephone directory with which one would relate merely for information and never need to engage with where and why and whence it had come to be the page it was. Scripture and 'sleeping partners' could not go together and the Holy Spirit was certainly not one of them.

So given sources had to be received by minds alive to what warranted them to be such. Truth was intrinsic to itself yet of a sort to need to deserve our recognition and co-operate with our discerning tests. We should see it like the whole river – a tide of revelatory 'given' making its way up the channels made for it by the downward flow of mountain streams originating in the reasonings and yearnings of the human soul, destined as these were, for the satisfying that historical revelation brought them. Truth would be the mutual integrity of these twin dimensions.

So there could not be right allegiance that was blind, docile or merely submissive. This ruled out a facile Biblicism. It also ruled out the Papacy. For, I concluded, whatever subtleties might surround the question when the Pope spoke 'infallibly,' the whole claim to do so offended the open-endedness of faith. If, with Newman, one wanted to terminate all 'private judgement,' all personal responsibility for belief, by first identifying and then surrendering to 'the one true Church,' to eat for evermore only out of her hand, one must realize that the decision to do so was inevitably an act of 'private judgement,' a decision one had oneself made, presumably on grounds of which one had been personally persuaded. Why should not these be susceptible of steady review? Apart from the enormous complexities of the claim to 'the one true Church,' with all the tangle of historical vicissitude and the over-playing of the ecclesiological hand at the at the risk of historical integrity, there was the basic impropriety anyway of wanting certitude and guarantee where there could only be the invitation to trust and be entrusted.

It was this which the Gospel proposed. The proper place of authority would be to 'know whom (not what) I had believed.' I suggested it was *properly* there in the words: 'This is my Son, my beloved, hear him.'[12] An authority worthy to be believed had indicated the trustworthy but only in the shape of a call to trusting. Less or more than this, I concluded, authority could not properly presume to say.

The Divinity School in Oxford is an architectural wonder. It was a thrilling place to read the essay (as custom then required) in the presence of the Regius Professor, H.L. Goudge, whose guest I had previously been at lunch in Tom Quad and with whom I walked in procession to the School. Since it was a token ceremony and he and others had approved the contents, there was no need to go to the bitter end. For me it was a goal that was sweet, something I had never thought to see from my mental window in the Turl.

It was, of course, far from exhausting all the issues, some of which maturer thoughts may venture in Chapter 9. I was to bring back to Oxford what ensued from sojourn in Beirut and from the experiences Chapter 4 will investigate in that 'sifting east.' If the reader will await the details of them presently, it will be convenient to complete here the Oxford associations to which their implications led.

We had left All Saints' Church, Beirut, the American University of Beirut and St Justin's House, in mid-1847, with the open-ended expectation of return. Meanwhile my hope was to devote some time to doctoral study of the intellectual issues in contemporary Islam as I had come to sense them in student friendships in Lebanon and beyond. That intention took shape in a submission for the Oxford D.Phil. of the topic: 'Islam in the 20th Century: the Relation of Christian Theology to Its Problems.' The idea was that there were clear parallels between what Christian believers had encountered in the 19th century from the likes of Darwin, Spencer and the 'higher critics' and the experience of Muslim intellectuals in the 20th. The formulation was, as I did not then realize, improperly broad, but it covered what I saw as my obligations. The onset of the 1948/49 armed conflict between the Arab world and the new Zionist State clearly made return to the east the more remote as the House had collapsed – its students being refugees and the Bishop's resources being diverted entirely to refugee relief. The Oxford sojourn took on a more durable guise.

It happened that Jesus College had the gift of the living of Longworth, a village ten miles from Carfax, and so within statutory limits for doctoral residence. It had just become vacant by the resignation of the Revd. R. Edmunds Jones, a classical scholar, who himself thirty and more years before, had succeeded the Revd. J.R. Illingworth, host to the annual reading-party of ecclesiastical dons who in 1890 had produced the *Lux Mundi* Essays. The College appointed me to the care of the parish. A strange amalgam then began of my antecedents in Bristol and the legacy of a theological initiative within our Church with which the founders of B.C.M.S. would have had little or no sympathy. I, for my part, had never had a mind to be theologically combative, feeling too keenly 'the mystery of things,' and having at least a will, if not a formula, for 'the comprehension of comprehensiveness.' The instinct to suspect that had surrounded my boyhood had not possessed me.

In any event, we were inhabiting that same Rectory where J.R. Illingworth had entertained his guests. There were older women in the Church who could remember having been servant-girls with Mrs Illingworth and could tell me vaguely where Gore, Moberly, Scott Holland, Walter Lock, and E.S. Talbot, had slept. We named the bedrooms in their honour. The house had nine of them. My bicycle went around the same lanes, where he – as I read – had taken his on spins in which he mentally chiselled the fine, chaste sentences of his several books on divine transcendence, Christian conscience, personality human and divine, and the rest. He had suffered long from a persistent eczema which kept him from normal Oxford circles and was something of a recluse, but when he died relays of village men carried his coffin to the church which lay down the lonely lane away from the main village.

I was not awaiting them to do the same for me. I was breathing the vanished air of a home and a place which, as a recent church historian has it, was a house of great Anglican significance.[13] How were we to co-inhabit across the generations? There was, of course, the routine pastoral ministry which no Islamic study had warrant to displace. I sometimes wondered what Illingworth would have made of my immersion in the Qur'an but surmised what it might have been if he had known my Beirut and lived at St Justin's. The claims of 'other faiths' were not on the map so squarely in his day except for the likes of Frederick D. Maurice.[14]

Inspired in part by the *Lux Mundi* window erected in the sanctuary of Longworth Church by American admirers after his death, we had a 'Parish Mission of Light' in our second year. For this there was a special hymn, which had partly in mind the 'darkness' of Palestine in 1948 and our own bitter tragedy of that autumn when our tiny daughter, Joy, aged eight weeks, died in her cot, and the village came somehow together in shared grief.

'O lighten, Lord, the darkness of our age
That gropes and falters in its fear and strife:
Shine through our gloom from out the sacred page
Where lives Thy story, Christ the light of life.

Break Thou, O Christ, upon our seeking minds,
Dayspring of truth, divine Incarnate light:
Come in Thy grace as when the watcher finds
Morning's new dawn disperse the brooding night.

So may Thy dawning here within our hearts
Shame out of hiding all our evil things,
Scatter the shadows from our homes and hearths,
The soul's recesses where the darkness clings.

Till in Thy light we too our light shall see
Finding release from ignorance and sin.
In Thee made wise and in Thy truth made free,
Children of light, we shall Thy kingdom win.

Thou art, O Christ, the joy of man's desire,
Thy splendour one in manger, cross and throne,
Let Thy light burn within our selves a fire,
The warmth be ours, the glory Thine alone.'

Like its predecessor in West Hall, Beirut (see below) we sang it to the tune: 'Saviour again, to Thy dear Name we raise,' this being a favourite hymn in the parish, where – for the choir's chief baritone – 'parm' on Palm Sunday (those 'people of the – ebrews') was always 'pal'm' as the spelling required.

Rustically, therefore, we tried to belong with our heritage and with those who shared it – for it was still a legend alive. For our part in the Rectory it seemed a work of piety to comprehend it theologically. I came to see how one of the crucial pre-occupations of *Lux Mundi* had to do with appreciating the Incarnation rightly and to see, further, how this impinged on Islamic theology. It was also closely linked with the controversy that lay behind the College at which I had studied at Bristol.

Did belief in Jesus as 'divine' require the sort of exemption from the conditions of time and place that would make his being 'human' essentially unreal? The protagonists of B.C.M.S. thought so, but without conceding thereby that his being 'human' was at stake. They were one with 19th century figures like Dr Pusey and Dean Liddon – in that respect. So they made their banner: 'The testimony of Jesus Christ' as 'the Word of God' in a way that required, for example, that when Jesus quoted Psalm 110.1 (as we have seen) he had infallibly underwritten the psalm's authorship by David, 9th century King of Israel and Judah, thus dogmatically over-riding what intelligent study of the psalm would honestly need to recognize. This position not only did violence to a text, it also disallowed usages that would have been natural to Jesus understood as truly human. It meant invoking his divinity in a manner uncongenial to the truth of it.

How and why uncongenial? Because it invoked a divine omniscience inconsistent with a genuine human quality and nature. There had been a long habit, in 19th century theology, and earlier, of assuming that 'divine nature' could not be consistently understood any other way. What Charles Gore did in *Lux Mundi* was to find the 'divine' and the 'human' more congruent with each other by seeing the essentially divine in the very self-expenditure that fully and veritably undertook the human as the human truly is. 'Very God and very man' were to be seen in full compatibility as a true and real condescension. Indeed, to understand the Incarnation any other way would be to distrust that it had happened. The limitation of human-ness did not endanger, still less compromise, the divine, precisely because it was self-limitation, the action of that grace by which God is God.

The old practitioners were unconvinced, fearful that something had been forfeited, or simply loyal to an old loyalty. Others hailed the new realism as enabling fuller integrity in New Testament study and a more intelligent allegiance to the ancient Creeds. If the central mystery was the Incarnation itself, there was no need to invoke the miraculous in some arbitrary form, so that sheer credulity, rather than reverent faith, should seem to be asked of believers. Indeed, had not the Temptations in the Wilderness ruled out the merely spectacular in the appeal of the Messiah?

Christology – as the technical term goes – i.e. expressing the Christhood of Jesus as the action of God, has always been the meeting-point of two interests. The one is the study of the actual Jesus, the other the study that asks: What is involved in God being God? The first ponders a personality, a life, a ministry and a passion, death and resurrection: the second an initiative, via the first, to undertake, within our human history, that which a love, proper to God, owes (we may boldly say) to our wrongness, our need to find forgiveness and to be redeemed. To speak otherwise of the unity of God would be empty theory. Christology is the other side of divine transcendence.[15]

V.

I have run ahead of my own mental story. I could not have written thus in my early thirties in Longworth but I was already much drawn to the thought of divine *kenosis* and Philippians 2. 5–11.[16] Some thinking might shrink from it as somehow diminishing the divine but, if we saw that it was all *self*-limitation then power, sovereignty, majesty, were in no way impugned. On the contrary, to deny the utmost of love to divine Lordship would be the deeper travesty. Aligning as far as my *simplicitas* could, with the legacy of *Lux Mundi* as Longworth presented it to me, involved a curious personal coincidence. Those discusants in the Rectory sixty years before had been much influenced by the Balliol philosopher, T.H. Green. He had been a significant factor also in my own philosophy in Lebanon.[17] Without him, we would not have been in Longworth.

Green had influenced Illingworth and Scott Holland in particular. They readily acknowledged their debt to him. He gave to the latter a deep sense of moral obligation, to the former a perception of the philosophical obligations of a true theologian. R.G. Collingwood wrote of him that 'it would be hard to tell from his works which Chair he occupied.'[18] He was unusual among dons in taking active part in the civic life and social needs of Oxford 'town.' Moral philosophy was his passionate concern. He was, therefore, troubled by what he saw as the dependence of Christian theology on 'the miraculous.' He wanted the human understanding of God to be independent of any argument from what was arbitrary, i.e. not integral to the ideal of the 'divine' and a responsible ethic. Further, and on the same account, he suspected the sacramental, if, becoming sacerdotal, it hinged on 'magic' and substituted some mystical 'sanctity' for genuine ethical obedience.

When his pupil, Scott Holland, decided to be ordained their high mutual esteem gave rise to a lively correspondence. After the event, Green wrote to Holland:

> 'You must not think that I have any animosity to the clerical profession, as such . . . My own strongest interests have always drawn me towards it . . . There can be no greater satisfaction to me than to think that I at all helped to lay the intellectual platform for your religious life . . . If I were only a breeder of heretics I should suspect my philosophy.'

He warned against what seemed to him

> '. . . an ecclesiastical pseudo-virtue . . . which in its social effects may become very mischievous. It is the sanctity of men who make religion their God instead of God their religion.'

He held that belief in sacred 'events' really derived from the 'ideas of which philosophy was the intellectual expression' rather than 'the ideas from any real happening of the events.' Hence he could not subscribe to the traditional creeds, though, in worship, he 'found no alienation.' He continued:

> 'You are one of those, I believe, to whom the revelation of God does not rest on miracles, though the miracles of our Lord seem to you naturally to arise from it. That being so, there is an essential agreement between us, if only your theology will let you think it.'[19]

'If you will allow your theology to think of it' was a proviso that had often weighed with me in coping through the early forties (1940–47) with the impact of Islam. Here in Longworth, as Green essayist, I was inheriting a deep 'negotiation' from an earlier generation with whom chance, or love, had bound me. How salutary that warning about clerical deviance from moral holiness into priestly self-importance: how necessary in Christology to get the association right between event and meaning, to see the 'naturalness' (to God) of what might otherwise be thought arbitrarily supernatural, lest fine souls and intelligences, like Green, would have cause for moral and spiritual demur. My own 'negotiation' over all that could be meant and should be confessed concerning 'God in Christ,' persisted long after our four grateful years in Longworth Rectory.

Soon after our departure a noted bit of Church history, part Tudor, part Georgian, was relinquished, sold, to pass out of ecclesiastical history. We had savoured it too briefly. It had been a summer and Christmas haven to our parents, to cousins of the boys. Our youngest, Christopher, had arrived there via the Radcliffe Infirmary Maternity ward. The timbers of the floor of the ample barn had crumbled into dust but with concrete laid down it furnished an ideal venue for the village children. With the Welsh Baptist Minister presiding, we launched 'the Longworth Forum' for delectable evenings of lectures in the capacious drawing-room, by the goodwill of celebrities abounding in the Oxford region, including John Betjeman and, also unforgettably J.T. Christie, Principal of Jesus College, entrancing a rustic audience with the poetry of Browning.

We were impecunious. Clergy ordained before the launching of the Clergy Pensions Board, took one third of the benefice income on retirement. This meant an unhappy vested interest of new incumbents in the demise of their predecessors. It also encouraged long persistence in office, there being no mandatory age of retirement. Longworth Rectory, however, had an orchard and there was a local fruiterer happy to buy the crop on the trees and market it. I secured some College teaching and marked a tally of Scripture Papers every summer in the School Certificate – not the most exciting way of supplementing income. The fine old house had its water supply from the well in the garden. It required some twenty minutes manual pumping daily to get the water into the attic cistern by means of a pump of the 'cow-tail' type. The garden even boasted a fig-tree and membership of the pig club in the village was a pastoral ploy in hope of getting closer to the local folk. Alas, the pig (named Lionel) died of erisypalis contacted in the sty, which – in my ignorance – I had failed first to disinfect. Having forfeited the post-war-time bacon ration to qualify for pig-food, it was one of the minor sorrows to have Lionel's carcase carried off to feed the Berkshire hounds – the best way of disposing of a lost tenant.

My D.Phil. was duly finished in the third year of our sojourn, supervised by Dr Ernest Payne, of Regents' Park College and orally examined by Professor H.A.R. Gibb and Canon Herbert Danby. We continued a fourth year at Longworth. St Justin's House, Beirut, sadly had receded into history, a casualty of the turbulence of the Middle East. There was no immediate prospect of return. Out of the blue early in 1947 there came an invitation to go to the Hartford Seminary in Connecticut, to become Editor of its

Muslim World Quarterly and Professor in its Department of Arabic Studies. The Journal, begun by Dr Samuel Zwemer in 1911, was one of the earliest in the field of inter-faith studies, while the Seminary's 'Area Studies' including India, Africa and Latin America preceded such developments by Universities which later superseded them.

The invitation, consequent on my Oxford studies, seemed in line with their logic. We hoped that beyond the five years of that contract the way back east might have clarified, the temptation to Americanize being gratefully felt but firmly resisted. I could at least perhaps repay Robert McElroy's grace. In late August of 1951 we departed from Longworth. The warm-hearted schoolmaster, under whom our John and Arnold had begun their path to learning, and the splendid organist of Longworth Church, and others, were on the quayside at Southampton to bid us farewell on the Queen Elizabeth (1) and our trans-Atlantic adventure began. It would be thirty years before we had a home in Oxfordshire again. After Hartford, Jerusalem, Canterbury, Cambridge and Cairo would possess us, with shorter periods in Nigeria, New York, and forays in India, Pakistan and Persia.

vi.

There was, to be sure, much in the twenty years from 1931 to 1951 for which Oxford was not responsible. Tranmere and Beirut belong to the chapters that follow. There was, however, as it seems to me, something symbolic about the association of my boyhood/freshman faith and the spiritual ancestry awaiting me in Longworth Rectory. It was perhaps an incidental tribute to the capacity of the Church of England to embrace its generations in communion. By and large my early mentors had been very different from the ones I later came to hold in awe by living with their local legend. The former, like the Oxford University Press in 1889, would have found *Lux Mundi* improper for publication. John Murray, however, accepted it and it ran through ten editions in the first year.

Lapsing years have brought different moods and modes of thought. Oxford philosophy drifted far away from the idealism of T.H. Green and lost itself in the wilderness of A.J. Ayer, reducing the knowable and the significant to the poverties of logical positivism. Theology too has been chastened in World Wars and has had to respond to Bultmann, Bonhoeffer, Wittgenstein and Heidigger and the literati of 'the stream of consciousness' novel. 'The light of the world,' precisely in being so inclusive a theme and being that 'in whose light we see light,' will always be at the heart of what is the crisis of faith.

'Where is the blitheness of faith?' Scott Holland asked in his opening essay, acknowledging that faith was often 'alarmed by its own perplexity.' 'Is faith,' he asked 'incriminated by the mere fact that it is in difficulties?' What impresses the reader still is the width and the frankness of his response. 'Our faith in Christ,' he insisted, 'must determine what, in the Bible, is vital to its own veracity.' We must be ready for the questions which had not been asked at the time when the historic Creeds were answering those that had been asked. They housed for us thus far a cumulative witness to that personal reality of God in Christ which was the heart of faith's conviction – the conviction every generation must possess with its own responsible integrity.[20]

Lux Mundi had little to say, and that dated, about the interliability of the several faiths of humanity. J.R. Illingworth's essay on 'The Incarnation and Development,' alluded tersely to the phenomenon of religious worship as being universal and to the rise of founders of genius and a detectable rhythm of decay after their demise.[21] As a group of Oxford dons, gathered amid the Malvern Hills to finalize their offerings to the world, they were responding to a western concern deriving from the western trauma of Darwin and the 'higher critics.' It was hardly to be expected that they would, or could, grapple with the complexities of faiths and finality, of development and truth, as they were only to be known in ventures beyond the west. Nevertheless, as they seemed to me through my window in the Turl and common lodging in Longworth, they confirmed in me the instinct that had led me back to Oxford from the experiences explored in Chapter 4. But first there had been 'the time to embrace,' Ordination and its sequel in the parish and the heart. We can defer to chapter 9 a fuller exercise of mind about what is thus far incomplete. There was more in the loom than the intellectual threads.

Chapter 3

A Time to Embrace

i.

'I would be afraid that one day that collar would choke you,' wrote the philosopher, Ludwig Wittgenstein, to a friend in Holy Orders.[1] 'Choke' was his word. Mine certainly 'identified' me as I made my way, Sunday p.m. from Manchester to Liverpool and on by ferry and bus to Higher Tranmere, duly to be present at Evensong as 'the new Curate.' It was March 8th, 1936, my twenty-third birthday – the earliest legal moment for 'the making of deacons.' For a brief while I was the youngest deacon in the Church of England – a purely fortuitous distinction.[2] What the evening congregation thought I do not know beyond, I suppose, a hopeful surmise. Or they may have been checking my antecedents and concluding in the manner of *Love's Labours Lost*, about the curate put up to play Alexander the Great:

> 'A good neighbour, i'faith and a very good bowler, but – for Alexander – alas! you see how 'tis a little o'er parted.'[3]

Ordination had conferred the part but how would it be enacted in the place where, in the strange ecclesiastical language, my 'title' was? The Service in the Bishop's Chapel, Manchester, was simple quietness itself. There were three of us, two sent by letters dimissory from Bishop Geoffrey Fisher, not minded himself for a Lenten Ordination, rare then and rarer now. Not to be confused with 'dismissory,' those 'letters' empowered the other Bishop to ordain us together with his own single candidate.[4]

Together we 'received the office of a deacon in the Church of God.' We heard the thrilling Gospel about 'loins girded and lamps burning' as of men 'waiting for their Lord.' We answered the several interrogations about believing ourselves 'truly called,' and finding 'in the Holy Scriptures all things necessary to salvation.' We pledged ourselves to discipline in personal life and ministry in terms appropriate to our *diakonia* in Christ. The slow maturing of my boyhood nurture, via Oxford and Bristol, through all the self-doubt and inner diffidence that had seemed to me inseparable from its validity, had received its formal seal and mandate. I knew it for a watershed, and yet I knew the analogy was false. For all that had tentatively, progressively, urged me towards it would gather what momentum it could, only in the forward flow that Tranmere would provide. Was it not in the very nature of ordination that naivete would yield to ripeness only in the going? I knew that something radical had happened, that it belonged with love to Christ and that, in purposefully enlisting all the future, it would live and happen only in the present – the present of Christ's 'real presence.' It was, in truth, 'a time to embrace.'

'The office and work of a priest in the Church of God' was to follow fifteen months later in Chester Cathedral, Geoffrey Fisher 'laying hands' on eight of us on Trinity Sunday, 1937. Had I known of John Donne's *Sonnets* at that time how well both occasions would have found my mind fitted to his words, the lines he addressed to one 'Mr Tilman after he had taken Orders.'

> 'Thou whose diviner soul hath caused thee now
> To put thy hand unto the lowly plough . . .
> What bringest thou home with thee? how is thy mind
> Affected in the vintage? Dost thou find
> New thoughts and stirrings in thee? and, as steel
> Touched with a loadstone, dost new motions feel?'

The poet phrased it all romantically and Tranmere had no claim to be more than a prosaic place. Yet he was right to press the question:

> 'Art thou the same material as before,
> Only the stamp is changed but no more?'

and right too in his high conclusion about the dignity he interrogated:

'Ambassador to God and destiny . . .
. . . to keep heaven's door.
Mary's prerogative was to bear Christ, so
'Tis preachers' to convey Him.'[5]

Time would have to tell. Did not the Latin Canon of the Mass have participants say: *Audemus dicere: Pater Noster.*? If it needed daring even to say the Lord's Prayer, how much more the word of grace, of absolution, of benediction and of peace – 'the Word of truth', 'in season and out of season.'?

It always seemed to be 'in-season' at St Catherine's. A sprawling parish of some 17,500 souls, it comprised packed rows of terrace houses between Borough Road, Birkenhead and Mersey Park with a rather more élite area, known as Devonshire Park, which took us down to the edge of 'Tranmere Rovers,' with whom we had no chaplaincy. There was a large Hospital next door and an Institute on the opposite side of the road which housed numerous activities. Half of the population soiled their hands, it was said, at Cammell Laird's shipyard on the River Mersey, while the other half made soap for them to wash in at Port Sunlight up the stream. The ridge of 'Higher Tranmere' commanded a fine view of the river and Liverpool beyond, with the majesty of the Cathedral of Liverpool slowly emerging on the skyline as the builders progressed.

There was a strong liturgical tradition from the previous régime and organizations in great profusion – two Sunday Schools, a Mother's Union branch, a lively Men's Fellowship, a Young people's Sunday p.m. Service, with a weeknight counterpart, a children's Monday Club, a Scout Troop (all levels) and a strong Boys' Brigade. There was also a steady Choir and a Day School up to the age of eleven, where the clergy functioned. Sundry smaller units fostered interest in ministries outside the parish and into the world, including the Industrial Christian Fellowship. There was disappointment in the Vestry if the congregation at Sunday Evensong fell below some four hundred and fifty. At the great Festivals of Christmas and Easter, Holy Communion took place at 6, 7 and 8 a.m. and with Morning Prayer.

The Parish Magazine was a sturdy monthly organ of these diverse activities and a busy forum of ideas and views.

To borrow a coinage anticipating Chapter 9 ahead, there was – one could say – a great 'on-behalf-ness' about the whole Church. It was vigorously there on behalf of the population in loyalty to the ancient Anglican principle of territorial liability for every soul alive within its bounds, for their due 'rites of passage' and the ministries that properly belong with them. There were visits to be made prior to baptism, interviews with intending brides and grooms and being with the bereaved in the immediacy of their grief and through its long aftermath.

This 'on-behalf-ness' derived from that divine counterpart in 'God in Christ,' the 'on-behalf-ness' which had brought the eternal Word into wordless babyhood, the man Christ Jesus to the cup in Gethsemane and the anguish of the Cross. We were only informants of the wondrous self-expenditure of God and called into conformity in our human selves. Ministry had to be an extension of the ever-brooding, ever-caring Holy Spirit taking of 'the things of Christ' so translating 'Emmanuel' into the homes and hearts of a crowded tiny patch of the world He had 'so loved.' The two 'on-behalf-nesses' came together most of all in Eucharist, in the sharing, one and all, of 'bread and wine.'

ii.

At the helm of this ample ship of grace was the Vicar, Henry Hill. He had come to Tranmere from Bristol, his native heath, five years before I joined him. He was in the warm prime of an energetic, compassionate, and genial ministry. I think we kindled to each other at my first coming for interview just before Christmas, 1935, though he told me he liked people to look one another in the eye ('the eyes negotiate') more than it was my self-deprecatory habit to do. My Principal at College in Bristol advised me, for obscure reason, to look elsewhere but I am for ever grateful that I trusted my own judgement. A fellow-Oxonian, Henry Hill was ready to commend me to the Bishop of Chester for ordination the coming Lent and I accepted. Was it that 'hill' and 'crag' seemed a likely combination, just as years later, singing the *Benedicite* at Longworth the 'Dews' and 'Frosts' were there in the pew, in the persons of a local family and the Churchwarden?

He was, I know, disappointed that I was not musical and he gave me to know that while the matter was good the sermon voice needed more variety. It was only later that Arabic made me realize what range the human tongue can command which normal English users never utilize. I took piano lessons locally and even bought a concertina in hope to be more adequate in leading worship and concerting street preaching for which, around those crowded streets, there were many occasions. But it was no use: the ear, the fingers, were not there. It is well to accept one's limitations.

These, however, were no bar to a growing friendship and mutual trust in which I aspired to a sort of 'Timothy status' with his leadership. We took a bus one day to Mold and spent a winter's day on the slopes of Moel Fammau. The Vicarage was a kindly haven after Evensong on Sundays until he or Mrs Hill would say, pretending some slip of the tongue: 'Must you stay, can't you go?' and I would repair to my 'rooms and board' at twenty-five shillings a week. The salary began at £220 a year, rising to £240 in the third year. The Vicarage was some hundred yards down Church Road on the opposite side from the Church. On Sundays, to mark the day as festive, he had the custom of wearing a tall, silk hat which he doffed in almost Dickensian style, as he greeted the converging worshippers.

Unlike some evangelicals, he did not hold aloof from other clergy but participated fully in Deanery Chapters, bringing his fellowship within a conceded comprehensiveness. This lesson stood me in good stead in later years. We had cordial relations with the neighbouring Methodists whose Chapel was affectionately known as 'the Pepper Pot' – for its architecture, not its temper. The Vicar's sermons were almost conversational in their directness, at least to me, wrestling at the time (as already recounted) with the vexed issues of authority and the credentials of truth. In the Lent of my introduction to the parish he was in the midst of a Lenten programme of 'lantern sermons' projecting the now long obsolete and cumbersome 4 by 4 slides of 'Pilgrim's Progress' and the like. We were still far from the banality and jadedness of the TV age. Parade Services of the Scouts and Boys' Brigade – in healthy rivalry – meant trumpeting processions to and fro.

The Vicar was a tireless visitor. When he wrote to me in Manchester before that crucial Sunday, he told me he was writing at 9 p.m. in the Vestry after several hours on the beat. On normal afternoons we went together, taking opposite sides of the road, armed discreetly with small cards (for filing) which could be almost hidden in the hand. On them would be merely the name of the householder, culled from Stubbs Directory and possibly out of date – for there was much mobility and a shifting population. But a name would at least give us a start and further data could be gleaned in conversation. On one such visit, he told me afterwards the following exchange occurred:

> H.H. 'I'm the Vicar from St Catherine's – your parish church. Called to say Hello! to let you know we're there and always hope to see you with us.'
> Householder: 'Oh!'
> H.H. 'Sorry, I'm not sure of your name' questioningly.
> She, curtly: 'Fortune.'
> H.H. 'I'm speaking to Mrs Fortune?' still enquiringly.
> She. 'No, Miss Fortune.'

The rest of the colloquy is unrecorded.

If we found adherents of other churches we wished them well, or left a Magazine, or a note about some impending event, and hoped to leave a sense of unity in Christ. Our main concern was the vast army of the unchurched, fewer then, no doubt, than now but still a deep anxiety to the pastoral mind. These visits would sometimes reveal the incidence of dire poverty, crippling loneliness, marital tension or child suffering. Baptisms might be one sequel or recruitment into one or other of the several interest groups the Parish had to offer. Ministry revealed itself to me as a lively form of openness to the human situation as it was in the fabric, or the chaos of ordinary lives. The Lord surely loves the minor characters having made so many of them. I came to see that Christ wanted from us and within us a kind of 'vicariousness' that engaged us for His sake with the commonality of life around us.

It was here that the 'collar' that might have 'choked' in fact availed to liberate. Ordination had been to 'the office' of ministry and I never ceased to shrink from the notion that faith and care could ever be 'official.' Any professionalism about 'Holy Orders' must surely be suspect. However, given that constant vigilance against distorted status, being entrusted with 'the part,' one had to let it take one over, yielding one's timid privacy into its public warrant. It rightly mattered to people that I was accredited, that I came to them from something organic which had been there long before me and would endure after me. Yet that abiding institutionalized concern of God with man and of man with God truly needed and recruited all that any 'I' could consecrate to its ends, even me with my Lancashire diction, my questing faith and all my idiosyncrasies. 'O'er parted' it might well be in respect of the Gospel of our Lord. Yet it was in the very nature of that Gospel to im'part' itself over 'the low lintel of the human heart.' Had it not been this way at the beginning with Mary, Mother of the Lord?

> 'We too (one cried) we too,
> We the unready, the perplexed, the cold,
> Must shape the Eternal in our thoughts anew,
> Cherish, possess, unfold . . .
> It is our passion to conceive Him thus,
> In mind, in sense, within our house of life . . .'[6]

– which brings me back to Harrowby Road, Thompson Street and Well Lane.

It brings me back, too, to the 'churching of women.' I imagine there are few so devoted to the incomparable Book of Common Prayer who would wish to retain that piece of it. Being next to a large Hospital with its Maternity Ward, our Church had to minister to what can only be called 'folk religion.' Regularly around 10 a.m. or otherwise by appointment, mothers would be discharged with their babies and immediately turn into St Catherine's for that 'office' of 'churching.' Did it exist on the basis of some superstition or was it a genuine giving of thanks? In the latter event, how incongruous to have it in utter womanly loneliness, with neither husband nor family to share in the gratefulness. And the 'Order' provided in the wisdom of Cranmer, or whoever devised it, spoke of 'the great danger of childbirth,' which had, no doubt, been formerly real, but even in the thirties had become less so. And it invited recital of Psalm 116 which had, to be sure, some wonderfully proper sentiments: 'Return then unto thy rest O my soul, for the Lord hath dealt bountifully with thee.' But it had some grievously improper ones. Why was a mother invited to say in that context: 'All men are liars.'? And what could she make of: 'Precious in the sight of the Lord is the death of his saints?'

It was perhaps here more than anywhere that I first sensed the painful ambivalence about so much in Hebrew psalmody and the Biblical Scriptures and began to wonder about the 'unity' of the Bible. Its texts would sustain one most fittingly and truly, but at times they would either obscure the meanings of Christ or leave one in dazed perplexity. I could defer the issue in Tranmere but not after I had come to measure Jerusalem. In the midst of sublime praise one would come upon emphatic enmity, or spiritual élitism as the psalmist savoured divine favouritism, or habitually identified his own enemies as also God's.

The Vicar normally took the 'churchings,' but from time to time, shrinking, they fell to me. There was, of course, opportunity in every extremity. One could find human rapport, enquire about the home, invite to more adequate, less superstitious, thanksgiving, and hopefully commend name, address and the 'good news,' rather than 'the great danger' of childbirth to the local parishes of the mothers. Yet over all the travail I had about this 'office,' one had to remember that there was a like superstition in the notion of *barakah* which brought those 'mothers of Salem' to Jesus long ago, for his 'touch' which might 'insure' their children against disease and 'the evil eye.'[7] Had he not over-ruled the disciples and said: 'Suffer them to come to me,' meeting them in the superstition his censure-minded inner circle had properly wanted to reject?

There was another grievous feature of my curacy, namely the week-long 'cemetery duty' at Flaybrick Hill or Bebington. This was a task which harshly underlined the reality of the 'unchurched.' The parishes of the deanery had to supply clergy to await any funerals that might be coming to the municipal graveyards. It was assumed by undertakers that some parson would be in attendance. Waiting in those cemetery chapels one could ruminate on the full measure of our corporate failure – we 'the priests of the Lord,' weeping now, not Joel-like, 'between the porch and the altar,' but between the unfrequented pew and the tenanted bier. One had no knowledge of the parties, of the deceased or the bereaved. The fact that the nexus was routine, perhaps on their side casual, proved that faith was either inarticulate or absent. Yet there they were in the crisis of death and grief, in a loaded and perhaps fleeting, contact with the things of God and the Christian comprehension of death and life. That clause 'as our hope is this our brother/sister doth' assumed deep proportions. Who could know?

One could at times surmise and glimpse how to relate the meaning of grace to the tenseness of the moment by the 'feel' of the congregation or any details one had been able to elicit from the undertaker in those brief moments of necessary manoeuvres around the hearse. If there were not a following funeral in the day-sheet, there would be time to mingle with the mourners on their way from the grave. One could, of course, commend them to their home parishes or even undertake some pastoral relation anyway. But how one yearned that the 'rite of final passage' might be more perceptively fulfilled. 'No man is an island . . . every man's death diminisheth me . . .' but why were we as a church as little 'involved in mankind' as these funeral occasions made us painfully to know? Why had we, or secularity, or both, made them to drift so far, or to want us only for a ceremony? There was for me in Tranmere nothing more desolating than 'cemetery week.'

Years later in my Pennine parish in the late seventies, there was a similar pattern at Huddersfield crematorium.

There was, however, far less incidence of such 'unknown' funerals. Moreover, there was a bi-annual service at the crematorium at which the families of all those involved in the previous six months were invited to attend. A great majority did so and the occasion was a grateful opportunity to reflect more deeply. I believe this was later discontinued by consent of clergy.

iii.

My main stay in all these perplexities in ministry was Henry Hill himself, his comradeship and experience. Only later did I realize that I had been partner to a crown of a career. He literally spent himself in Tranmere and eighteen months after I left for Beirut, he moved to St Luke's, Hampstead, where after a brief sojourn he died of cancer in 1941. Untrumpeted in the counsels or annals of the Church, he was a sterling exemplar of the stuff of which she is made, the very pulse of her durability. When by 1956 *The Call of the Minaret* was published it was imperative I dedicate it to his memory in company with Bishop Graham-Brown of Jerusalem, whom I had found, in the interval my second 'father in God.' I believe they, beyond the veil, were happy in the association.

We junior clergy in the Chester Diocese had more formal and official nurture from the Examining Chaplains, for whom we wrote sermons – submitted, not for their good but for ours, by way of comment and criticism. Bishop Tubbs, among them, Dean of Chester and former Bishop in Rangoon, enjoined me to remember that more of my hearers read the *Daily Sketch* than did *The Times*, i.e. 'Be sparing with theology.' He was unaware of that business with the Ellerton. Another Chaplain was Michael Ramsey, with whom I was destined to be so deeply involved in Canterbury when he was Archbishop and I was Warden of the Central College. I have no record of any communication from him in Lincoln where he was then Sub-Warden of the theological College, but I have no doubt he reported to the Bishop.[8]

Another ministry of the Diocese to us was Retreat at Hawarden, at one of which I came to know George Appleton, then on leave from Burma, who guided our meditation. How we drew in the aura of Gladstone in that place with his immense energies as repute told them and his strange habits of self-flagellation in struggle with his own sanctity. It was in retreats that I was squarely confronted with the subject of 'confession,' which – anyway – neighbouring parish usages had not allowed me to overlook. Was 'general confession' in the offices all that was rightful for the self and 'general absolution' in the liturgy the sum of priestly duty: '*He* pardons and absolves . . .' How were those 'who truly repent' properly to know themselves as such? I knew that the questions went deep and that a dismal sequence of 'sinning and repenting' only inwardly had somehow to be halted sacramentally. But could it be halted in what Protestants derided as 'auricular confession,' listing one's self-reproach into a hidden, official, absolving ear? I was keenly aware that such self-narration might only need yet another 'confession' to acknowledge the hidden satisfaction of it, the sense of self which must always attend on self-abnegation. Simone Weil tried the utmost in self-detachment to the point of dire austerity, but it was well observed of her that 'she was not detached from her detachment.'[9] Aside from this secret 'rift within the lute,' the compromise of congratulation over 'confession,' how was one to do justice to what Emily Dickinson described as 'the cellars of the soul.?'[10] I had not yet heard of Scott Holland among those famed *Lux Mundi* 'Luxites' of the previous Chapter but had I done so, I think I would have concurred with what he wrote:

> 'I cannot conceive myself using confession without putting myself in relation to sin in a way to confuse it . . . All sort of motives would be creeping about me, intricate tanglings, my taking colour from what was around me . . . I have an obstinacy of reserve in me with which I can come into contact with God but cannot let it suffuse itself through communication.'[11]

Here my faith and ministry were negotiating with one of

life's most urgent issues: 'Create in me a clean heart, O God.' I had my own share of inner compromise, sins of body, mind and soul. Was I incriminated the more in not trying to put them into so many words in another's hearing? Or would that exercise be only a device, even a pitfall? And what of my being on the hearing end of another's effort to come clean? How could I detach the active role of private absolution from the private knowledge of the identical need of it?

Counsel, by all means, and many were the occasions to venture it, and assurance of divine forgiveness in the context of a will to 'no-subterfuge' about that hidden self. But could one honestly believe that it could ever be truthfully 'unhidden'? In the Canterbury context years later, I acknowledged the wisdom of the dictum about priestly confession: 'All may, none must, some should,' and there was always the solace of knowing that there would always be clergy confidently affording to the faithful what my reluctance – I will not say 'withheld' – but could not cherish.

The Diocesan, beyond the parochial, factor quite properly made me aware of the issue of 'the Reserved Sacrament.' It may be assumed that we did not 'reserve' the elements at St Catherine's. The practical needs of 'the Communion of the Sick' could be cared for either by taking the bread and wine, where feasible and without undue delay, directly from the sanctuary thus underlining the sense of the fellowship there for absentees, or by consecration of the elements in the sick room. This too might take more of our time, but fulfill what our time was for, as a 'means of grace.' But reservation with a view to adoration was to misread the very nature of Holy Communion. To make a spectacle was to negate a sacrament. 'Take and eat, take and drink' – these commands were inseparable from the meaning of the Eucharist.[12] There would be an implicit idolatry in elevating, carrying around with attendant genuflections, that which belonged essentially with the food analogy of faith. The 'Presence' such veneration might acknowledge was to be known, as of old in Emmaus, 'in the *breaking* of the bread.' What was then for *witness* was surely the wounds alone.

Such firm conviction, however, was not called to be quarrelsome about what it disallowed. Remember the mothers of Salem! There could be a sense that 'means of grace' could be, for pities' sake, where our fallibility believed to find them. Nevertheless, such tolerance of diversity gave no liberty to be party to what was liable to be a travesty.

Ministry, for good or ill, and given the long vicissitudes of the history that had transmitted it, could not be exempted from misconception. In negotiating my way through all these usages and the asperities they might sometimes generate, I became sure that priesthood should be vigilant against pretension. One feature of sacramentalism in Tranmere which rejoiced me as authentic was that at Holy Communion we did not retain the chalice in our priestly hands as if it did not truly belong with all. The old rubric anyway had charged us to deliver it 'into their hands.' With those who were handicapped or frail it was another matter, but otherwise would one preside over a hospitable table at home and hold cup in one's own hands to the lips of a guest? The chalice only belonged with us because it belonged with them. Retention by the priest *might* symbolize that it was theirs on sufferance or essentially a perquisite of ours. The matter might perhaps be inconsequential but once one had perceived the danger insistent one had to be.

Our nurture by the Examining Chaplains proceeded in guided reading on which essays were required. We were commended to Kenneth Kirk's *The Vision of God* (abridged), Peter Green's studies on moral problems and Hastings Rashdall: *Conscience and Christ.* For my own part I purchased *Northern Catholicism*, a volume commemorating in 1933 the centenary of Keble's Assize Sermon., the accepted signal of the Oxford Movement. I found myself asking then, and since, how he could interpret the reform of the iniquitously immoral revenues of the Irish bishoprics a fit occasion for lament at 'secularization,' and of defence of the rights of 'the ark of God' against unholy hands, or argue distressfully that herein was an occasion concerning which (as his text went) he would 'not cease to pray' for the legislators of the deed.[13] There was much here for me of inner negotiation with conscience and truth. In the light of the textual context, was Samuel not at odds with himself in peevishly denouncing fledging Jewish kingship yet loftily accommodating it? Who was to know what tensions of *amour propre* lay behind his handling of the issues as the chronicler conveyed them? Was the Church fighting for its due order on the right front vis-à-vis the State? Was Catholic Emancipation four years earlier something reprobate? Had the Church no valid, forward-looking cognizance of all the implications of a reformed House of Commons after 1832? Was Keble conniving with damage-containment when 'damage' deserved a wiser analysis? All too often the Church, for its own truth's sake, had had to concede ground it once thought it vital to defend. Had 1833 a discerning celebration in 1933? It might have been better to opt for the date of Keble's publication of his *Hymns for the Christian Year.* 'New every morning is the love' and 'Blest are the pure in heart' meant more to me than 1 Samuel 12.23 and Keble's effort to rest 'National Apostacy' upon it. Or was I, in fact, just 'a turbulent deacon.'? Essays anyway were not required on *Northern Catholicism*. Perhaps I have said too much about the 'turbulence' of my mind. There was solace in the young people and one in particular.

iv.

It was natural that the youth of the parish should be my special care with Henry Hill in fatherly supervision. The Young People's Service Fellowship consisted of a Sunday p.m. worship and a Thursday evening theme and discussion. The annual calendar-card of the latter (October to June) had four panels: Facing Life, Facing Christ, Facing Life with Christ, Facing Life for Christ. The first was meant to deal with issues in the current scene, social, political, sexual, ethical; the second with faith and commitment; the third with devotion and prayer; the fourth with mission and practical discipleship. The aim throughout was to draw each and all to personal faith in Jesus as Saviour and Lord, and then to grow in all that such conviction demanded of us. Confirmation preparation and post-Confirmation care moved within it. We ranged widely and meant earnestly. The shadows of Nazism grew darker around us, and gas-masks were distributed in schools with their sinister profile on the unknown. *Videmus nunc in aenigmata*, said the Latin of 1 Corinthians 13.12 and perhaps it would always be that way. We had to live in the present.

A party of the Y.P.S.F. attended the Keswick Convention of July, 1937, girls in a rented house, boys in a field-camp. We ran a Boys' Camp in Conway for the younger fry and in the summer of 1938 ventured on a Beach Mission in Penmaenmawr. When C.S.S.M. declined to sponsor us we made our own banner: 'Children's Services' and spent two weeks 'evangelizing,' the girls and women of the party in housing, the boys again in camp. It was here that some began their own initiation into witness. Two members of my years later found their way to ordination, while a third, with whom I spent hours in New Testament Greek, later joined the local Brethren Hall and became a missionary in Singapore. Vicar Hill came to the grand finale on the beach to vet and bless our fledgling efforts, a Tranmere by the sea.

My pledge about 'overseas' was never out of mind in the parish as the end of my three years or so came in sight. The final location, however, was far to seek and the quest passed through many vicissitudes too tedious for rehearsal here. The sphere turned in part upon the auspices and about these I was long unclear. In the event it was agreed that I should pursue my ministry within the jurisdiction of the Bishop in Jerusalem and within the British Syrian Mission and its Bible School. The dual setting needed careful definition and entailed one major crisis. This being weathered and the course set fair, my plans were made to depart for Lebanon before the end of January, 1939. The Bishop of Chester gave me his blessing – he had, as I was later to discover, a formidable elder sister (he being the last of the Fisher siblings) in Palestine, who became, affectionately, '*the* archbishop' as soon as her brother did.

The parish farewelled me with a massive Arabic Bible, a

Hebrew New Testament and a French Bible, all suited to a task ahead. I was able to present my anticipations, with lantern slides, to a crowded gathering and for my farewell sermon chose the words of 2. Corinthians 2.3: 'My joy is the joy of you all.' The time of one embrace had ended to give way to another in the Middle East, lasting, with interludes into the eighties. Between them there was a third. It was decisive to all else.

V.

Locomotion around Tranmere was always by bicycle. Neither the Vicar nor I possessed cars. Bus and ferry were available for quarries further afield. When I went to Penmaenmawr for the July mission of 1938, I went by tandem bicycle. The rear saddle was not vacant. Melita pedalled with me. We had discovered each other in the parish – a risky thing to do. It is usual in narratives like the present one, to enthuse briefly over personal romance, to assume that every one knows what one ought to be discreet enough to leave to silence. Readers do not want to be told what they can well imagine nor to be told again how wonderful love was – and is.

Let me not imply that love-discovery was other for us than what it has been a myriad times. Yet if we are exploring how faith and life negotiate, love, too, demands to be explored as bearing crucially on both. In times when so much is 'betrayed with a kiss,' the kiss of casual sexuality in treachery to genuine love, it is urgent to affirm, from within, the mysteries of marriage and what it meant to me to say, as it were, with Dickens' David Copperfield: 'She filled a vacancy within my heart which closed upon her.'

In current terms the workings of my mind may seem odd and unduly deferential to family and vocation. I could never feel that embracing ministry and embracing love were separate things. The second ought certainly to be deferred until the first had been transacted. Only after 'priest's Orders,' the rubric ran, lest studies and discipline should be disturbed. I had been ordained priest at Trinity,

1937. There was no need to be precipitate about the liberty to act but by 1939 I would be due to go overseas. Two things mattered to me. The one was that it was right for my parents to know and meet and love my destined partner. The reader may exclaim: 'How improperly solicitous!' To me it did not seem so. My parents were in their sixties, my mother a victim of chronic rheumatoid arthritis, allegedly contracted after my birth. I did not know what might obtain, via Hitler or circumstance, by the mid-forties.

My other concern was that I could not invite a partner into my life in mission unless she had an independent sense of that vocation. I had been given to believe that 'a call' should not depend upon affection, but rather stand in its own credentials. Perhaps I was wrong in this – in assuming that authentic calling might not emerge from original attraction. My faith was negotiating with itself over the deepest things and that was how it went.

Let it not seem from this preamble that my love moved only by this logic. Quite the contrary. I discovered a love that allowed of both provisoes but lived by its own warrant. It grew upon me during the summer of 1937. I was twenty-four, Melita twenty-two. The point came when my thoughts needed to be told her. I did not know if, but suspected that, they would be returned. She had been recruited to the Sunday School teaching for which I was responsible. I sensed we could, hopefully, be one in the mathematics which reckons one plus one as one. I decided to venture but with discretion proper to the Parish scene, the Vicar being away on holiday.

She came at my request to the Vestry one Saturday 'to talk about mission' a fair enough ambit. I asked her about vocation and when she confirmed it I said: 'Do you think we might fulfil it together?' It was a sacred moment, the glow of which remained through all the years. A small pad lay on the Vestry desk. I wrote on separate sheets the same words: 'Father, glorify Thy Name' from our Lord's prayer in John 12.28. We each signed each of them and we each kept one. Mine now lies with her grave, battered with the years of wallet-care. We talked more and went away to wonder and to ponder.

When we met some ten days later everything was affirmative. A difficult way lay ahead. By the following April she would need to resign her secretarial job and embark on College studies. Her father, John Wesley Arnold, a Liverpool city-missionary, had died earlier in 1937. Fees would be a problem. Her mother was ready, but also loathe, to yield up a younger daughter to an overseas vocation. The issues of where and how, in which I was currently involved, involved her also and us both mutually. One enquiry she made produced a firm negative on medical grounds because of a serious childhood illness. She sent me a note with the harsh news which simply read: 'We said we were willing: we must prove so.' Putting everything in the balance this note, nevertheless, endeared her to me the more. The morning I received it I wandered around Tranmere like a piece of driftwood on the sea. Holding our motto in place we had to hold ourselves in abeyance through several weeks. At length, as noted already, my own destination clarified. Without this love-intrusion into the story the Middle East it would never have been. I owed entirely to her the destination that was to mean so much in the pattern of our lives.

Paradoxically, the uncertainties played a crucial part in our one certainty and things began to fall into place. Melita began her studies at Mount Hermon College, in Streatham in late April, 1938, two years from which would bring her to the spring of 1940, by which time – it was anticipated – I would have passed a whole year and more in initiation in Lebanon. We were engaged coincidentally with her departure for College, at Easter 1938, so that there could be some formal juncture about our finances.

It meant, alas, the separations which were so often to be required of us by the exigencies of what united us. My occasional trips to Streatham deepened our authenticity, and there came the tandem riding and the delectable summer including Penmaenmawr. In the interludes of the beach mission, we roamed the hilly hinterland. With autumn came another separation and my chance, amid the alarums of Munich, to be closer to Mother Arnold in her Tranmere homestead, helping her to batten down against the possibility of air raids. Christmas re-united us before my departure for Lebanon at the end of January. I had the satisfaction of knowing that Melita was thoroughly and mutually at home with my family, via numerous excursions to Blackpool and that my parent's home would be part of her fortitude during the long deferment of marriage we knew to be necessitated by the calendar the mission set for us. Indeed, at the time of my departure, she had not been formally accepted, pending College completion, but the Mission knew that I would no longer be available to them in the event she did not follow.

We travelled to London together on the Monday after my final Tranmere Sunday, she to return to Streatham, me to entrain for Trieste, there to board my Italian boat for Beirut. At the Swiss/Italian border stop – assured that there was time – I left the train to mail a card to her, only to find the train departed when I returned. My baggage had gone on ahead to be retrieved at Milan when I caught up with it. Such are the escapades of the love-lorn. What happened after the voyage comes in Chapter 4, though there was one grievous crisis, not *about* us but *around* us, which I defer to chapter 11.

Sixteen months elapsed before Melita reached Beirut in May, 1940, via the last ship to do the crossing from France before Italy's entry into the War closed the Mediterranean to all civil shipping. It was a narrow thing. The Mission's requirement about Arabic study involved a further postponement, with the one of us in Jerusalem completing that, the other in Damascus awaiting it. There was one final hitch. The French Consul in Jerusalem, tense with the Vichy régime in Syria/Lebanon after the Fall of France, at first denied me a visa to return. Jerusalem or Beirut – which would the venue be? Who should travel where? Happily the Consul relented. Melita and I were at last wedded in All Saints' Church, Beirut, our beloved Graham-Brown officiating, on December 31st, 1940, three years and five months after our first conditional troth, its pre-marriage anticipations fulfilled, its weddedness all ahead. The wonder had precariously eventuated in a world at war. We were painfully aware of the risks and costs of our survival.

We made the first of our homes in a rented house alongside the Lebanon Bible Institute in Shimlan, and were immersed in the double trust of the School and of All Saints Church, Beirut. In late June came the evacuation of civilians from Lebanon and we found ourselves part of the Church Missionary Society's Hospital in Gaza where our first-born, John, arrived. Arnold, his first brother was born two years later in Beirut, by which time we had begun the Palestinian Hostel at the University. Not till July, 1948, did they acquire a tiny sister, Joy, of Longworth, born in the historic Rectory and tragically leaving us after eight fleeting weeks to lie in Longworth Churchyard. Christopher was born in Oxford nearly three years later and half a year before we departed for Hartford, Connecticut, U.S.A. By that time we had contrived four very different housings and some eleven more would follow. It would be tedious to list them merely for a catalogue. The wonder was the partnership and how successive jobs and ministries, for the most part, demanded both of us.

That in Gaza was perhaps the most demanding. A rented flat, within walking distance of the Hospital, it fronted on to the Hisham Mosque. Pacing that distance together under a full harvest moon the night when mother-labour was beginning remains vivid in my memory. The flat was a haven for cockroaches. We would find them when we entered with the lamp from the street. It was a routine chore to despatch them with a hefty shoe wielded like a hammer. Baby hygiene was not easy in that setting. Through the years of hostelry in Beirut the common hearth (if we may so speak of wood-burning stoves) of budding students and tiny youngsters was benediction. Home-making was something we were allowed to learn by much varied practice as exigencies demanded. But reminiscence must here give way to reflection. How should faith, literally, negotiate, interpret, understand, receive this sweet, incredible, overwhelming thing that marriage constituted, the mystery life was granted as in trust?

vi.

The Lord, as Isaac Singer somewhere observed, may have been all too frugal in giving us humans intelligence, He was surely generous, even prodigal, in giving us passions and emotions. Those which belong physically and sacramentally (the adverbs inter-hold) with our sexuality are the most intimate and enlivening of all. This we knew in the strange reverence, the blissful tenderness, which possessed us mutually when 'our eyes' – and so much else – 'negotiated there.' How the world became a different place because the other was in it. How it has not been the same place since death supervened to terminate the fifty-one years, from troth to parting, both at Easter. What is this meaning that inheres in touch and sight, in embrace and intercourse? How does the possessed belong in the possession, the giver in the given? Perhaps the clue was never so expressed as in Shakespeare's lines:

> 'So they loved, as love in twain
> Had the essence but in one:
> Two distincts, division none:
> Number there in love was slain . . .
> So between them love did shine,
> Either was the other's mine . . .'[14]

'Each the other's mine' – how right that can be through a whole life of loyal union in which – as with us – the entire sexuality of each is held for the other, undiverted, unbetrayed, in total mutual reliance, and all set within what is revered, acknowledged, joyfully accepted, as the economy of God. So, at least, was our negotiation with the mystery we had come to know when we knew each other as two in love, and as we 'knew' each other in the sense the Bible meant in telling us that Adam 'knew his wife,' (Genesis 4.1) or Paul in his counsel to the Christians in Thessalonica (1 Thess. 4.4).

For, in Christian marriage, the partnership of love bestows on either party a status, a dignity, a quality (in the old Latin sense) so that each becomes, abidingly, the 'thine' and 'mine' of the other. This status, joyfully bestowed, then becomes the bond, the setting, the surety, in which it is fulfilled, and the fulfilling is enabled by the pledging. It is then a matter of 'being what you are,' as in ordination or any other acquiring of significance. The weddedness is at once a fact and an achieving, the one, as grammarians might say, a present simple, the other a present continuous. The point is that the achieving is truly empowered by the status, just as the status – no merely formal, legal thing – is realized in the transacting it hallows.

The analogy of the arch in architecture can come to our help in comprehension of true marriage. The arch is a device for making what it has to do a means of doing it. The very weight it bears solidifies it for such bearing. It springs necessarily from two separate walls or columns. Marriage never overrides or cancels our individuation, what we apprehend with Dylan Thomas as a 'small bone-bound island' in which 'we learn all we know' and 'all . . . is inseparable from the island.'[15] Lovers remain their separate selves, conserving, contributing, all that heredity, nurture and aptitude can bring to the arch they will create.

Inherent in that always separate personhood there lies, however, a 'tendency towards' – a 'vacant space within the heart,' an instinct, sexual, physical, spiritual, intellectual, to seek and find 'the other.' Those are the arms of the potential arch. We should be wary of surmising that they have no destiny, unless some other vocation authentically awaits them. We should even more be wary of supposing that they have a destiny that does violence to the organic nature of our human frame, the very organs located – not as Yeats vulgarly derided them – 'in the place of excrement,' but rather in the place of dignity and hallowing. Copulation can only rightly be an intimacy of wonder, a culminating transaction of mutual delight, requiring and expressing the utmost in self-exposure, self-imparting.

The limbs of the arch that seek each other are held in their seeking by the keystone, by the vows of troth, by the bliss of marriage. That locking of the arch does not imprison except to fulfill; it ties only to liberate. It both holds and is held. What yields into it stands because of it. Then the arch holds up its world. It creates space for home and children, it supports security. What entails upon it of tasks and vicissitudes finds it able for them. It is toughened by its tribulations, consolidated by its burdens – if such they can be called. For the arch, or the dome – the arch in rotation – finds them part of its own meaning. They are only there because it is there and the two are one thing.

So, at least, we discovered in five decades of discovery. There was 'a first fine careless rapture' to be sure and many mundane passages. Do not suppose I romanticize. Some twenty months after Christopher's birth, Melita was diagnosed with tuberculosis and immediate sanatorium treatment was imperative. It was Christmas Eve. There followed ten months in Gaylord Hospital, Connecticut. Fully recovered, the Superintendent discharged her as 'a model patient who had contributed helpfully to the healing of fellow patients.' An anonymous friend helped us with the fees and her four lovers visited her delightedly, debating together over the forty mile return journey what to have for supper. The Study Programme and some episcopal travels involved us in long separations in the fifties and the seventies, but these were no more than the masonry belonging with the arch. It stayed.

When in the mid-eighties a series of minor strokes impaired first her responses, then her speaking, and finally her mobility, nothing impaired the abiding positives of our retrospect and our communion. When Melita died after four years of wheel-chaired fragility and was laid to rest on the north side of Ascott Church, we sang at a Memorial Thanksgiving the hymn we had used at our wedding forty-eight years earlier, with its needless interrogative:

> 'Hast thou not seen
> How thy heart's wishes have been
> Granted in what He ordaineth?'

We added a further verse recalling what needs Chapter 5 for the clue:

'Praise to the Lord when to tasks undesired
He doth send thee,
Making of sorrows and trials occasion to mend thee,
Then in His care His devices to bear,
Measures of grace He doth lend thee.'

and also to 'All my hope on God is founded,' the apt insertion:

'Home and child and troth upholding,
Grace the arch of life secured,
Christ the Lord its spaces filling
With the joy of sweet accord.
Death unbinds mortal minds –
Faith their bond unbroken finds.'

In a now familiar hymn, Jack Winslow, whom we were to come to know in Canterbury, sang to 'the Lord of all power . . . wisdom . . . bounty . . . and being.' It seemed right to add on the same occasion:

'Lord of all mercy, we yield You again
The gift of Your giving our joy to sustain,
The love in our being You willed to entwine,
In making, re-taking, Your wisdom's design.'

vii.

Have I been rash or pretentious in writing thus on negotiation, as it seemed to us, between faith and life in this most vital realm of both? Is there something immodest in reflection on the truth-dimension of what most ennobles, rejoices and evokes our human-ness? Could there be a conspiracy of silence about what most engages human story? Would not such a silence be ignoring how far Christian marriage is maligned, despised or simply misconstrued, in the climate of our time? Sexuality has become a part of trivia, inconsequential, promiscuous, irresponsible, commercial, a debased currency of brazenness. Perhaps it is only the openness, the publicity, the media-mediation, that are more blatant, more intrusive. Victorian parlours were not innocent of sexuality and their novelists are often accused of skirting evasively around it.[16] Now we have it no longer in multiple disguise but in the naked and the genital, the flagrant and flamboyant. We have forfeited the deeply religious ingredient of reticence, of awe, of mystery, and honest wonderment.

It is, then, the more urgent to set down the testimony of vital faith and faithful life and the peace they speak into our angry, anxious turmoil of the passionate in selves. Only when we truly love is the universal pattern in us. For what such love identifies as desire is where the real is. 'The sweetest wife on sweetest marriage day' is where our capacities for loving are best identified – to be translated outward into reverence for every other marriage and a heart for all that, measured by this touchstone, is impoverished or tawdry, elusive or denied. Love between us becomes a sacrament of the beneficence of God. By these lights, to sense other attraction is to pray for its fulfilment – not in lust and appetite, there or here – but in the same terms as one's own. To register human beauty anywhere is to conceive, not lustfully *with* it, but gratefully *for* it the destiny meant. The married-ness of others receives the reverent tribute of one's own blessedness, or their marriageability the salutation of our good faith.

It is the fool who argues that marriage makes the permanent relation the last relation. It is precisely its bondedness which opens it out to home-based community and a disendangered circle of friendships and society. It makes us dead to sexual competition but in no way dead to interhuman-ness. 'Happily ever after' is not the artificially imposed conclusion Victorian readers demanded of their novelists.[15] It is more truly the potential of a trust for which 'to have and to hold' is never into some nebulous, neutral, fictional perpetuity arbitrarily supposed, but only in the steadiness of a love that daily wills it and attains it.

Given mutual faith, and given *the* faith (chapters 9 and 10), this is no empty notion. 'The things we do after the flesh,' as even fierce old Ignatius insisted, in his *Epistle to the Ephesians*, 'are spiritual, for we do all things in Jesus Christ.'[17] For whereas in nature the body affords the place, in grace it is the place – the holy context – which decides the body.

In writing so, I realize that I engross the Christian case, as our experience underwrites it, in the whole sad complex of the failed marriage, the broken home, the unrequited loneliness, the deprived childhood, the travestied sexuality, that beset the human scene. That was precisely the reason for making the case that alone takes the measure of how desolating these tragedies must seem. To care for the meaning of our sexuality is not, thereby, to despise or disown the short-fallings it must identify. Quite the contrary: it is to come by just the perspectives and the energies by which to know them for what they are.

It must follow that instead of mere remonstrance or superiority, there has to be in all relation to the world in Christ, a vicariousness, an undertaking of the wrong, its necessary indictment, its strenuous redemption. The 'on-behalf-ness' we noted earlier has no more urgent sphere than that presented by the vagaries, the miseries, the tribulations, of misguided and frustrated sex. These certainly demand *à priori* the making, the ensuring, the sustaining, of true marital arches over the homing of society. They demand much more. For it is precisely the nature of the tragedy that that solution is often far to seek and the ruins exist because the arch was never there.

When Augustus Caesar – he of the census at Bethlehem – legislated against the unmarried citizens of Rome, he declared they were, in some sort, 'the slayers of the people.' That reproach might belong with some homosexuals. It is at odds with the contemporary menace of the awesome spate of human population. What might Caesar say of unmarried parents – single or vanished? 'The night my father got me,' sang the poet, 'his mind was not on me.' How could they indulge a transient pleasure negligent of the liability in which it implicitly involved them? Biologically there is no such thing as a 'single parent.' The copulation was always there and, with it, whatever a future might entail. By the Christian sacramental measure haphazardness and sex become incompatible. Yet Jesus befriended prostitutes and believed them retrievable. For him they were still capable of the alabaster box of precious ointment. Bystanders in the Gospel might see their devotion as 'this waste'. Jesus saw it as the sweet reversal of 'the waste' that was their former living.

Such hopefulness is part of the witness by which its necessity is identified. Our culture, where it is hideously at odds with its own benediction and its heritage, must be denied in its illusions if it is ever to be retrieved into its truth – the truth that lives in gentle troth secured everywhere in hearts that truly love and loyally abide. This is a very ancient Gospel. It is the only good news there is. For the rest, as Thomas à Kempis had it of the Lord he loved: 'If I cannot see Thee present, I will mourn Thee absent.'[18]

Meanwhile, the Church – and all who will – have to take up in vicariousness the toll of what distorted sexuality has willed upon society. Such was – and is – the logic of a long embrace. The body, as the poet knew, is

> '. . . Where the high senses hold their spiritual state,
> Sued by earth's embassies,
> And sign, approve, accept, conceive, create.'[19]

Most of all is it so in and through marriage, in the intimacy of 'true minds' and of 'the one flesh.' Music, it has been said, is what happens in you when you are reminded by the instruments. So too is that other indefinable mystery that 'negotiates' through body, mind and spirit, in the instrumentality all three must bring to its theme and harmony.

These paragraphs have attempted no characterization of her who was all to me through more than half a century. One cannot contain experience in adjectives or attempt some verbal photograph of how it was. James Joyce, in the last of his stories collected in *Dubliners*, has his 'Gabriel,' the husband, say:

> 'Moments of their life together broke like stars upon his memory . . . moments that no one knew of, nor ever could know of . . . For the years had not quenched his soul nor hers. Their children, his writing, her household cares had not quenched their souls' tender fire. In one letter he had

> written to her then he had said: "Why is it that words like these seem to me so dull and cold? Is it because there is no word tender enough to be your name?" '[20]

Or, as Goethe had it:

> 'Holy's our name for such a blessed state,
> Which too is mine when upon her I wait.'[21]

Chapter 4

The Sifting East

i.

Early in a late January morning, 1939, the Italian ship Galileo, ex Trieste, having called at Brindisi, Larnaca, [Alexandria] and Haifa, round the headland of Ras Beirut and docked in the inner harbour among the business houses and the wharves of the Lebanese capital, against the gleaming backdrop of the snows on Mount Sunnin. My eastern baptism had begun. Sifting is an apt word to describe what was to happen to my sense of mission, to my perceptions of the task of personal Christian faith within the transactions of culture and community to which inner loyalty had brought it. 'I am soft sift in an hour-glass,' was how the poet saw himself.[1] But the hour-glass allows its grains no option. Time only uses them for a measure. Mine was to be a sifting about meaning.

The next day found me housed amid the mountain snows in Shimlan, a straggling village below the narrow road which led south along the ridge from Aley, its junction with the main Beirut/Damascus highway twisting its way towards the crest of the Lebanon range. The minor road passed through Suq al-Gharb, 'the market of the west' – which west I did not know, unless it were the seaward view across the pine woods and vine-terraces towards the coastal road for Sidon and Tyre on the littoral where, years later, the Beirut airport would bring to earth its tally of processing aircraft – a more inexorable form of the European nexus than the Phoenicians had known.

Lebanon, with its allies in Alexandria and Carthage, had long been a mediator between the east and south and north of the great 'middle sea.' Had it not, in fact, given the northward continent its name?[2] I would have to wait to be initiated into the modern trauma of its vocation as a land –

itself a composite of creeds – negotiating between the great hinterland of Arabism and Islam and the legacies of Greece and Rome.

My immediate pre-occupation had to be with the language of that destiny. Arabic study began forthwith, crucial as it obviously was to the more private task to which I was committed. This was a dual thing from the beginning. Chapter 11 will be a better place to tell how it had been precariously contrived. I was under the authority of the Bishop in Jerusalem to serve as Chaplain of All Saints', Beirut and also under the direction of the British Syrian Mission at whose Lebanon Bible Institute I had arrived. Prior to the events of 1941 the worshipping community at All Saints was small. Services were 'intermittent,' and did not require residence in Beirut. The congregation was composed mainly of shipping agents, academics from the American University, teachers from numerous schools and some retired folk. A certain 'sifting' (of me) had to happen when I needed to appreciate that there were diversities of Anglican usages in liturgy to be acknowledged in a situation where the faithful could not go round the corner to find what was more congenial and, by so doing, preserve unaffected loyalties.

The Bible Institute had only recently been launched under the guidance of the Revd. Evan Harries, a New Zealander and a Presbyterian. It was not in competition with the long established Near East School of Theology (affectionately known as 'the Nest'). but was designed to train village evangelists for what it saw as the more pressing needs of personal witness. Strongly Bible based, it was content to leave more elaborate theology to the academic realm where it did not aspire. The Mission had lately been through a process of self-examination on this score and had come down firmly on the priority of evangelism, and 'sound doctrine,' over a theology more responsive to perplexity. Within three years I was to find myself minded – I hope rightly – to reverse the reckonings.

> 'Two roads diverged . . .
> I could not travel both and be one traveller.'[3]

That conviction, however, only came slowly and, meanwhile my reception in Shimlan was at once warm, loving and exacting. I was rapidly at home with the twenty or so budding evangelists and especially with the Lebanese Tutor, George Etr, who was my initial Arabic teacher with a zeal that exaggerated his ideas of my capacity to absorb his ministrations. There was no place in my heart for that aloofness or pre-possession of superiority of which 'Europeans' are invariably accused by eastern academics. I was never thinking with Tennyson

> 'Better fifty years of Europe than a cycle of Cathay'[4]

or Araby. Quite the contrary. I was entranced with the beauty of the land and avid for an intimacy with its people and its soul.

George's efforts were geared to the more formal grammar teaching I had from Sitt Miriam Mishalani, a frail spinster with a meticulous mind, who lived in the village. As she was house-bound and a communicant she was later able to check my diction when I celebrated Arabic Holy Communion. We often sat on a concrete bench outside her cottage, looking down into the Mediterranean haze. Between them the two endeared me to their language, so that – despite its demands on *mens* and *vox* – I grew enamoured of its fascinating consistency, the discipline of its syntax and the range of its vocabulary. There was a tradition in the Institute that required verse recitation after breakfast and this encouraged me to venture into memorizing. Or in the spring sunshine I could wander down the mountain tracks and be unheard mouthing the linguistic rudiments of my vocation, pausing to savour the fragrant cyclamen and anemones that interspersed the stones. Painfully if slowly I began to operate in the simple idiom of the Institute in preparation for the Summer School to which I would be going in Jerusalem.

The impact of that journey belongs to Chapter 6. I had, in all, two summer schools there and a further autumn term in 1940, under the Arabist, the Revd. Eric F.F. Bishop, an inveterate enthusiast and a tireless friend of Palestinians, whose mentorship through a long retirement I greatly valued. There was one traumatic hiatus in the story of my 'Arabizing' which I reserve for Chapter 11, and also a half-year sojourn in Gaza, occasioned by the Allied Campaign in Lebanon in the high summer of 1941. In due course I was able to participate directly in the Arabic tuition in the Institute and take up the role intended for me well before the end of the three-year probationary period for which the Mission had contracted. It paid no salaries but it did afford us home and maintenance and a 'pocket' allowance for other expenses. Incentive for Arabic study – had it been needed – was sagely, if sternly, supplied by the Mission in its ruling out marriage until I had attained 'the third stage' of Arabizing, but that is part of the story of Chapter 3.

Modest as my competence was it did introduce me to the hard perplexities of 'fulfilling the Gospel' – as Paul expressed it (Romans 15.19) – in the itinerant shape assumed, for the most part, by the trainees at the Institute. My identity with them in hope and affection was complete and the experience precious. George Etr and I walked from Shimlan to Sidon in one day to visit his native village. In the summer of 1939, prior to the Jerusalem sojourn, some six of us went on a trek through the villages across the range, calling first – as custom required – on the local *mukhtars*, chatting and singing where we could and sleeping by night on the flat roofs of hospitable folk. It was a tense time politically as Europe drifted into war and I was briefly arrested as a dubious quantity in such 'native' company, until a more senior *gendarme* assumed me harmless.

But was I not a dubious quantity within myself? The question deepened during the time in Gaza. The Christian Hospital there had a high, and deserved, reputation. As often with mission homes of healing it was popularly named for its long serving earlier mainstay, Dr Sterling. 'Sterling' was the place to which sick villagers, accompanied by anxious relatives, made their wistful way from their abodes all along what was tragically to be known as 'the Gaza Strip.' They would return gratefully endeared to those whose care and skill they had received. For a whole half-year it was my job, as 'Gaza Chaplain,' to go with the 'evangelists' to re-visit these old patients and their neighbours, through the wide perimeter of the 'legend of Sterling.' Remembrance of the Hospital was our entree. We would sit for hours receiving and being received, exchanging greetings and 'holding forth the word,' regaled from those large red melons with which in season the Gaza region abounds – almost miraculously luscious from the dry, sandy soil.

In hospital too, there were lantern slides about the life of Jesus to which patients, listlessly or curiously, submitted as evening gave them respite from the ministrations of nurses or the attentions of Alfred Hargreaves, the skilled, and irrepressible doctor-in-charge. We also had morning prayers in the Chapel to which arriving out-patients were welcome, along with the nurses and orderlies. I had been enjoined previously to bring some punctual discipline into this exercise, for the doctor had the gift of words. As experience lengthened I felt that more than punctual awareness was involved. How ought saving truth to hold a captive audience? In what form should ministries of meaning properly belong with ministries of care? Was a hospital ward a right location for a preacher?

Manifestly it would never have sufficed to say: 'Deeds speak.' People will understand that 'God is love' simply by savouring a genuine human love of them in their emergency. Not at all. How could they? When meeting the unfamiliar we reach for the familiar, the furniture of our usual minds. Doubtless dimly aware that these medicos worked long hours and drew no salaries and could enjoy pay, luxury and prestige elsewhere, the 'lay' mind concludes that they must be doing it for merit, in order to stand well with God. Or others, more malignly prompted, assume they are a cover for imperial politics, paymastered by the 'European' 'interest.'[5]

So we must be careful always to make it plain that if 'we love,' it is 'because God first loved us.' (1 John 4.19) The Gospel will not be visible except it be sometimes also audible. There is something authentic in that hyphen joining 'surgeon' with 'evangelist.' In his/her context, the one would not be without the other. Therefore, the nexus of the village-itineraries with the hospital centre was due and right. 'How is Mustafa since he left us?' might be rightly joined with: 'Does Mustafa love the Lord?' If the Hospital embodied its hallowing via its Chapel it was right that the Chapel should be articulate with that faith. It would never be right to obscure, still less to forego, the Christian 'interest' in the mind and heart as well as in the surgery and the bandages. The will for an inclusion of all in 'the hearing of the Word' could never be renounced by the will for their inclusion in the healing of the sicknesses.

Yet, whether in Gaza or Lebanon, the question persisted. Was personal evangelism the right reading of vocation? How viable was the liberty of response which it assumed for the private self of the listener, bound – as all were – into a complex of tethers, by poverty, illiteracy, stolidity, group loyalty and inward fear? Ought not ventured ministries of truth to be allied with larger perspectives of life and wider dimensions of significance? Did there not need to be, because of 'God in Christ reconciling the world,' a bearing of that trust upon the whole ethos of Islam, rather than – perhaps forlornly, perhaps unduly – upon the individual? To be sure, the personal equation would always be crucial in the things of faith, but could that equation be rightly broached in evangelism without patient reference to all that held the personal equation in its grasp and reach? Might that indicate a broader field of relevance than Shimlan assumed?

I was not to know for half a dozen years how tragic those villages around Gaza were to become – Khan Yunis, Beersheba, Rafa, Fujallah, Jabaliyyah, Majdal and the rest. The war of 1948 would roll over them. 'Abd al-Nasir would make his name among Army officers in battle running through them. In that sense they would be the seed-bed of the 1952 Revolution in Cairo. Their grim vicissitudes would culminate in Israeli occupation after 1967 and they would come to symbolize the futility of human hope. They were there, in their simple economies, their ancient patterns of husbandry, their eternal melons. Other philosophies were around that saw only a vacant landscape or nomads who could

'. . . fold their tents like the Arabs,
And as silently steal away.'[6]

These perceptions were hidden from me in 1941 but what might their unread demands mean for a career in itinerant evangelism? Must not one strive to belong with human crisis in all its implications and might not that vocation require other terms of reference than those of the Bible Institute? The sifting in my mind was far from 'soft.' I could never abandon belief in the openness of grace to all nor the truth of the person as the clue to its embrace. 'Whosoever will may come' would always be the ensign of the Church, but how was their 'willing' best concerted and deserved?

Then there were the problematics – more besetting in the present context than, for example, it had been in Tranmere – of 'rival' Scriptures and mutual incomprehension, so hard either to avoid or to overcome in the limitations of village conversation. Our Christian witness would be at once caught up in questions of authority, of meaning and its interpretation which the situation could hardly undertake, given the limitations of the encounter on either side. There would be the exchange of quotations: Jesus was, and was not, 'the Word made flesh.' His 'divinity' was a false distortion of his role as a 'mere' prophet. Our sins need no 'saviour' sent from heaven to 'enable God to forgive.' God had a prerogative of mercy and needed no such 'devices.' The Scriptures we brought were, anyway, faulted, 'corrupted' if not 'abrogated.' The Qur'an sufficed.

It was not simply that such impasse was wearying: it was that it seemed to call for relating differently, less simplistically, more vitally. It seemed to argue aiming to set the entire issue into larger terms. Chapter 8 is intended below to take up all that was here at stake for me. The French Arabist, Louis Massignon (1883–1962) had written of 'Arabs . . . distinguished by an intransigent concept of transcendence' when he was 'trying to re-think the Incarnation in Arabic terms.'[7] The back and forth of day-to-day meeting struggled with its own inconclusiveness even when it did not descend into polemic. It was almost like playing tennis with the ball back and forth from court to court. If only we could let the net down! That would escape the futility of winners and losers but it would also have been the end of that sort of game. Yet what other sort was there which would bring us together not in competition but in communication and relate us together on more viable terms, perhaps of scholarship but certainly of mutuality, more engaging than those of the itinerant evangelist? Perhaps the Near East School of Theology – skilled, or stilled, in erudition as the Bible Institute saw it – had its point.

At all events it was my sense of things that was being sifted. I would never surrender the convictions that cry: 'Woe be to me, if I preach not the Gospel.' But how to do so? I had to fall back on the diversity of 'gifts,' the contrast in vocations. When in the summer of 1942, after three and a half years, we moved into a new chapter, it was with genuine gratitude both backward to our many debts and forward to our further hopes. The break was entirely friendly and after coming under 'single' (not 'new') episcopal 'management,' I continued to go to help in Shimlan as a volunteer from Beirut. What was it that began in 1942 and led through five sifting years to our first sad experience of ecclesiastical 'redundancy'?

ii.

There were two factors. The first was the leadership of Bishop Graham-Brown, the second the impact of the American University of Beirut. The story is how they came together. The Bishop I held in awed affection from the time in 1938 when I tried – successfully – to overcome his hesitation about the B.S.M. appointment. He had very close relations with many of the Mission's members but he was sensitive to the possible strains in my dual obligation. My sense of him deepened when, during my 1940 study in Jerusalem, he invited me to serve as his Chaplain and I saw him in action in many of the pressing demands of his task in mandated Palestine under war conditions, and with the Arab Church.

The schools of the Bishopric were close to his heart. He hoped that if Jews and Arabs were schooled together in youth they would resolve their politics in maturity. That the vision would be grimly disproved in the long sequel did not make it the less worthy. Graham Brown was anxious that the graduates of the schools of the Bishopric – St George's and Bishop Gobat's in Jerusalem, St Luke's in Haifa and the Bishop's School in Amman, and others – might maintain the tradition of reverence in learning and of vocation in life when they went on to the A.U.B. That University was almost invariably their goal, if possible, with its high repute, its Arabic and English quality and its splendid locale. Once he was assured that he would not be suborning us from the British Syrian Mission, he invited Melita and me to establish a residential hostel to which former pupils might go.

In a meeting with the University's President Bayard Dodge, it was agreed that I would be enrolled as an Adjunct Professor (any accredited residence requiring such Faculty status in its 'manager'). This would ensure a modest salary, since All Saints' Church paid none. Its funds could, however, provide our share in the rent of the two storey house required, while hostel fees would take care of the rest and of its running costs. We spent the summer of 1942 acquiring needed furnishing and equipment and started out on the great adventure in the Fall. Justin Martyr, a 2nd century Palestinian Christian who had always retained the philosopher's robe after becoming Christian and therefore symbolized scholarly faith, seemed the right figure to invoke for patronage. We could not, however, be 'Justin Martyr House.' So we canonized him and St Justin's House came into proudly modest existence. That it would be a casualty of the Palestine/Israel War of 1948 was hidden from our eyes.

Even so, it was baptized in tragedy. Bishop Graham Brown was killed in late November when, his chauffeur-driven car was struck by a train at an unguarded level-crossing on the newly built Haifa/Beirut railway which criss-crossed the coast road perilously at many points. He was returning to Jerusalem after dedicating St Justin's in two separate Services, one for the civilian church community and one for the academics. We were orphaned in our very infancy. It was a struggle to survive. The House-Chapel in which he had prayed never lost – while it had being – the savour of his presence.

We began with eleven members. After a testing year in English teaching, I moved into philosophy and exciting things followed. War time recruitment explained the anomaly for I was philosophically 'raw,' becoming, no less oddly 'acting Head of the Department' three years later, when Charles Malik, the Professor, moved into diplomacy and became Lebanon's first Ambassador in Washington. War is responsible for many vagaries. I spent an urgent summer in 1943, aiming to absorb Locke and Berkeley, Kant and Nietzsche, William James and William Ernest Hocking. These mentors of the Sophomore mind would have to cohabit with the discipline of a House with twice daily Chapel and informal studies within whatever wider circle might have room for it. It was to be gladly and modestly present in the context the University generously gave it, though with some initial hesitation, in case it might prove an uneasy adjunct, albeit too small to do much harm. The venture – and that suspicion – can only be understood against the background of the A.U.B.'s own story.

iii.

'It is a complex fate, being an American,' the novelist Henry James once wrote.[8] In his view, Americans were always being obliged to self-scrutiny because of European civilization, so much older, so much more venerable. That sense of things brought him, and many others – T.S. Eliot and Ezra Pound among them – to find permanent haven among Europeans. The complexity of being American in the Near and Middle East[9] was of a different order and the A.U.B. was its most paradoxical example. Its inauguration in 1866 with 'College Hall' was a gesture of genuine Christian aspiration and benediction. Inside the same Hall in 1984 the eighth President, Malcolm Kerr, was brutally assassinated by a mad gunman supposedly taking revenge on its alleged machinations or simply in a blast of mindless hatred.

In the forties, when St Justin's began, there had been – as Abraham Lincoln would have phrased it – 'four-score and seven years' of educational service. Much of the political, legal, medical and commercial leadership of Lebanon, Syria and Palestine had passed through and from its doors. Despite war conditions they were halcyon days. The dark spectres were below the horizon. It was manned by idealist professors and administrators who had invested their whole lives, some to two or three generations, in a loving commitment to an adopted country which, in generous measure, had adopted them. It was a nursery of Arabic renaissance, funded exclusively by voluntary sources and free of political entanglement which only the wilfully malicious could deny.

Its situation, however, was inevitably ambivalent – a circumstance which, given the location, could only intensify with time and circumstance. It, too, had known the 'sifting' of the East. Beginning life as the 'Syrian Protestant College,' it had been a progeny of the American Presbyterian Mission, one of whose veterans, Henry Jessup, wrote in 1893:

> 'Education is only a means to an end in Christian missions and that end is to lead men to Christ and teach them to become Christian peoples and nations. When it goes beyond this, and claims to be an end in itself, that mere intellectual and scientific eminence are objects worthy of the Christian missionary . . . then we do not hesitate to say that such a mission has stepped out of the Christian and missionary sphere into one purely secular, scientific and worldly. Such a work might be done by a Heidelberg or a Cambridge or a Harvard . . . but not by a missionary society labouring for spiritual ends.'[10]

But could 'spiritual ends' be so categorically, or unilaterally, exempted from the sciences, or isolated from other areas of the growing mind? And what of the veritable patchwork of creeds and loyalties in the Lebanese scene? Which was 'the Christian' identity and could education be separate recruitment?

Slowly the institution sensed the dimensions of its *métier* and began to re-define its concepts, detaching itself officially, though not ungratefully, from its 'mission' matrix. Its first President, Daniel Bliss, explained its independence notably.

> 'The College is for all conditions and classes of men, without reference to color, nationality, race or religion . . . Christian, Jew, Muslim or heathen, may enter and enjoy all the advantages of the institution and go out believing in one God, or many gods or no god: but it will be impossible for anyone to continue with us long without knowing what we believe to be the truth and our reasons for that belief.'[11]

The sense of identifiable and accessible truth was clear but it must make its own way in open forum and in a prudent, realist sense of how divisive loyalties would be unless the forum preserved a careful neutrality. The fact of religions at odds was compelling reason for avoiding to disturb their respective hold on identities. Many theological issues were left to silence in that stance, but then theology *per se* was at a necessary discount. Only philosophy in its more discursive or academic way, would be free to raise the vital questions as to truth, meaning, knowledge and its credentials, life and its dilemmas, death and its unravelling.[12]

It was a role to which 'philosophy' at St Justin's could be content to aspire, accepting the perplexing abeyance of 'witness' and theology, except insofar as these could be contrived within its own domain, via discussion groups and Chapel, to which, no doubt, teaching 'fall-out' could contribute. There was no subterfuge here and the understanding of the relationship availed. The first negotiation between President and Bishop had been formal rather than cordial as the former needed to know what quality there might be in the infant hostel. It warmed with the years. In 1945 I was surprised to be invited to take the West Hall Services, which annually in February were the one occasion when the University allowed 'spiritual aims' to take some articulate Christian form. I wrote a hymn for the series of addresses (Tune: Ellers) which was meant explicitly to be implicitly Christian, for that paradox was inherent in the situation.

> 'Here take our minds, our faltering minds, O Lord,
> Quicken and guide them in the tasks of thought,
> Upon their dullness be Thy Spirit poured
> Till, learning truth, they love Thee as they ought.
>
> Here take our hopes, our youthful hopes, that call
> Beyond the ruin of these years of strife.
> Give them a strength no evil can appal
> And let them shape the deeds of daily life.
>
> Here take our wills, our wayward wills, that choose
> The barren paths of selfishness and sin:
> Enslaving choices teach them to refuse,
> Theirs be the freedom of Thy rule within.
>
> Here take ourselves, our stubborn selves, O Lord,
> Make fit our thoughts, inspire our hearts we pray:
> Roused be our souls to hear the sounding chord
> Which calls us to Thy Life, Thy Truth, Thy Way.'

It was, at least, honest in its due constraints.

The normal University Chapel Services, three weekly, were taken by Professors according to rota and fell to me about once a semester. They were broadly consonant with third President, Bayard Dodge's distinction between the University's task and that of the religions. He declared

> 'Protestantism means religious freedom and as a Protestant institution we wish to give our students freedom of worship and freedom of belief . . . It is for the mosque, synagogue or church to provide the practical formalities (sic) of organized religion . . . Working with God we wish every student to be religious.'[13]

It would be via philosophy – if at all – and perhaps through literature that everything left there to silence might be aired, pondered, explored and resolved. One had to accept the ethos of the institution and appreciate the logic of the pressures to which it knew itself liable. The meaning of my Ordination was being sifted, its Blackpool/

Oxford/Tranmere origins disconcertingly searched afresh beyond what Shimlan and Gaza had begun. The All Saints aspect of the triple 'charge' remained constant and some University personnel belonged to it. At St Justin's we could complement it.

Happily University philosophy was headed by Charles Malik, an outstanding (Greek Orthodox) Lebanese product of A.U.B. itself and of Harvard. He lectured weekly to some 160 sophomores with *élan* and eloquence. Twice weekly they met in three groups for open discussion based on the lectures, on W.E. Hocking's admirable *Types of Philosophy* and on reading hand-outs from Plato's *Dialogues*, to Bertrand Russell's *A Free Man's Worship*. These more than sufficed for theology also and delved into daunting questions like those shortly to inundate the Palestinians among them. To listen to Charles Malik in full cry was what it must have been like to attend on Demosthenes. He was still youthful, often dramatic, always challenging, cajoling, exciting his hearers. We took on separately where he left off. In more intimate Junior and Senior classes Courses in Christian Ethics, the History of Medieval Thought and the English 17th Century World, there were occasions to take yet deeper stock of where philosophers had been and why and thus where we were ourselves and why. It was exhilarating and formidable in its demands.

For my part personally, as mentioned in Chapter 3, it led to the Green Moral Philosophy Essay and, thereby, to the quest for a D.Phil. More importantly it was some kind of mediation to the minds of Muslims, Jews and Druzes and to a range of differing Christians, not in any kind of indoctrination but in the open forum of study and encounter, heart to heart, for which I had half gropingly been yearning without knowing where the answer lay.

St Justin's, as well as being a sweet intra-marital venture, (for it needed us both) was a steady learning process which brought us closer to what any Christian presence had to be in its deference to diversity, its will to realism, its tasks of mind and its acceptance of a likeness, however remote, to the perceived way of 'the Word made flesh.' The A.U.B. was indeed a sifting institution and if there was a sifting also in ourselves there might be hope there was also a sifting in the stream of youth who passed that way, the grim future mercifully hidden from their eyes.

In the summer of 1947, with the Green Essay and much else under our belt, we committed St Justin's House to new leadership and headed towards Oxford in hope of further study on the intellectual issues of contemporary Islam as Muslim youth – as we could now understand – was facing them. The All Saints' Chaplaincy would become a separate, now funded, ministry with no more than a benevolent eye on the Hostel. How long our absence would be we could not know but it was intended to lead us back to more of the same, only wiser, in due course. The narrative of what ensued in England was told in chapter 2. Within a year, owing to the Arab/Israeli War St Justin's House had perforce to close. Its normal clientèle were refugees. Bishop Weston Stewart diverted all his resources to refugee relief. He made it clear to me that the door back again for the foreseeable future was unlikely to re-open. It was the first of our three bitter redundancies, the first of three dismantlings of enterprises we dearly loved and sadly lamented. Of such stuff are siftings made. The furnishings we had tenderly gathered were abruptly dispersed and the House that had been home to students and host to numerous soldiers and civilians, and a humble forum for the bewildered young, passed into a forgotten history.

iv.

There were other desperate siftings to come and since these Chapters turn not on chronology but on themes, it is fitting to ask about the fortunes of the old Justinians in the lapsing years. Some found their way into teaching or commerce in the new world, others in Jordan in the same sense. Two went to their pharmacy and the bitter destiny of the Gaza Strip, another into the trauma of leadership at the University of Bir Zeit, later an embattled target of Israeli oppression on the West Bank. One, by contrast, entered the Israeli diplomatic service, concluding as the Israeli Ambassador in Singapore and later devoted his generous energies to the work of the Alliance Israelite Universelle.[14] Two others bear special significance, sojourning in the House as they did for three successive years. The one was Kamal Nasir, the other Tawfiq Sayigh.

On April 10th, 1973, on Brighton Station, returning from being interviewed for the post of Reader at the University of Sussex, I picked up an evening paper and was appalled to read that Kamal, with two other Palestinian activists, had been brutally murdered by Israeli assassins (later officially decorated) in a terrorist attack on an apartment in Beirut. Later the mangled bodies were grimly pictured in the Press. Kamal Nasir belonged to a noted Anglican family, Butrus Nasir was a senior Arab priest in Ramallah when I first knew him. Musa Nasir served for a time as Foreign Minister of Jordan. Kamal was a lively Justinian, with a flair for poetry and a strong love of his Arab heritage. He was not a terrorist – except by charge of those who see their opponents only in that guise. But he was a patriot and strove in his writing to give voice to Palestinian dignity and hope. Of him and his two Muslim companions in death, Nadwa Tuqan wrote:

> 'Motherland, for your sake their blood was spilled
> Like rosary beads of rubies . . .
> And words fall
> Much as their bodies fell – corpses distorted . . .
> Gone are those we loved
> Before their vessel ever anchored,
> Before their eyes caught sight of the distant port,
> Palestine,
> In the seasons of your irremediable mourning.'[15]

He was in his fiftieth year. I had not seen him since his graduation.

Tawfiq Sayigh was a gentler soul. His poetry breathed a more subtle strain of wistfulness and inner destitution. I remember from our friendship in the forties a certain detachment in his attitudes as if the set of his heart was more for rumination than for conversation. He seemed to approach the world, not with a cold suspicion but rather with a kind of wariness that could not allow itself to trust too readily lest the sequel should prove acceptance too naive. That sequel would so desperately justify the caution was not then apparent but perhaps there was already, about what made him a poet, a prescience tragically confirmed. The climax of the Second War World, building up to the dramatic European finale in May, 1945, concealed from all but the most perceptive what would follow for the Palestinian world from the realization of the Holocaust. Victory would align world politics in new shifts of authority and these would be laden with urgent emotions of guilt, anger, reproach and anxiety. The Arab East, whose history had so often been prescribed by European factors, would enter on a continuing saga of that factor in the tragic form of 'the Zionist Imperative,' with Palestinians its primary sufferers.

On every count of youth, insight, imagination and the art of words – Tawfiq Sayigh was well endowed to give them voice. A further asset was his instinctive sympathy with modern western literature and especially with Franz Kafka and T.S. Eliot. The latter's *The Four Quartets* he translated and published in Arabic. He found in Eliot's 'free verse,' breaking away from stilted convention and relying less on rhyme and more on teasing imagery, a stimulus much to be emulated on the part of Arab poetry. Such 'free' style he encouraged in the journal *Al-Hiwar*, ('Dialogue') which he founded and edited in the sixties. Inevitably all such ventures of Arab initiative on the part of authors associated with western education came under suspicion of 'cultural freedom' being no more than a cloke, allegedly, for American 'interests.' Sayigh felt, perhaps more sensitively than most, the irony of such calumny. It came to be for him only another dimension of the denial of legitimacy which exile from a 'native' land had spelled for him after 1948. From being briefly Director of the United States Information Center and Library in Beirut, he had left in 1951 for Harvard. Short teaching assignments followed in both Oxford and Cambridge, England and he spent three years as Lecturer in Arabic Literature in the University of London, before his major poesysing in Lebanon in the sixties. Dismayed by their indecisiveness, and shattered in the summer of 1967, he moved to California where he died, in an elevator, on the Campus of its University at Berkeley at the beginning of 1971.

The Lebanese poet, Khalil Jibran, on whom he wrote a study in Arabic *New Light on Jibran*,[16] intrigued him but he could find no haven or solace in Jibran's strange capacity for mystic fantasy. His own themes revolved around a spiritual exile in which alienation, unrequited love and sheer adversity seemed to deny all authentic hope. Events 'had made him a vagabond,' as if a passenger on a vessel to whom disembarkation is denied at every port. He is one for whom 'every thread is cut,' and 'every land is hostile.' The 'wasteland' analogy, so definitive in the early Eliot, echoes through all his *qasidahs*, but – unlike his Anglo-American mentor – there was for him no 'homing' from one habitat into another, no refuge in the kind of Anglican adoption which contrived *The Criterion* out of *The Wasteland*.[17] The antecedents of Eliot's Europeanism were not there and there was no 'Palestine' in Eliot's inner equation.

The Christian associations were deeply present but – by the sixties – only in the interrogative.[18] *Qasidah 2* asked:

> 'What, then, is the thing I call "I"?
> And "my lord my Lord"
> What is the thing You call your servant.?'

There haunts all theism a great 'but.' Reputedly, 'God cares,' 'God sympathizes,' 'God sees,' but how does this reputing square with manifest inaction, this alleged redeeming by the Saviour, with the pathos of an unrelieved despair? Has the Christ truly 'risen from the dead,' or is the shroud still round Him? Is He no less a captive than the poet who interrogates Him? There are hints here of Oscar Wilde's plea for a 'hand to the drowning' on another sea than Galilee, of D.H. Lawrence 'resurrection' of the disillusioned Lord. Cripples in modern Bethesda lie by waters no hope troubles.[19] Sayigh noted with grim irony the tear-shape of the Sea of Galilee where, at Cana, 'the water turned to wine tasted water to my lips.' The yearning of the unresolved exile of intelligence and heart alike is the more telling for its New Testament allusions. How could it be otherwise in a Christian Palestinianism? The poetry to which St Justin's House was nursery would measure how close it had been to the unsuspected meanings of graduation into life.

V.

The life of the House, however, as we lived it, was still innocent of these dimensions. It is only in retrospect that I see how they contributed to my perceptions of any western Christian presence in the context they were so soon to darken. Two considerations seem to emerge from the history of the American University of Beirut and from my own eight year retrospect when we left Beirut in the summer of 1947. The one was the degree to which good-will, hope, even relationship itself, seemed to be enmeshed, entangled, enveloped, in instinctive enmities, suspicions, questionings, that lay like a crippling prejudice on all exchanges. The other was the inherent disqualification of the very core of Christianity which lay at the very core of Islam and its finality. At times the two came together in a sort of impasse, feasibly relieved by courtesy and practicalities, never truly overcome, and always liable to harden.

It was the puzzle, not to say the pain, of this impasse that I carried with me into the project of studies which brought us back to Oxford in the autumn of 1947. In Chapter 2, gathering Oxoniana, as it were, in one sequence, I left to silence the material of my D.Phil. studies. It is time to review them now. For they had everything to do with the eastern years through which they had passed. When, .in due course, they led on to the job at Hartford, Connecticut, it was still the same logic I was pursuing. The travel away had been physical only: it was in no way academic or spiritual. Indeed, whoever has once learned it ever leaves it? is the real 'eastern question.'

Need intellectual relations between westerners and easterners in what was dubbed 'the Near' and 'the Middle' between them be always dogged with doubt of the good intention? Was the insistent self-sufficiency of Islam for ever impervious to Christian community of mind? Were the ultimates of either always to be in that doldrum of neglect or suspicion, or both, which seemed their customary fate? Would there always have to be either a conspiracy of suspicion politically, or a conspiracy of silence theologically, denying the heart exchange that should obtain between them?

Perhaps the very word 'conspiracy,' sinister as it was, could provide a clue. It did, after all, mean – originally – 'to breathe together.' This, literally, we had been doing all the time – the same air, the same Mediterranean, the same mountains. Lebanon, in that sense, was a conspiring country. Why should mutuality be sold out to distrust, beset by the drift to negativity, baulked by instinctive scepticism of the good intention? The American University had survived by a tolerance that was avid for its benefits but denied it the ultimate relevance the context required. When the good intention became, or seemed to become, itself a victim of the forces of distrust,[20] even the tolerance failed. There had been no doubt of it in halcyon days. Yet 'the conspiracy theory' was always at work, finding education a mere 'front' for politics and religious concern an intrusion into Islam's sufficient world.

What, then, might 'breathing together' mean insofar as a will to intellectual integrity could understand it? The student world in Lebanon had been my immediate climate. My question was: How could what was genuinely participatory, as youth knew it and as philosophy explored it, be deepened into religious sympathies which ruling forces of suspicion, stereotype, and dismissive distrust were always decrying and denying? As briefly outlined earlier, it seemed well to focus on what Muslims were writing for their own reading in respect of the problems of faith and conduct. Hence the phrasing of my D.Phil. proposal. Apologetic, on the part of any religious custodians, is liable to be self-satisfied or self-exonerating, if it is directed to outsiders. This was why I was wanting to discover the self-critical in Islam rather than the sort of self-admiring which emanated, for example, from the presses of Pakistan after its establishment in a spate of articles on 'Islam and . . .' with an exclusive array of topics – peace, justice, sex, education, human welfare – on which it had the potential, essential panacea. When honestly probed, might one not discern in all these issues, separately probed by light of the faith in question, but not privatized within that faith as if the worlds were disparate, a realm of inter-sympathy? Christian theology, during the 19th century had registered its own traumas of faith and Scripture, of things divine and things scientific. Calendars of incidence might not tally and there would always be the sharp contrast in the fact that the challenge was domestic in the West, not an 'import,' as largely for Muslims, and so dogged by political emotions.[21] Could Islam and Christian theology in any way 'inter-sympathize' around them? This is what I set out to discover in hope of eluding, if not removing, the besetting inhibitions of political distrust and the prejudice of familiar polemic. I was convinced that we should acknowledge the impasse for what it was and refuse to concede that it was all there ever could be.

The territory I had thus far known was confined to Lebanon and Palestine. Reading would have to enlarge it urgently. 1947 was a time of turmoil in Islam in the sub-continent, with the dominant Muslim League set on independent statehood for the Muslim majority areas. I realized that state-creation in Pakistan would constitute a profound verdict on Islam, about Islam, on the part of a vital segment of its people. Creating statehood, against all the logic of a unitary India, not only spoke volumes about how Islam saw itself but would necessarily generate volumes more in debate about what the 'Islamic' in the statehood meant – not to say volumes more about the viability of millions of Muslims more, denied by state-creation itself the allegedly indispensable condition of survival.

It was agreed that my studies should be confined to material in Arabic sources and to that relating outside the Arab Muslim mind insofar as it had expressed itself in English or could be reached in translation. This allowed me to include Turkey as well as India-Pakistan. Journals, such as that of the Al-Azhar in Cairo, and *Liwa' al-Islam* in Lahore, were part of the field together with numerous books of leading scholars and/or movements of renewal. From Jalal al-Din al-Afghani, via Muhammad 'Abduh, to Tawfiq al-Hakim and Taha Husain, I tried to digest the mind of contemporary Egypt, in company with the mentors of Turkish Islam like Zia Gökalp, and of Asian Islam in the persons of Ahmad Khan, Amir Ali, Khuda Bukhsh and Maulana Azad. What was finally distilled into my dissertation as a measure of Islamic modernity-in-mind was published some fourteen years later, much condensed and up-dated, by the Edinburgh University Press in its 'Islamic Surveys' Series, no. 3: as *Counsels in Contemporary Islam*. There is no point here in reviewing it again and, after four tumultuous decades, it would all need doing again.

What of 'the relevance of Christian theology' which was the other half of the proposal? I was well aware that the verdict of many would be: 'None at all,' since Christian theology with its Christology was Islamically flawed from the start and had absolutely nothing to offer. Was not true theism about 'unity,' *Tawhid*? Not to have it absolute would be like proposing a treatise on navigation without reference to wind and tide. Yet navigators from Ulysses to Columbus would have been lost without the stars. Astronomy too was inseparable from their ability to negotiate the waters. That, by analogy, was how Christianity had seen the place of 'the truth of Christ' within 'the truth of God.' Any 'relevance' about this or that in *any* theology would always turn on what 'the art of faith' ought to include, on how we chose the analogies by which we measured it for ourselves. In what sense, perhaps we should ask, were we navigators at all? What was the relation between authority to believe and belief in authority? Did the question even arise or were believers somehow made so, kept so, proved so, by warrant for which they had no responsibility?

The great spokesmen like Muhammad 'Abduh and Muhammad Iqbal, key figures in Cairo and Lahore, seemed entirely ready to hold faith and reason, piety and philosophy, in tandem provided that no tension was allowed to register between them. The central question, it seemed to me, was whether Islamic faith and Muslim life were required to be in mutual negotiation at all. If so, were any areas reserved from debate? Might only law be at issue while theology was immune? In what terms might, or might not, the Qur'an be involved? Who might appropriately undertake the task and what should be their relation to the whole community? I ventured to append to my dissertation an Appendix about the *Lux Mundi* phenomenon in Christian theology written in a form slanted towards Muslim thinking. I suppose it was an odd sort of 'Made in Longworth' tag on the whole tapestry. How did initiatives of mind within the Islamic world cohere around coteries of thought that had sensed a duty of religious response? What liberty might they assume, attain or permit themselves? How was continuity to be ensured, given that change was required?

This initiated me further into the concepts of *Ijma*ʿ and *Ijtihad*, of 'consensus' and 'initiative,' in Sunni Islam – the organs of Islamic adaptation the canons of which were themselves at issue. I realized that there was sharp argument not only about 'reform,' but also about the status of 'reformers.' What needs to be thought? Who is warranted to think it? My painstaking induction into this fascinating world of the Muslim mind in its self-expression between the eighteen-eighties and the nineteen-forties brought two impressions firmly home. The one was that we were indeed 'conspiring,' breathing the same religious air of studied trusteeship of belief, the same themes in mental liability for faith. The other was how disparate the two faiths were, or had become, in how the trust of doctrine was conceived. The fact was that the two faiths, if we may so speak, were very differently tethered to their content and I realized that it was their content which prescribed the tether. A theology that included a Christology as inseparable from its being a theology at all would always be at odds with a theism that, in the name of divine unity, rigorously excluded one. The dissertation had to end on a realist note. There might well be a Christian relevance to Islamic theology but it could only be by hope of radical ventures between us of which – for all the common territories and separate tasks we shared – there was little evident sign.

Looking back after forty years I am intrigued to find that I wondered whether 'the most useful beginning was not to make the very existence of the problem (of communication) a means of Christian grace through the very quality of the self-expression it might evoke.' I even found a strange analogy between the pains demanded of Christian thinking in being drawn through Islamic reckoning and what John Donne saw the exigencies of verse doing to his interior experience when there he tried to give it voice. He wrote:

> '. . . as the earth's inward narrow, crooked lanes
> Do purge sea water's fretful salt away
> I thought if I could draw my pains
> Through rime's vexation, I should them allay . . .'[22]

Accepting exigencies as an enabling discipline rather than as a weary obstacle might be a way of refining traditional Christian frustration about a theology alongside Islam, drawing all that was inimical (or seemed so) through a different idiom and finding the poetry that might replace the prose of old controversy.

I am surprised, in retrospect, at how little I then drew out what seemed to be to me later the positive areas of inter-theology which were present in the entire concept of creation, of a 'sacramental earth' entrusted to a human 'dominion,' and of a divine stake in that 'dominion' vested in the actuality of prophethood and 'guidance,' as clear evidence of a divine/human inter-relevance. All these, it now seems to me, were crucial to a full mediation of either theology to the other once it was realized that these dimensions made it impossible they should be mutually exclusive. I detected in 1950 what I called 'a lack of adequate human realism' in Islam and this would remain one of the vital issues for theology *per se*, inasmuch as what we may, or must, believe about God will always belong with what we can, or should, believe about man. 'There would be no thoughts of divine redemption,' I wrote, 'where there was every confidence in human attainment.' 'Islamic revelation is addressed to those who are conceived to need a knowledge of what to do rather than a power whereby they may.'

My D.Phil. venture had greatly served me in exploring Islam and had left me with many unresolved questions about the whether, and how, of an inter-theology that would be genuine, vital and constructive, but I was somehow convinced that the hope should neither be denied nor abandoned. The search for it must continue and, one-sided though they might often seem to be, all the ventures must, and would, be made, being neither sanguine nor in despair. It was only some quarter-century later that Marshall Hodgson, in his erudite and ambitious *The Venture of Islam*, laid down the, to him, categorical and total incompatibility of the two faiths and the futility of thinking otherwise. 'For Christians,' he opined

> '. . . being based on revelation means being in response to redemptive love as it is confronted through the presence of a divine human life and the sacramental fellowship of which that is the source. For Muslims, being based on revelation means being in response to a total moral challenge as it is confronted in an explicit divine message handed on through a loyal human community.'[23]

Even accepting that this summary was all, about either, was not 'redemptive Love a total moral challenge?' Was not 'human community,' either way, reciprocal to 'divine message.'? Was there not about Quranic reading of the natural order a sacramental human trust capable of the presence of 'divine human life.'? The several crucial factors here – 'revelation,' 'message,' 'community' – things at once 'divine/human' and in association – could not 'confront' inwardly, as they did, were they thought only to confront each other in hostility across some exclusion zone. What was common in those factors had already crossed it.

vi.

It was this conviction that went with us as we travelled in the late summer of 1951 to Hartford Seminary, Connecticut, U.S.A. for teaching in its Islamic Department and Editorship of its journal, *The Muslim World Quarterly*. Despite family sorrow, we had been blissfully happy in Longworth and it would have been delight to remain. There was also in the spring of 1951 a call to return to Tranmere as Vicar in the Parish of our dreams. There had come, however, to be a logic in the shape of things that demanded we stay with the eastern bent of such vocation as we had. There would have been little continuity in forsaking what Beirut had hardly left reversible, reinforced as commitment had been by the Longworth reading and writing. A physical return to a now non-existent Justiniana was impossible. It seemed right, therefore, to accept a five-year assignment to Islamic things at a centre long dedicated to them in the new world. The contractual limit was important. We did not know what in five years might transpire but we were aware of the danger of finding the U.S. so congenial that we might have no mind to leave it.

Congenial we certainly found it but never to the point of extinguishing for us the priority of the Middle East and of posting there whenever it might so eventuate. I simply transferred my Oxford Islamica to the Oxford-like portals of the Hartford School. It would still be 'the sifting East,' now mediated through the task of teaching its Arabic, Muslim dimensions and hopefully still serving it at one remove. I had to go on with the completed D.Phil. as if the Examiners had rejected it. For life still had it in critical dialogue.

Though the invitation to Hartford came to our country Rectory 'out of the blue,' there was some rhyme and reason in it. Hartford was looking for a successor to Dr Edwin Calverley in both his roles as Professor and Editor. It was searching for a 'doctorate-borne' contender, or, rather, in my case, invitee. While in Longworth I had been recruited as Secretary to a small group convening intermittently to study Islamic topics within the Church of England's Church Assembly. We met, mostly, in a fascinating house in Lord North Street, in the very bosom of parliamentary Westminster, at the home of Canon McLeod Campbell, General Secretary of the Assembly's Missionary Council. To this body came a Council Member of Hartford. The rest followed. President Russell Henry Stafford of Hartford, met me at (his) the Author's Club in Whitehall, where he overwhelmed me with his presentation of the quality of the Seminary, his inflated notions of the way in which my scholarship would emphatically enhance it, and his apology for what he feared was the meagre-ness of the stipend which, he said, might yet be upgraded. I was in no mood of bargaining but only of perplexity. The salary was already many times greater than our pittances at Longworth. I was rather deterred than attracted by his enthusiasm and hyperbole until counsel from around persuaded me how rightly to read his style.

There were hazards to be negotiated around Melita's history of tuberculosis but these were overcome and at length the die was cast. Other things being equal, there was something appropriate, via the A.U.B. and going back to Robert McElroy and Oxford Americana, about a venture across the Atlantic, given that it had this explicit eastern bias. With those loyal Longworthies farewelling us at Southampton on *The Queen Elizabeth* (No. 1), we were on the way to discoveries of *Moby Dick*, and Emily Dickinson, Robert Frost and William Faulkner and all the other enrichments of literature, friendship and culture which the American ethos holds in store for all who will discern them wisely.

I soon found a steady connection, as volunteer assistant at St James' Church, West Hartford, with Douglas Kennedy as Rector, and through the kindness of Bishop Walter Gray – of whom more in Chapter 5 – in licensing me in his Diocese of Connecticut. We coincided with the years in which St James moved from its first site on South Main Street to a new location on Farmington Avenue with an impressive campaign of parish-pledging and fund-raising. Once again I was to find things academic and things pastoral merging together as I believe they always should.

It would seem that there was a right continuity shaping between St Justin's, Longworth, and now Hartford, a certain unity of intent which was a great solace and encouragement. I was allowed a year's overlap with Edwin Calverley in respect of the editorial part of my assignment and for this I was deeply grateful. The *Quarterly*, in fact, helped to focus my thoughts further than Longworth had done simply by dint of the necessity to preside over a 'a Christian organ of Muslim studies.' What, precisely, was it aiming to do? Its origins, as the brain-child of Dr Samuel Zwemer, were strongly missionary, but could, it, should it, be also a journal of truly academic Islamics? To be sure, Islam itself was never asking for a merely academic interest. It did not see itself as there to be examined: it demanded to be followed. Too many in western academia had been prone to neutralize it in mere dissection – though, so doing, they estranged themselves from its disciples no less sharply than the missionaries. Might not Islam be properly susceptible of fair, perceptive, reverent treatment from within a faith not its own but as a faith in its own right? Could it even be seen as a 'world' ready for the openness of genuine inter-thought, at once scholarly and religious? Might it be the vocation of the journal to proceed upon that confidence and perhaps, by so doing, actually merit it?

When the Quarterly passed fully into my duty, where it remained until 1960, I began to introduce editorials based on Quranic verses like 'There is no refuge from God except in Him,'[24] to explore their theological implications as a Christian might. I would later be accused from several quarters of trying to 'Christianize' Islam, or willing on it what did not belong. This was not the case. I was simply trying freely to possess the Qur'an, in *all* its implications in a way that – as it seemed to me – Christians had long failed to do out of their explicit distrust of its status or their sheer unfamiliarity. It seemed right to go with it as far as it might take the mind, without staying to resolve all the attendant questions of status in the abstract. Let there be brought to it, not in barren controversy but in careful hope, all the positives of Christian faith and see where they might end. Why is there no affirmative word to hold what 'prejudice' implies the other way – a word to suggest spiritual sympathy finding itself justified.? For me, this seemed to happen in numerous ways and it was later to give rise to two books in the seventies that benefitted from the intervening tests of time and experience.[25]

What, after all, I asked myself, was the alternative? Either to entrench polemic or to stay satisfied with analysis without soul. For the latter, I recalled, Wordsworth had some warning words:

> To . . . 'pore and dwindle as we pore,
> Viewing all objects unremittingly
> In disconnection, dead and spiritless:
> And still dividing and dividing still,
> Break down all grandeur . . . while littleness
> May yet become more little, waging thus
> An impious warfare with the very life
> Of our own souls.'[26]

Everything would turn on the temper we brought, either to the other. We would have to begin and end where our souls were, with mind in keen attendance on them.

The Hartford sojourn was enriching in several grateful ways. There came in 1953 the Colloquium of Muslim/Christian study organized jointly by Princeton University's Department of Oriental Languages and Literatures and the Library of Congress and meeting on the campus of the University. Warm friendships were there for the finding which later helped me in my travels. Then in 1954 came the offer of a Travelling Fellowship from the Rockefeller Foundation, admitting of some eight weeks on the road in the Middle East. The *per diem* allowance was, by my standards, more than adequate: it enabled me to bring the family across to England where they spent Melita's first summer out of sanatorium while I widened, territorially, my familiarity with the East. Flying to Beirut (my first air-borne venture) I went on by road, rail or plane, to Istanbul, Ankara, Aleppo, Damascus, Baghdad, Amman, Cairo, Tripoli, Tunis, Algiers, Tlemcen, Fez and Tangier. In several places impromptu studies were concerted and my horizons were greatly extended. Baghdad was particularly rewarding with the close friendship I encountered among the Shi'ah at Al-Kazimain. I had to wait until 1956/57 and the initiation of the Study Programme of the Near East Council of Churches to discover the world of Persian Islam, but crossing the Bosphorus by ferry from Europe to Asia, to discover The Blue Mosque and Haghia Sophia in company with Lyman MacCallum,[27] and to gather Quranic calligraphic verses in the suqs of Aleppo, truly complemented the ventures of book-mind which Hartford had sponsored. Along the way, especially in Cairo and Fez, I was able to waylay figures who had only been names to me from the time of my dissertation.

The whole journey armed me for the two final years the agreement with Hartford had to run and, at the same time, hinted to me the pattern which the future might take, albeit in a form still to be revealed.

Debts incurred in America are by nature irrepayable. Were this Chapter a narrative it would have to lengthen itself inordinately and lose its main thread. The spontaneity of hospitality, the vitality of human things, the incentive to adventure, the will to participate – all these were refreshingly alive for the enlivening of the stolid Englishness that was liable to suspect a robust imagination and a tireless urge to be at grips with every problem. I was able in measure to repair my sad English ignorance of American literature and philosophy and to enjoy the unstinted generosity of colleagues and associates on campus and beyond.

Certainly the U.S. sojourn was entirely responsible both for the genesis and publication of *The Call of the Minaret*. For my part it was a strange case of stumbling into print. A small group for Christian study of Islam used to meet, mainly in New York, to which I was invited. They were people responsible either for teaching or for administration and some had long retrospects of ministry across Asia and Africa. They thought that some kind of 'manual' was necessary and that the effort of producing it might focus their ideas. It would reflect the change of scene and temper since Temple Gairdner's *The Reproach of Islam*, written in

1909. I was invited to make a draft. The commission was exciting and I found the material growing as I pondered it. The result became much more than the group had envisioned but they bore with it, reflected on it and withdrew from any primary responsibility for how it would emerge. The title was meant to indicate that there truly was a 'call' to Christian mind and soul from the mosque which could only be answered by perceptive, open reckoning with what it constituted for the faithful Muslim. The clear, peremptory clauses of the muezzin seemed a right, courteous and inclusive framework for a study of Islam in its doctrine, liturgy, law and devotion – all in the immediate setting of mid-20th century life. The writing coincided with my first acquaintance with Harvard via the Conference which produced *Islam and the West*,[28] and was enriched by numerous other stimuli, not least the several Summer Conferences of outgoing recruits at Meadville, Pennsylvania.

Unknown to me, one of the group took the text off to the Editor, for religious books, of the Oxford University Press, New York. He showed enthusiasm and I was informed that the book was on the way. I was not to know that it would have a quarter century of life, be also paperbacked and find a revised, up-dated career thirty years later. Its positive quest into the minaret's Muslim meaning, insofar as the outsider could perceive it, had also to be a translation into Christian hearing. If there was a neighbourhood of sound, there was also an economy of transcendent claim. The former could too easily be registered in annoyance about broken sleep, or in the scant indifference of the too familiar. Beyond these, there surely had to be a sense of meaning truly inviting ministry, a summons which had a claim on those to whom it was not addressed precisely because it was so imperative to those it did.

The book's third section, 'Minaret and Christian,' tried to explore what that call might entail in respect of thought, witness, attention, service and interpretation. Canon Max Warren, then General Secretary of the Church Missionary Society, gave the book almost lyrical acceptance in a double issue of his Newsletter, though he sobered me later by observing that 'the Irish were given to strange enthusiasms.' In time Muslim reviews came saluting what they saw as its positive, just portrayal of Islam even if they had reservations about any conceivable Christian 'ministry' concerning it. For my part, the book was 'bread on the waters,' no more than a turn in the long road that had begun sixteen years earlier and would continue decades more. The book's inscription to Henry Hill and Graham Brown showed how far back my debts reached. The immediate ones belonged in Hartford and New York and perhaps it is right to see the book's longevity as a token of all I owed them.

The author might well have been thought something of a hypocrite had he remained outside the Middle East, securely out of earshot of his own theme – though by 1956 there had come to be an imposing Mosque in Massachusetts Avenue, Washington, D.C. Islam has now a much more prominent presence in the U.S.A. and Europe than was the case then. The minaret had been part of our mental landscape in Gaza, Beirut and Jerusalem. There was point in letting it be so again. In any event, gladly renewable as the contract with Hartford was ready to be, or alternative ones elsewhere in the ever hospitable America, we had always assumed ourselves in transit as non-resident. This was not a logic we would have forced upon events. Events themselves connived. Initiatives taken by the Jerusalem Diocese and the Near East Council of Churches developed into a joint appointment which would make me the latter's Study Secretary, as a Residentiary Canon of the Cathedral of St George, in Jerusalem. Our departure from Hartford was as logical and regretful as it had been from Longworth.

vii.

The 1954 journey had given me some inkling of what might be afoot. Institutes of Christian study of 'other faiths' were being developed at the time in a variety of Asian capitals. Possibilities varied enormously and it was clear that the Middle East was in no shape to admit of institutionalized Muslim/Christian study – outside existing Schools or Seminaries of Theology. e.g. in Cairo and Beirut. Any programme must of necessity be one of inciting local courses and resources, encouraging study via guiding publications, and possibly convening summer Schools. The care of any such programme must necessarily be peripatetic, involving constant travel to local venues, if it was to be at 'grass-roots.' It would also be very precarious. The summer of 1956 saw the gathering Suez Crisis – no augury of settled content, with the comings and goings of 'the Canal-Users Association' and other futilities and culminating in the criminal folly of the Suez invasion by connivance of Ben Gurion, Anthony Eden and Guy Monet.

We were faced with a hard decision when we arrived back in England that summer, committed to the new enterprise. What home could such a 'minaret-call' admit? Moreover, John and Arnold were at a crucial stage in their school life, adjusting from the U.S.A. and prospecting towards Cambridge and Oxford where they eventually arrived. Melita and I decided that we would set up home in England and that I would 'do the beat' alone for ten and a half months, with six blissful weeks of reunion in the English summer. It was the hardest decision of our lives. We sustained it for three yearly stints, by which time it seemed evident on all counts that the Study Programme should go to other hands and that we should resume a single household. The way we did so belongs to Chapter 5.

It is hard to tell which of us suffered the more. Certainly the loneliness told on Melita's spirit and she did not have the constant stimulus that fell to me of travel and engrossing tasks. I, for my part, never had more reason to notch off days, day by day, in my diary, like some Crusoe on his tree – some three hundred plus of them till we could meet again. The benediction of what I have explored in Chapter 3 was with us unfailingly throughout. Fortunately, despite my sundry ports of call, we were able to sustain each other with steady letter-writing. Readers will understand the dedication of these Chapters. Many queried our decision but vocation required it and authority seemed to go along.

So, in September, 1956, I set out via the Institute at Bossey of the World Council of Churches, to make my way to Jerusalem. Archbishop Geoffrey Fisher was kind enough to call me to Lambeth to enquire into my hopes and to bless the new venture. He talked pertinently about theology between faiths and I was awed and encouraged by his concern. We had not met since at Tranmere after a Confirmation (Melita's) he gave me his blessing for Jerusalem in 1938. If, as reputed, he was truly a workaholic he had discernment in his malady. I was soon to discover how much reason Lambeth Palace had to shake an angry fist across the Thames at the Houses of Westminster.

The 'residentiary' Canonry at St George's was soon to prove a misnomer. I had less than a quarter of my time during the three years in 'residence,' spending in fact many weary weeks in Beirut as a better springboard from which to foray – as I did – to Istanbul, Baghdad, Cairo, Amman and Cyprus and Khartoum. But Jerusalem (the Old City, then in Jordan) was always the venue for summer Schools, the first of which convened in July, 1958, to be continued every year until 1967 (After 1959 I shared in them from Canterbury) Some sixty gathered every year from the whole dispersion. Variously housed, they combined some 'pilgrimage' dimension with lively Biblical study, Islamics and Christian theology in tandem. Among the scholars who could be recruited to this venture was Dr Daud Rahbar whom I had come to know in Ankara and who brought a rich personal experience of both faiths to his very able scholarship, and his own particular stress on the 'worshippable' as the clue to theology.[29] His friendship remains among the most cherished memories of those lonely years.

The Suez Crisis, of course, greatly prejudiced western relationships across the Arab world, though – able to get to Cairo as early as May, 1957 – I was touched by the warmth of human welcome despite my British guilt.[30] It had seemed imperative to me that we should strenuously disown the crooked folly of our British policy and affirm an Arab/English solidarity in Christ despite it. Accordingly, in Beirut in November, the Revd. 'Aql 'Aql and I issued a strong statement to that effect, repudiating the duplicity and the violence and dissociating ourselves wholly from its implications.[31]

'Odds' are always to be reckoned with if one has loving ends. There were times when 'this was all folly' stole over me in a pain of futility. Islam, people told me, is, was and would remain, impervious to Christian meanings. It had everything already and what we wanted to interpret into it would always be vetoed by its adamant assurance, its entrenched theology of unexamined, unexaminable, unity. At such times, I had to fall back on my conviction that Christian relation there had to be, that there were features of the Islamic soul and mind which *were* consonant with things unique in Christ and that this Semitic 'consanguinity' had to be made evident so that estrangement might be overcome.

To be sure we had our high days. There was a notably successful 'school' in late November, 1956, in Beirut which served to put the Programme 'on the map,' and a lively beginning to it in Isfahan the following May. It was there under a Persian sky and the aura of the Persian domes, I discovered the Sufi invocation of 'the Name that is written on the leaves of the olive' and, mystified as to its first meaning, wondered how it might fit with Gethsemane. That was the kind of thing that was always happening when one hearkened to the Qur'an or the writings of the Muslim *Aqtab*, the 'masters of devotion.'

I had occasion also, by invitation, to spread my wings further still with journeys into Pakistan and India as well as a six week sojourn in Ghana, Nigeria and Sierra Leone. These forays were meant to link the N.E.C.C. initiative with its counterparts elsewhere. They also helped to develop my own perspectives by contacts wider than Arab Islam afforded. It was thus that I came to meet and talk with figures like Maulana Abu-l-'Ala al-Maududi and Dr Allah Bukhsh Brohi. The great Iqbal had, of course, died well before those late fifties but I remember vividly a visit to his tomb beside the celebrated Badshahi Mosque in Lahore where I read an inscription in four languages. 'Do they not reflect on the Qur'an or do their hearts have locks upon them?' (47.24) Evidently the Qur'an was aware of an inattention that imprisoned its meanings and demanded to be awakened. Our 'theology of attention' equally clearly had some mandate to be such.[32]

The other central plank of the Study Programme was an issue, almost monthly through those three years and beyond called 'Operation Reach,' very widely circulated and carrying a Bible study and a presentation of some central feature of Islam for reflection and testing in the circle of experience the recipients enjoyed. The hope was that human relationships would be alerted, warmed and informed by its contents. Certainly for me the steady business of producing it was a constant spur to ideas and connections. I kept a notebook of impressions and of the sundry 'catechisms' to which I was subjected in my travels from both Christians and Muslims and these were all grist to the mill.[33]

Amid so many vagaries and imponderables, it is hard to know what the Study Programme accomplished. It renewed and deepened the sense earlier acknowledged of massive incomprehensions waiting on Muslim/Christian mutuality of mind. Chapter 8 below is a better place than here, in longer retrospect, to assemble in theological terms the *raison d'être*, the *raison de non être*, of the community we sought. By the late summer of 1959, other loyalties had to intervene, my Jerusalem 'stall' was left vacant and the N.E.C.C. cast around for the future. It would be a whole decade before I would be back again in the same 'territory' in place and theme and it would then be out of Cairo and in episcopal harness – at once both a complication and an adaptation of its first incarnation. 'Operation Reach' would give way to 'Emmaus Furlongs' and 'Grace Cup,' as study prods and products, no longer of the Council but of the Dioceses. The story belongs to Chapter 6. The reunion of August, 1959 was all the sweeter for the absences we had endured and in the knowledge that they would no longer be always impending like shadows on tomorrow. There was always that strange verse in the Qur'an about 'God mastering what He had in hand.'[34] It was faith's courage to believe that perhaps we had been part of it. Meanwhile, what could be more thrilling than the as-yet unclouded sky of Canterbury?

A large part of the wistfulness of those years was how to negotiate loneliness. What did one do with those surges of longing and emotion pulsing through one's very being? The very fidelity which occasioned them had to have them in its care. They had to be translated into trysts of heart which could be as if there were no intervening distance. It was the anniversaries and great festivals which were most difficult. Christmas, 1956, I spent on the campus in Izmir of the Amerikan Kiz Koleji where Christmas lunch was taken at different stages up and down the campus and we were invited to compose limericks. Services I shared with Samuel Bird, my fellow-deacon of 1936, who had exiled himself in the Izmir Chaplaincy. Christmas, 1957 found me in Lagos, that of 1958 in Lahore. New Year's Eve was our wedding anniversary. I spent the last few hours of 1956 and the first of 1957, snatching sleep in Ankara railway station, watching the cleaners with their busy brooms and waiting for a decent breakfast hour at which to descend upon my host. Later, on reaching Beirut, I learned that those hours had coincided with my father's passing in Blackpool a few days short of his seventy-ninth year. The same Eve two years later found me in a train in Sind en route for the Quetta Eye Hospital's seasonal clinic in Shikapur.

There were lifts of heart and mind along the way. One of the most memorable was the beauty of the phosphorescent light along the lips of the prow's waves as we sailed through the pond-like waters of the Persian Gulf en route to Muscat and then turning in among the grim, black hills of the harbour, later to visit the grave of Bishop Valpy French on one of its rock-girt beaches.[35] My most memorable cold I encountered in inland Turkey, at Konya, saluting both Paul and his Iconium adventures (Acts 13.51–14.6) and the snow-clad Mausoleum of Jalal al-Din Rumi, founder of the famous Mawlawiya Order of Sufism, with its conical tower strangely resembling the traditional headgear of Armenian clergy.

Or one would find oneself climbing to some peak-top

hermitage amid the awesome grandeur of the mountains of Ethiopia where no female foot might tread, or trying to absorb, with the help of Hassan Dehqani-Tafti, the architectural glories of *Naksh-i-Jihan*, 'the design of the world' in the heart of Isfahan.[36] There was a magic in the association of these several worlds, what they had been, what they might yet be, and their urgent necessity to converse by dint of an Islam that had a mind, and of a church stretched, to respond. Contriving itineraries was more than negotiating with calendars and priming the pumps of opportunity: it was contriving mediation between communities and minds, between legacies for what they honestly were and meanings for what they might yet be.

When we made long journeys by car in the States, especially up to Maine and beyond or across from Connecticut to Colorado,[37] our tiny Chris would ask, prospectively: 'How many nights in it?' 'Nights' there often were in the pursuit of the Study Programme, some of them sleepless in airports, some of them metaphorical in searchings of the heart, some of them spiritual at the very core of faith. I reserve to Chapter 6 the days and nights in the meaning of Jerusalem. Had I not noted at the end of *The Call of the Minaret* that, after Mecca and Medina, the two most sacred mosques and minarets were those across the valley from Gethsemane? The ventures of the three succeeding years seemed to be living in that inter-space.

Chapter 5

Forfeit in Canterbury

i.

'Know, Selim, that there is a monastery
Which standeth as an outhouse to the town.
There will we banquet ("lodge?") them.'[1]

Archbishop Geoffrey Fisher, with much pioneering by Canon Walter France, had the same idea. Housing whom? – clergy from the wide Anglican dispersion. Why? because all were in need of theological depth and width, all were apt for richer fellowship in the things of worship and ministry, all were potential material for the emerging leadership of church administration and spiritual direction. A 'Central College of the Anglican Communion' had become in the forties an urgent symbolic and practical necessity and as soon as post-war occasion allowed he was persuaded of the duty to bring it into being.

And 'the outhouse'? Indeed – the precincts of the original monastery the first Archbishop, Augustine, had established soon after his arrival on a mission from Pope Gregory in 597 A.D. in sequel to the 'conversion' of the King of Kent and his people. An 'outhouse,' to be sure, in the days of playwright, Christopher Marlowe, of Elizabethan Canterbury but renewed in the mid-19th century as a house of prayer and study through whose emissaries much of that Anglican Communion in Asia and Africa had been given birth.

'There will we dislodge them' was the decision of Anglican Primates during the tenure of Archbishop Michael Ramsey in 1967. The decision to close the College was a sorry failure of vision and resolve, a forfeiture of an interfolded destiny linking Bede's *Ecclesiastical History of the English People*, beyond the trauma of monastic dissolution, via the renewals of the Oxford sacramentalists, to the life and times of Michael Ramsey. The brief vocation of the College was a beacon light in recent Anglican history. Its forlorn demise was my deepest private story, a harsh, unwanted redundancy, entailing a sense of dereliction whose sources were official and against which all personal positive efforts after continuity were disallowed.

The Abbey at Canterbury was, of course, no stranger to sad vicissitudes. The last abbot, at the dissolution under Thomas Cromwell, died – it is said of a broken heart – within two years. The College had inherited his 'grace-cup,' a delightful remnant which we brought out on state-occasions, such as archiepiscopal visits, though it was never filled again.[2] Renewal came when Edward Coleridge and A.J.B. Beresford Hope, M.P. for Maidstone, concerted the formation of the Missionary College in 1848, reconstructing ruins which had fallen foul of intervening centuries and had become a quarry for the house-builders of Canterbury in Stuart and Hanoverian times. The Central College became a natural successor a whole century later. Thus far no new resurrection is in sight.

The story of what was forfeited, and why, inevitably became a strenuous part of my faith's debate with the meaning of the debacle, my life's negotiation with its bitterest passage. For, after a year as Fellow and another as Sub-Warden, I had become Warden of the College at the beginning of 1961 on the departure of the first Central College Warden, Kenneth Sansbury, to become Bishop of Singapore and Malaysia. My eight years to the summer of 1967 were a time of excitingly congenial endeavour and warm, wide fellowship. Who, in right mind, could fail to kindle to the task of interpreting Canterbury – legend, tradition, architecture, heritage, ethos and vocation – to a variety of her proper sons and daughters who looked to her from the ends of the earth? It was precisely the authenticity of the concept and the promise of its implementation that made the termination so painful an experience, contrived as it was, not by insuperable circumstances, or unnegotiable factors, but by a negative lack of will, a languidness that let the vision die. We had reason, in the event, to recall Marlowe's own motto: *Quod me nutrit, me destruit,* 'That which was my nurture becomes my destruction.' If the story has a logic of reproach it is told here more in a mood of melancholy. There is no need to exaggerate what itself has full measure.

ii.

St Augustine's, as a missionary College, from the 1848 inauguration, filled a noble role in Anglican history with a succession of well-remembered Wardens down to the thirties of this century. Its founders had modelled it on the pattern of an Oxbridge College, with a Governing Body of Warden and Fellows, appointed for a specified period by the two Archbishops of Canterbury and York and the Bishop of London. This stipulation, intended to ensure due accountability was to have an ironic quality in 1967. The Foundation under Edward Coleridge retrieved the ruins from their quarry-like fate and from the cock-fights, auctions and other civic usages which had secularized them in the eighteenth century and from the ravages of earthquake and storm. The first Court became the College 'Quad,' the old Hall the new library, the guest hall of the Abbey the Dining Hall of the College and the northern cloister rooms for students. Only a modest endowment attached to the College itself – a circumstance liable to prove its Achilles heel. Its viability depended on its use by missionary societies, mainly the (then entitled) Society for the Propagation of the Gospel, who by sending students ensured it a *métier* and by paying their fees an income. All was ordered under a Charter granted by Queen Victoria. The major ruins of the great Abbey and other parts of the original monastery remained as they were, though now recovered from profanity and able to tell their legend mutely. The Tudor walling where Henry viii had courted and played tennis with Anne Boleyn was integrated partly into a new Museum and the Gateway Chamber where their daughter, Queen Elizabeth, had slept and whither Charles Stuart (later the 1st) had escorted his French bride, Henrietta Maria, on her arrival at Dover, became the College Common Room. The old and sometimes bitter rivalry with the Cathedral, the house of 'secular monks,' the shrine of Thomas Becket, Martyr, and the beneficiary of neighbouring dissolution, was relegated to the past as the College strove to discharge, outside the walls, its new ministry in the nurture and discipline of missionary scholarship and devotion.

Eloquent measure of its success lives in the Crypt Chapel below the College Chapel that lies between the Dining Hall and the Warden's Lodge. Its walls are lined completely with small stone tablets commemorating its 'graduates,' the men it sent into the worlds of Asia and Africa. They carry the date of departure which often coincided with Ordination, and the date of death. The eloquence is in the span those dates allow. Few had more than a decade before death overtook them. Expectancy of ministry was brief, given the perils of climate and sickness as they were in Victorian ventures into swamps and forests and slums. Yet it is clear that there was never wanting a succession, a sequence going where death had thinned the ranks. 'Here we offer and present ourselves . . .' become no trivial formula in Eucharist inside that shrine of a much maligned century of English mission to the world. It was this costly tradition which, in part, had given origin to what more prosaic ecclesiasticism would call 'the Anglican Communion.' It was these student-priests who had pledged a stake in Canterbury to nascent Christianity for which Cranmer's Prayer Book and Keble's *Lyra Anglicana* would become possessions tethering to a distant sanctuary the heart's affection.

The régime in old St Augustine's was doubtless spartan and austere but there was an *ésprit de corps* across the years that had voice in a long series of Warden's 'Occasional Papers,' which are a mine of minutiae about the comings and goings, the ordaining and the dying, of these Augustinians. Bede, in his *Ecclesiastical History*, records how the first Archbishop, seemingly a timorous soul, relayed back to his Pope Gregory the questions that beset his mission.[3] A much more sustained and voluminous correspondence found its way into the 19th century archives in the intercourse of the College with its dispersion. All their self-interrogation as experience yielded the basic dilemmas and issues of a missionary intention across the world became a legacy to a later time and to a successor institution appropriately lodged in the same hallowed precincts.[4]

For it was becoming apparent to perceptive souls by the thirties of this century that the pattern was changing. The first *métier* of St Augustine's College had in measure fulfilled itself in the genesis and ripening of churches looking to Canterbury in the bishoprics to which it was the loved mother. Other agencies too had fulfilled themselves in different areas from those of St Augustine's 'graduates,' notably through the energies of the Church Missionary Society. Vital as society-based ventures had been, it was increasingly apparent that direction and administration needed to pass from *ad hoc* Committees in London, to diocesan structures in each and every local Christianity. Such structures would pre-suppose local, national leadership. That leadership would need fuller initiation into faith and order, into communion and discipline, than the often-circumscribed matrix of particular mission had provided. 'Ministry to such ministry' had become the urgent and crucial need of each, the vital right of all. Would not Canterbury, with its fourteen centuries of retrospect and its immediate century past of sacrifice to have the churches exist, be the right imaginative centre for such a 'ministry to ministry,' such a discharge of obligation within a Communion truly alert to its contemporary reality?

iii.

Archbishop Geoffrey Fisher, the first much-travelled modern Archbishop of Canterbury, rapidly became aware of these needs when he succeeded William Temple in 1945. His early journeys abroad convinced him of the urgency of the diocesanization of the Anglican allegiance, so that newly created Provinces, notably in Africa, should no longer be led by English Primates but fully entrusted to men of the local soil, tuned to the local ethos. It became a central plank of his policy to inaugurate these structures, setting them free from official reference to Canterbury and entrusting to them their own independence in office, liturgy, canon law and discipline.

Two immediate imperatives became promptly clear. One was the level of theological education and competence, the other the necessity of inclusive, mutually tolerant churchmanships. Both could best be met in a house of prayer, study and fellowship, which pooled a diversity of needs in a single unity of mutual discovery and exploration. Standards of training left something to be desired, since worthy pastoral 'carers,' lively archdeacons, potential bishops, in many places, enjoyed only a modicum of academic learning and were still far from being the local Hookers, or Herberts, or Gores, or Temples, of their own culture. Such they would need to become, not by imitative assimilation but by a genuine flowering of their innate capacity with and through 'the riches of Christ,' more fully discovered in a context that both transmitted all that was Englishly theirs while liberating all that was natively so. Such would be the meaning and actuality of 'oneness in Christ,' where we, being His, 'all things are ours'. (1 Corinthians 3.23).

Geoffrey Fisher's thinking along these lines, and the alerting of the Communion at large to these hopes, owed much to the enterprise of Walter France, a Secretary in the S.P.G. and formerly a missionary in Japan. He knew the situation intimately from the inside and he deplored the pattern by which overseas bishops were liable to send their promising clergy to a variety of colleges in England, often on the basis of their own familiarity. Why should such 'futurands,' he asked, not be brought together in one place to mutual profit? Ought there not to be a house of study designed for their particular needs, rather than asking them to fend as best they could in institutions contrived for the needs of English ordinands – a quite different commodity? He pressed the point in a University Sermon in Cambridge on June 1st, 1941, the occasion being a recollection of that strange Victorian institution of 1841, the Overseas Bishoprics Fund, devised to finance them, innocent as they were of the sort of funding available to bishops in English dioceses. Bishoprics could only be properly constituted in British territory – hence the special measures necessary to the establishment of the Jerusalem Bishopric in the very year of the Fund's inauguration.[5] The irony of the situation was not lost on the preacher. He spoke of 'the new era . . . concerned with the whole architecture of church life,' where bishops and clergy of local origin 'must have continued access to all Christian knowledge in liturgiology, history, canon law, and pastoral and moral theology.' Rhetorically, he asked: 'Is that mind wholly dead which sees in the church overseas little more than a far-off, picturesque nursery where the children may be admired, but where the wisdom and agonies of adult life are not to be expected?' He urged that the centenary should be marked by an active expectation and nurture of indigenous leadership.[6]

Five years earlier in *The East and West Review* he had argued that emergent nationalisms should not be allowed to isolate or pervert local churches. To deter and dissuade cultural separatism and encourage a local universality of mind and temper, clergy everywhere – and through them laity in each place – must be offered a full, scholarly experience of their whole heritage. This, he said, required a College in England designed to equip them for a liberation of their culture into full articularity in Christ via a comprehension of the wholeness of the Church. He added 'religious drama' to the list of requisites. His case was entirely consonant with his New Testament, inasmuch as its Epistles required that they many should be one and the one many and had been indited to that incorporating end. Unity was in true diversity – a common mind variously fulfilled.

His phrasing of the vision anticipated almost exactly what the Central College became.

> '. . . a small College, preferably in England, capable of receiving thirty or forty students, staffed perhaps by four men, each a specialist, each capable of directing study and guiding research, would soon become more than an academy. It would become a centre of scholarship to which the Church in all lands could turn for information, and perhaps for counsel. It would be a meeting round for men of many races, not only studying together and sharing their heritage

> of tradition and experience, but forming links which might be strong in binding the churches together and preventing national isolation . . . a vision of great mutual enrichment, and not least to the Mother Church.'[7]

It is well to detail this formulation, if only as a measure of what was so cruelly cast away about three decades after it was written. To be sure, as his son later assured me, Walter France was a 'romantic,' but he had truly sensed and stated what the times demanded. Perhaps he was a trifle negative in seeing 'nationalism' as only tending to isolate and not also potentially to enrich, and the feeling of 'Englishness,' implicit in his locating of the College, as the best security for things Anglican, though instinctive to him, would need to be adjusted[8] – as indeed it was when the vision was attained.

Walter France had pioneered a project, chartered a concept and dreamed a dream. After the end of the Second World War, Geoffrey Fisher was entirely ready for the logic of the case France had made. It coincided with what Fisher perceived the Anglican Communion requiring of his primacy. He found a ready agreement from the Presiding Bishop of the American Church, Henry Knox Sherrill and also in the Bishop of its first Diocese, Connecticut, Walter H. Gray. They may not have known that seven decades earlier the beloved conferees at Longworth and *Lux Mundi* had pictured 'an Anglican Oratorian Community' where they would 'say their offices, discuss and read, and keep their hours together.'[9]

The Lambeth Conference of 1948 resolved to implement the ideas of Fisher and France and a Lambeth Conference thereby became the mentor and referee of the whole concept – a point which was ignored in 1966–67 on the very eve of the next Lambeth. The 1948 decision ran:

> 'In the opinion of the Conference the establishment of a Central College for the Anglican Communion is highly desirable and steps should immediately be taken to establish the College, if possible at St Augustine's, Canterbury.'[10]

When remitted to a Conference Committee, this resolve was confirmed, the value of the Canterbury location stressed and strong emphasis laid on representativeness in churchmanship and due strength in scholarship. It envisaged a central library adequate to undergird research and respond to enquiry. It agreed to seek generous endowment for the implementation of the whole.

Four years later, under Kenneth Sansbury, a pupil of Walter France, the Central College opened its doors. The Victorian Charter had been revised in the intervening years to admit of the *métier*, making priest-students admissible from all quarters. The College remained a Corporate Body appointed by the two English Archbishops and the Bishop of London, though – as I know from my own case in the Wardenship in 1961 – Fisher consulted all his fellow Primates, as of their right and not of mere courtesy. The College's *raison d'être* was thus adjusted from that of furnishing recruits *to* the dispersion into that of welcoming and enheartening clergy *from* it, all the while savouring the genuine continuity between the two roles.

Unhappily, the 'generous endowment' never materialized. With, at best, some twelve per cent of its operating costs from its own endowment, the College would subsist by dint of grants from the Anglican Communion to enable it to receive the clergy that communion sent to it, just as Societies had earlier enabled it to subsist by financing the recruits they sent for training. Either way it was a precarious subsistence. It is, however, salutary for an institution to be viable only by virtue of what it can achieve and fulfill, rather than by the comfort of bequests. The cost, however, was a complete vulnerability when the will to sustenance failed. That imagination and generosity in harness gave it only a life-lease of fifteen years must always be to the reproach of all concerned.

iv.

But that is to anticipate. The financing was in the trust of the whole Communion, every diocese contributing, however modestly, so that it could be the possession of all. The major weight fell, appropriately on the Churches of the

West, the United States, England and the Provinces of the Commonwealth. Numbers grew steadily during the fifties and the Lambeth Conference of 1958 minuted as follows:

> 'The Committee has examined with care the Report submitted to the Archbishops and Bishops of the Anglican Communion, and desires first of all to express its appreciation of the fact that so much has been achieved in so short a time. There is considerable evidence to show that the College is meeting a real need in the Anglican Communion, and in spite of initial handicaps and difficulties its life is firmly established.'

It noted, however, two 'main difficulties.'

> 'The College has been handicapped by having no capital resources of its own, either to complete the work of establishment or to act as a cushion to meet rising costs. The Committee is satisfied that every economy is shown in ordinary expenditure, and so far the budget has just been balanced every year. But there is no margin even for modest modernization, let alone necessary extension.'

What the signatory, Walter H. Gray, there identified persisted to the end, with grants from the Communion agreed in the Conference often falling behind either in amount or schedule or both.

The Committee's second 'difficulty' had to do with Provinces and dioceses making adequate use of the College by nominating clergy. On that point the situation steadily improved in the years that followed, though, of course, the two 'difficulties' were inter-locking. The Resolution of the Committee went on:

> 'If the Conference approves the continuation of the College *until the next Lambeth Conference*, it is essential that bishops should ensure that suitable men are set free for a period to take advantage of the opportunity. Generous bursaries are available to suitable men . . . But, if the College is to fulfill its proper task, every part of the Anglican Communion needs to be represented.'[11]

Within three years of Lambeth, 1958 that representativeness had been achieved. That its internal finances received such tribute was due to the yeoman, voluntary labour of the Bursar, Edward Chandler, who served the College through its entire career, a man of gentle diligence and total dedication. It was no fault of his, or of ours as a Corporate Body, that by the next Lambeth in 1968 there was no College to assess, to praise or scrutinize. In 1958, as in Dickens' *Great Expectations*, we 'discerned no . . . parting from her,'[12] though aware of how poised on unpredictables the future would be.

I had joined the College the year after Lambeth, 1958, after nomination by the Warden and appointment by the three appointers under the Charter. It was thought that my experience across the Middle East and my time in the American Church would all be relevant to its task while my theological 'stable' – to use a horsing metaphor – was thought apt for the balance and appeal of the College. For our part, Melita and the boys and I were eager for family unity after the long separations of the years with the Near East Christian Council's Study Programme. We settled into No. 9, Vernon Place, then a College property and sixteen months later into the Warden's Lodge. The Honorary Canonry of the Cathedral which Geoffrey Fisher attached to the post was throughout to me an awesome privilege, though I have often wondered, with Robert Louis Stevenson, how 'any man can dare lift up his voice in a cathedral,' since no words can ever match the silent sermon of stone and glass, of arch and line, of towering vault and the haunting presence of the centuries.

I found the patterns due and right – the daily Offices in Chapel, on Saturdays in the Crypt, the Eucharist in all the languages and liturgies of the churches represented, the stimulus of corporate Bible Study and the task of lecturing, whether in doctrine or culture or exegesis, and – over all – the comradeship of unitary diversity. The understanding was that the dispersion nominated its own clergy. In the case of the Episcopal Church, U.S.A. there was a nominating committee, in New York, which vetted all applicants, ensuring six a year, whom we accepted without more ado. Nigeria also usually attained a six-strong contingent. Elsewhere we would have to concert with individual bishops.

Bursaries were available but travel costs had to be conjured out of the air by various means. The British 'Society for the Promoting of Christian Knowledge' was generous among English sources of *ad hoc* funding. The understanding was that no priest-students of less than five years' standing would be accepted – this in order to ensure that experience had been gained and study-issues ministerially faced – nor were any judged too senior in years, or set in habit, to benefit by the College in terms that could be invested in their life-expectancy.

This made for a lively diversity of expertise and perplexity, so that Chicago could rub shoulders with Tokyo and Ibadan with Isfahan and India with the Caribbean. We tended to find that the older the person the more likely to be deferential to 'mission traditions,' wedded to western norms, and reluctant to indigenize. It was the younger men who were more likely to get the measure of their own cultural liberties in Christ while at the same time absorbing the heritage that was theirs by free adoption alongside that of birth and making. We had no mind to imply that the Lord could only aptly be praised under a gothic arch or with the melodies of Bach and Handel. Yet in esteeming wattle huts and the booming drum, we had no mind to suggest that these were 'good enough' for 'natives' to use them.

We re-named our 'houses,' thus far, unimaginatively A.B. C.D. as Azariah, Brent, Crowther, and Temple – an eminent Indian Bishop of Dornakal, a noted Canadian/American Bishop, the first Anglican African Bishop and one whose Primacy at Canterbury had been tragically abridged by death.

The dining Hall of the College was a place of modest fare, replete with historical memory as Guest Hall of the monastery and with many hidden secrets of its more dissolute years until duly repossessed by the to-be-priest-students of our immediate ancestry. In the Middle Ages there had been widespread use of monastic guest-halls as inns, with comedians on hand for entertainment. So central was such hospitality to transients that grantees of dissolved monasteries after dissolution were required to maintain comparable open house. We did not emulate the directive which ran:

> 'The Customary at St Augustine's directed that no waiter carried more than three dishes at once. The refectory being the common dining hall, no singularity in eating or drinking is allowed, no noise to be made. For instance, if there are nuts, they are not to be cracked with the teeth . . . Should he spill anything he has to go and do penance. He is not to make signs across the refectory if strangers are not present, nor to look about or watch what others are doing. He is not to lean on the table. His tongue and eyes are to be kept in check and the greatest modesty observed.'[13]

While modesty was indeed esteemed among us, we ignored the old rubric about Augustinian cloisters:

> 'Let no one dare to ask about the gossip of the world, nor tell it,'

and the one concerning corporal punishment, enjoining bowed head and covered eyes on the part of all others while it was being inflicted on the culprit. Nor again were we in the régime in which 'hay on the floor and beds of straw were renewed only once a year.'[14] Rather, the new order window-ed in the stone mullions of the open cloisters, so that – unlike the medieval scribes – no 'fingers froze.' However, it was explained to Americans, used to continental 'lows' and ample house-warmth, that, in the more moderate English winter and the inferior heating systems, 'many are cold but few are frozen.'

We did draw, however, on ancient history for its precedents around the problems of culture. Was the African drum inherently infused with tribal war and pagan dance, or could it be duly baptized into the call to worship, the due equivalent of that very English thing – the bell? Was libation irretrievably part of ancestor worship or could it be drafted into the reverence of Christian prayer? What of ancestor worship *per se*? Was it, in fact, 'worship' at all, or potentially at least a dimension of grateful piety? If devotion was not to be captive to the culture that brought it, imitative rather than creative, must it not find authentic expression in what belonged with local haunt and ethos?

Bede's *Ecclesiastical History*, already noted, gave us to know that the 7th century in Kent had faced the same problems. Gregory had recommended that the old shrines and temples – and the paths the 'natives' trod towards them – should be retained so that familiarity would serve the new Christian faith. But they were to be disowned by the removal of all pagan symbols and by the sprinkling of holy water to exorcise the demons of superstition so making possible the installation of 'the true and only Cross.' Continuity and discontinuity – were not the issues comparable, even if we had reason to dispute the supposed efficacy of 'holy water.'[15]

These, and other topics in doctrine, history, ethics, and liturgics, became the material of dissertations undertaken for the College Diploma on the part of those with the necessary competence to undertake research and independent thought. Others, no less pastorally effective, but lacking academic skills, received a College Certificate of Residence. for everyone expected to take some creditation home. The distinction was invidious perhaps and needed care in its application but it registered faithfully the disparities which plainly existed in the standards of ministerial capacities across the whole Communion. Both sorts of salutation were awarded on Diploma Day at the end of the academic year at a service usually held in the ruined crypt of the Abbey open to the sky.

As for 'not asking about the gossip of the world,' there was hardly a theme in faith or life that could not be articulate in those haunts, where history was like 'a green fuse' pushing, spring-like, through our veins. There was a mingling of pastoralia from Lagos to Madras, from Seattle to Manila. Only China, sadly, for reasons beyond our scope, was absent from our society. Nor were we an exclusively Anglican community. Via World Council schemes of scholarships, or other means, Orthodoxy from the south of India or from the Balkans, was represented, and occasional scholars from Europe. A Franciscan Islamicist found a haven with us, and the otherwise wholly clerical community was leavened with a small infusion of 'senior ordinands' who brought experience in a variety of posts and skills to our enrichment during their preparation for – mainly but not exclusively – English Holy Orders.

The Church of England was the part of the Anglican Communion that used the College least. Clerical 'leaves of absence' were rarer then and liable to be taken abroad. We sought to remedy that situation by the development of 'Open Weeks' each term. English Diocesans were invited to nominate clergy for invitation and to pay their travel while we undertook their accommodation from Monday p.m. to Friday after lunch. We could manage up to fourteen, the Warden's Lodge had spare rooms when sons were away at College, or Fellows could oblige. These 'Open Weeks' coincided with special lectures by invited experts of whom the College had a generous panel, just as it did of speakers for the Thursday evening 'Common Room,' in the famous Gateway Chamber.

The 'Open Weeks' served two purposes, They infused a breath of C. of E. into our living and forged friendships, which – in turn – had the potential to meet another need, namely where to 'bestow' our members during the Christmas and Easter vacations, when the College closed its kitchen and the members anyway needed to travel. Anglo-Saxons might have resources to go across to Europe – perhaps never so adjacent again, but brethren from Asia and Africa could, through 'Open Weeks,' discover homes hospitable to them in the interludes – to the great profit of the parishes.

The disparity in wherewithal, just noted, was one of the side-problems for we embraced a wide diversity of living stipends and standards, as between Baltimore and Harare. For the most part, these were manageable, with patience and goodwill, and it was salutary for the affluent to appreciate the privations of their brethren, and to respond accordingly, the English, of course, being somewhere in between.

Another issue for vigilance of a harder sort was implicit in our situation. It was no secret that the Central College was meant to serve a future leadership. Did attendance, therefore, mean that 'x' was a man marked for a day when he might say: *Noli episcopari*, and nevertheless consent? By no means. Yet the thought could hardly be suppressed. It was urgent that, whatever might, or might not, transpire, we must be and remain a company of 'the holy and humble in heart,' blessing the Lord either way. In point of fact, ex Central College priests have been bishops and archbishops in every part of the Communion, including the martyr Archbishop of Uganda, Janina Luwum, and his colleague, the Bishop of Mbale. It was on this count that the biographer of Geoffrey Fisher could write:

> 'The Archbishop was gratified to discover, on his extensive travels, how many clergy holding positions of great responsibility had passed through the College.'[16]

It could not have been so without the presence, in many cases of wives and families. The College had facilities for some *en famille*, others with wives alone. This meant great enrichment all round and gave Melita and other Fellows' wives a ministry in the various arts of being wedded to a cleric. When in 1968, while temporarily in Nigeria, we travelled to the home and parish of Isaiah Alegbeleye, we found a hanging sign outside his vicarage advertising home-made cakes, by a cake-maker 'U.K. trained-expert.' The sign referred to makeshift ventures in the 'Lady Warden's kitchen.'

The College's ministry to the Communion was fulfilled not only in the residential academic year of three terms from early October to late June, but also in residential Summer Schools, of which there were normally three every summer, of twelve days each. These were largely in the care of Canon Leonard Schiff, ex India, since I was away every year of my wardenship, except 1967, in Summer Schooling in Jerusalem. Each School would comprise three area-topics and recruited from a wide circuit of interest. When the College was disbanded the Summer Schools were retrieved in Cantess, the Ecumenical Summer Schools at Canterbury.

In its entire vocation the Central College could be described as a sustained negotiation between original Englishness and authentic Anglicanism, the fullness of a world community with a local matrix in time and place. It was a negotiation that had to be lived as well as studied. Our liturgies were in no way restricted to those of the Church of England. We were Anglican extraterritoriality hard by the mother Cathedral, whose very presence on the skyline was inspiration, not to speak of its music, its windows, its precincts and its Crypt. Churchmanship for us all was comprehensive and participatory. The *Liturgy for Africa* allowed a greater scope for creation and ecology than Crammer had been able or alert to provide. Worship could be lifted from the immediate pre-occupations of the 16th century, with its noble heroism, into patterns open to the crises of the 20th as our human reach disclosed them. The very title of 'The Book of *Common* Prayer' seemed to approve ventures beyond its forms once what was truly 'common' had come to be more widely experienced. Likewise the fidelity to sound doctrine, which the Book in its necessary 'uniformity' had been intended to ensure, needed to pass into the loyal care of a wider reach of mind and spirit. In its founding concepts, its modest attainments and its proven promise, the College could be said to constitute both the symbol and an organ of Anglican fulfilment in love with 'the mind of Christ.' Why, then, should it have been allowed to lapse, cut off in its vigour and consigned to history.?

v.

The reasons were partly financial and partly personal. The former are the easier to explore. From the time of the 1948 and 1958 Lambeth Conferences and the Toronto Congress which convened in 1963, the principle of a common charge on member churches had been made central to the financing of inter-Anglican projects, of which the Central College was the first. But structures to ensure the policy were slow to materialize. At the time of the closure of the Central College, there was no Anglican Synod, though from the sixties an 'Executive Officer' had been secured in the person of Bishop Stephen Bayne.[17] That Office was the next claimant of the inter-funds, with the Jerusalem Archbishopric another and a new Anglican Centre in Rome anticipating the same status. The Central College had, literally, to 'eat out of the hand' of its Communion – a legally chartered body in its own right and yet operable only as the organ of the Communion that, via Lambeth, had authorized both its rationale and its livelihood. With that status it was honour bound to let the 'maintenance' flow to it from that pledged financing and not go out for itself to 'raise' finances on its own account, most likely – if more directly – from the same sources. This principle was honoured to the end. The Corporate Body did not see itself as a fund concerting profession, but a teaching, caring entity fit to be made and kept viable by its official status as the Communion's Central College – though sundry lecture fees and incidentals were diverted into its Library purchasing from teaching members.

Financial viability, though pledged, was rarely fully forthcoming, or was behind the clock, so that budgeting was always precarious. For my part, I offered for election to the C. of E. Church Assembly and the Convocation of Canterbury and, on election, tried to use what persuasions I could to untie the strings that ran via the Assembly to 'the Central Board of Finance.' Accountants sometimes lack imagination and 'the Board' never fully acquiesced in being drawn upon by decisions taken inter-Anglican-wise, which cut across its own system of authority.

Those in the third, or the two-thirds, world who stood to gain most by its availability were the least able to contribute to its continuance. Those most able to pay for it were, therefore, the most obligated to be generous. It was an embarrassing equation in that the 'haves' (materially) were required to be magnanimous about the 'have-nots' (likewise materially). It was difficult for the latter to exhort the former, if the former, for any reason, faltered in their perceptions about the latter.

There was one factor particularly in relation to the American Church which we could never overcome, especially after the departure from office of Geoffrey Fisher and Walter Gray. It had to do with the piper and the tune. Those who pay like to administer. Some misgivings arose in the U.S.A. about increasing the funding (as necessity required with the passing years and through agreed budget studies which the College provided regularly) without organizing some committee structure to supervise the College and its life. Here we faced a dilemma. Any such committee would need to be as worldwide as the Communion. To be realist it would need to meet, say, twice annually. This would involve an expenditure diverted from the bursary and travel charges of the College, so – in default of new money – drastically reducing the priest-student intake. Ought we to expend funds on people debating the College and, by so doing, contract the very subject of their counsels? Ought it not to be possible, in Christ, to trust each other.? Were funds anyway, in ecumenical circles, rightly expended on officialdom? Here, however, lay our vulnerability.

Every effort was made to have the concepts and workings of the College amenable to scrutiny and advice. The London Committee, chaired by Bishop R.R. Williams of Leicester, in part fulfilled this function in England. Its Minutes were available across the waters. When I was in the U.S.A. lecturing, or otherwise, I took occasion always to meet with the American Committee for admissions in order to bring its members as far as possible into the analysis and to learn their mind. The College autumn Term had perforce to be arranged before its participants were on hand, the rest of the academic year was always subject to their critique and ordering. At the end of each year, the whole student body was invited to comment and to advise about changes or initiatives for their successors. In this way the administration of the funding was as democratic as that funding could logically admit of, in all good faith.

In the event, this did not suffice. With the defaulting of promised moneys the finances became more urgent and it became clear that the main sources were loathe to make them good and plan effectively and decisively for their increase. At their meeting in Jerusalem in May, 1966, the Primates decided that the Central College would close that summer. The African and Asian Primates could only deplore: as, inevitably, petitionaries in matters of finance, they could hardly press insistently for the sustaining of an entity which they were in no position significantly to fund. For their part, and for lack of energetic counter-counsel, the western participants either wearied or approved.

The reason for the decision was only a financial one, communicated to Warden and Fellows by Archbishop Michael Ramsey as such. He simply indicated that from the given date the Anglican Communion could, would, no longer finance its College-creature. The question of the Lambeth mandate to be the Central College was neither mooted nor addressed. It was on this point that our response was immediate. Did the decision mean that the Primates had over-ruled their own Lambeth and decreed the end of what had, in 1958, been voted to continue 'until the next Lambeth.'? No it did not, explicitly: implicitly, it did, since without finance – it was assumed – the College could no longer function even if it retained an official warrant to do so.

This was the sorry subterfuge of the decision. If the College was simply deprived of its 'hand to eat from,' to which it had been ever loyal, it would devise other hands – hitherto improper to it – from which it would fight to continue. By 1966 we had as many as four hundred former priest-students, all of whom were endeared to its vocation and many of whom were in positions of influence in dioceses and parishes. We would be free to 'work out our own salvation.' Plans were drawn up for a letter to 'all whom it may (it surely will) concern' about our need, our situation and our hopes. Meanwhile, we protested to Michael Ramsey that priest-students were already in 'the pipe-line' for 1966/67 with plans and promises made. We secured a reprieve on that account for that year, hoping to prolong the time to allow Lambeth, 1968, to speak its mind. As a matter of courtesy, our circular-letter was submitted to the Archbishop. His response this time was unequivocal. We were to desist from any such saving operation. The financial decision was to be taken as a termination of the concept and the end of the dream. That was the gist though those were not his words. The upshot seemed to indicate precisely what had embarrassed the Jerusalem discussion, namely how to lay off the expenditures while not, except *de facto*, impugning the principle and dismaying the beneficiaries too pointedly. It was a strange kind of negotiation between having and not having, between the reservations and the ideals of 'inter-dependence in the body of Christ' – as the current phrasing was.

In Canterbury we of the Corporate Body were left with the immediately painful experience of responding to numerous letters from everywhere, deploring grape-vine news of our impending demise, enquiring why it had been thus decided, urging our own vigorous self-help, offering to share, and enquiring when it would be launched. There was a note of anger and of incredulity in many of those letters. All a Warden could do was to explain that we were required to lie down and die. When Lambeth came a year later there was no official discussion of a *fait accompli*.

vi.

It is difficult to write about the role and personality of Archbishop Michael Ramsey. There were undoubtedly hurdles to be taken and problems to be resolved which were not of his making and which called for strenuous leadership and a careful strategy. It was from him that these would need to be forthcoming as the *Primus inter Pares* of the whole Communion and as the Archbishop locally involved and with most at stake. The simple truth was that those personal resources, or their steady deployment, were not forthcoming. He was aware, of course, that the Central College had been a particular concern of his predecessor but he had inherited it and its claims stood in far more than the personal commitment of a retired activist, greatly disappointed by its demise.[18]

I had several sessions with him in the Old Palace during the sombre months preceding the end. He was generous with his time and yet strangely capable of somehow evacuating issues of their dimensions of anguish or crisis, if he was not interested. I still feel the pain of one quiet occasion in his study when I ventured to bare my heart to him. I remember saying: 'Your Grace, those buildings are at the heart of Anglican history – the Abbey, the Missionary College, the Central College. If one *métier* has again been abandoned, what is to become of them – in your Diocese, with so much sacramental in them from the long past?' When he replied, quite tersely, but not unkindly: 'You can take in lodgers,' I was so overcome I had to restrain tears in his presence. I did not know what exactly he meant, unless it was that we could keep the kitchen staff employed and tide over until other times. It was all a far cry from the *angst* I felt about all that was in forfeit. It was the more searing an experience by the fact that he seemed to find it all somehow inconsequential.

I often wondered how far he was really appraised of the actual levels of academic competence then prevailing in the Anglican ministry world-wide. His own orbit, prior to his tenure in Canterbury, had been Cambridge, Durham, York – hardly a complete background for an Archbishop in Canterbury. His attitude was often donnish in its perceptions. One analogy he used with me about the financial exigencies was that the product on offer was not worth the price tag attached. It was in itself a depressing use of terms in that context. In a letter he observed that 'to think in terms of the provision of a top level faculty' would make 'the expense greater still.' Did he assume, as they might in Cambridge, that talent could only be had where good money was? If so, how was that the spirituality which so marked his character? And was not all this 'inter-dependence in the body of Christ' and, therefore, a 'labour of love'? It is true that the Corporate Body was a modest group – though four of us had doctorates.[19] We were, anyway, ministering to the clientele, and the clientele embodied what the Anglican ministry was and was likely to remain.

I had to try hard to bring this perception of ours home to him. It was true that our Diploma and Certificate were not 'graduate' stuff. Nevertheless, the writers were enlarged, re-charged, and renewed and we had not failed them.

The irony was that the actual level of our clergy intake was on the point of having a vital fillip from a new factor.

Many capable, academically exciting and excited clergy were very willing, from India and Hong Kong, from the U.S.A. and elsewhere, to share in an inter-Anglican family during a sabbatical, but could they combine it with the acquisition of a new Degree? We had, until 1966, to say No. They often went where they could have that added feature. The new University of Kent at Canterbury, with which we negotiated, agreed that candidates with suitable pre-requisites could combine residence with us with an M.A. in theology by dissertation in one year. In 1966–67, one Canadian priest did so. Had this facility been 'on the map' a little longer and duly publicized, one significant factor in our recruitment would have been met and the level of scholarship raised. To be sure, loyalty to the actual situation would have dictated that we remain operative in whatever terms, however lowly, the Anglican ministry required, but our 'repute' as Michael Ramsey was minded to esteem, or dis-esteem, it would have been enhanced. The opportunity passed – a casualty of the demise.

We were, no doubt, fit to be queried if thought of in terms of a house of reference for every problem, a sort of think-tank for every perplexity. That might have come, in some measure, had we had a longer occasion to aspire after it. We were after all no older than a teenager when we ceased to breathe. It is hard not to feel that survival would have been eminently possible, eminently desirable, given the long investment of vision and hope, had there been actively in place an archiepiscopal determination eminently so resolved.

It was always puzzling how to understand His Grace or, as one observer put it, 'to get far down into his undoubted depth of mind and heart.' He had a disconcerting way of seeming to be able to set aside that to which his thought did not kindle, to be absent as well as present at the same time. This was very evident on the annual occasion when he came to College, for dinner and an informal conclave in the Gateway Chamber, where he would be open to questions. Geoffrey Fisher would handle these times with great aplomb, even loquacity, fielding questions with gusto and serious delight. Michael's approach was reserved, at times monosyllabic. When asked, for example, how he saw himself and his Office, he replied: 'I see myself as a kind of patriarch.' Was he making jocular reverence to his image as more venerable than his years? Was a capital 'P' meant, or a small case 'p'? Much of importance turned on the ambivalence but he would not elaborate. The question was simply left dead. He gave what seemed to us a curt and imperceptive reply to the intriguing question whether the office he held and its place in the whole Anglican Communion would always need an English occupant. The real problematics deserved some sensitive exposition. In spite of all, there was, I am sure, a deep bond between us, fatherly affection on his part, genuine, if sometimes puzzled, affection on mine. His biographer, Owen Chadwick, kindly exonerated him from all responsibility for the end of the College, 'in the circumstances,' though conceding that it was seen by some as a major miscarriage in his career.[20]

vii.

He sometimes seemed strangely oblivious of what became of us in the dispersing Faculty. He knew that it was open to me to develop existing links with Union Seminary, New York. One Fellow we could ourselves place in the one living the College had care of – conveniently vacant – at Fordwich near by. For the rest we were left to fend for ourselves. There were times in that final summer when my thoughts drifted to the solace of Shakespeare in recalling the feelings of the faithful retainers of *Timon of Athens:*

> 'Yet do our hearts wear Timon's (Michael's) livery.
> That see I by our faces: we are Fellows still,
> Serving alike in sorrow. Leak'd is our bark
> And we, poor mates, stand on the dying deck . . .
> We must all part – into this sea of air.'[21]

It fell to me to indite the last of the long series of 'Occasional Papers,' numbered no. 415, to interpret, as far as words could, what had overtaken us. My American sojourns brought Robert Frost to mind with his plea:

> 'Ah, when to the heart of a man
> Was it ever less than a treason
> To yield . . . and accept the end
> Of a love or a season?'[22]

'Treason' was not too strong a word, unless – in accepting our quietus – we were to disown what it had always symbolized and the love we had brought to it. If faith and life are truly conversing they cannot hold at bay either romance or betrayal.

So the final Warden's Letter concluded:

> 'We say farewell to one another, dispersed from our calling but still loyal to it in our hearts. There have been other dissolutions here before . . . "Man's last and highest leave-taking," said Meister Eckhart, "is leaving God for God." We leave what we have known of Him for what we shall yet know, leave the God we have found in the mercy hitherto, for Him we shall learn in the mercy henceforth. It is our calling not only to trust God *for* salvation but to trust Him *with* it. Only so "shall all manner of thing be well."'

Faith has to know, and to acknowledge the measure of what was cast away, the worth of what was forfeited. That was the reason for the extended narration here of the concept, the rise and the termination of the Central College. There is no honesty in love which is not honest with reproach. *Nostra culpa.*[23]

My Melita felt the departure from Canterbury as keenly as I for she had been joyfully fulfilled there and the loss of the College tenure meant also the loss of a home. We packed books and belongings in cardboard boxes in the basement for despatch when we could know where. There were few who could have thought of the College in the terms of Mark Twain's wry humour: 'I did not attend the funeral but I wrote a nice letter saying I approved of it,' unless it were those who had eager eyes on the destiny of the revered walls and amenities.[24] For us personally it was wry comfort too to think in terms of what A.N. Whitehead had once remarked: 'It belongs to the depth of the religious spirit to have felt forsaken.'[25] Or was the right logic in the odd observation of Washington Irving: 'I have found in travelling in a stage-coach that it is often a comfort to shift one's position and be bruised in another place.' What that 'other place' would be we had to wait to know and bruising it would prove, with yet another redundancy in train. Canterbury had been a wonderful 'stage' – indeed superb, inasmuch as many told me that I had the finest study in the Church of England, looking out on a fabric of history and the flint-stone, Tudor chequered, walling of the garden with its two splendid lime trees and the trim lawns, devotedly cared for by Laxton, the maintenance man, and Stannard the gardener and Stanley Terry, the porter.

Canterbury via the College had brought us a wealth of friends, invitees to the functions of the college we shared with the community at large. For us two, privately, coinciding as the closure did with family anxieties such as come to all, we knew the poet's words:

> 'The spirit and the flesh cried out for more,
> We two together, in a darkening day . . .
> In the deep middle of ourselves we lay.'[26]

We have only occasionally been back to Canterbury since and it has seemed then a different place. In mid-September 1967 we left for Union Seminary, New York, to follow this in the first half of 1968 with a Visiting Professorship at the University of Ibadan in its Department of Theology and Arabic, and then, through 1969 a Bye-Fellowship for writing at Gonville and Caius College, Cambridge, pending what might yet unfold in more settled terms.

These were necessary practical measures. How inwardly was faith to negotiate around this piece of life? 'Here we have no continuing city,' might be apposite from Hebrews 13.14. Or should we simply agree with Bishop Stephen Bayne that 'Anglican history was littered with the wreckage of departed dreams' and reflect that another had been added? Or, would it be more fitting to recall how Dorothy Sayers, in her play about a maimed master-builder at Canterbury in *The Zeal of Thy House*, had counselled him

'. . . when God came to test of mortal time
In nature of a man whom time supplants,
He made no reservation of Himself . . .
But in good time let time supplant Him too . . .
Thus shalt thou know the Master Architect
Who planned so well, He may depart and leave
The work to others.'[27]

Who and where and how the 'others' might be would have to wait.

Or perhaps the wisest course would be to invoke thanksgiving as the way of 'rejoicing in the Lord alway,' to revert to that relic of a 'grace-cup' which at times of celebration or of parting had been passed round among the brothers. Like every venerable institution, St Augustine's had its 'Graces,' some composed for its Central College incarnation. Here are three in the conviction that nothing is lost if we can make it an oblation.

'Lord, who wast known in the breaking of bread and in whose breaking bread is known for a pledge and sacrament of fellowship: Hallow, we pray Thee, this our board and College for the glory of Thy blessed Name.'

'Lord, whose compassions fail not, give us grace so to recognize and receive Thy mercies that we may fashion our own selves after the same pattern of kindliness and care, through Jesus Christ our Lord.'

'Be present, merciful Father, with us Thy children who acknowledge Thy providence in their provision, Thy bounty in their supply, Thy bonds in their fellowship, that so they may know Thy hallowing in their receiving through Jesus Christ our Lord.'

Chapter 6

Unease in Zion

i.

'. . . I reach Jerusalem . . .
. . . it elates me . . .
To void the stuffing of my travel-scrip
And share with thee whatever Jewry yields.'

So Karshish, the Arab physician of Robert Browning's poetic dialogue.[1] Not here 'what Jewry yields' only but also the Anglican 'presence' – English and Palestinian – which I found there in midsummer, 1939, in uneasy partnership amid the ever deepening unease of the British Mandate. After the thrill of my first sojourn, our – or my – travels brought us to Jerusalem, for a shorter or a longer time in each of the years 1940, 1945, 1956 to 1966, 1970 to 1977, 1980, 1982, 1992. Truly, as medieval pilgrims knew, 'the road to Jerusalem is in the heart' whether or not the road is taken. How ought faith and life to negotiate with the vicissitudes of that half century, with the supreme theme of Zionist fulfilment and the costly ironies of Zion? What in that vexing context of the inner story of Anglicans in the bewildering complexities of 'the Holy Land,' as the *ecclesia* moving in, through and then beyond Mandatory circumstance into the trauma of Palestinian tribulation and Israeli triumph, a church aspiring after a oneness in Christ against all the odds of time and place? It will be well to take the ecclesiastical unease first, keeping always in mind how far it was prey to all that made 'the peace of Jerusalem' so far to seek, so acrimonious even in the seeking.

'It elates' was Browning's word, not mine. We may suspect the same about the psalmist. There are few things in holy writ more ironical than Psalm 122. Either the poet meant it but only in his dream, or he was fending off the bitterness of delusion. There was little adequate or durable in the restoration of walls by Nehemiah – if that was what the psalmist meant to hail. Was 'prosperity' ever the mark, or the benison, of true lovers of Jerusalem in any century, least of all in ours? What was this 'unity with itself,' as Coverdale rendered the puzzling Hebrew of v.3, where others have 'rebuilt . . . solid and unbroken,' or 'firmly bound together,' or '. . . reconsolidated,' or '. . . one united whole'?[2] *Cujus participio ejus in idipsum*, runs the Vulgate. Or, as the N.E.B. thinks, does it mean 'built to be a city where people come together in unity.'? If so, we have to ask who 'the tribes' of v.4 are and whose 'the thrones' of v.5. The very greeting of 'Peace,' (v.8) is for 'brethren and companions' sakes.' But who are they, to warrant the Septuagint's: 'whose fellowship is taken together'? The entire irony of 'the Holy City' is explicit in its most familiar hymn of admiration and salute. The psalm's orchestral themes are anticipation, courtesy, reverence, excitement, aspiration, resolve, confidence and celebration – all of them ambiguous.

For long ages there used to be two fascinating approaches to Jerusalem. Since the terrain tilts to the east, it is prosaic to come uphill for the west. From the Jordan valley, via Bethany, however, cresting the eastward slopes of the Mount of Olives, a breath-taking panorama awaited the eye, now much diminished in its drama by visual distractions. From the north, the Nablus road used to afford a sudden revelation of the domes and towers as it climbed the breast of a hill now levelled into highways and suburbia. It still did so when taxi from Haifa, after passage of the border at Ras al-Naqurah out of Lebanon, brought me to summer school of Arabic in Jerusalem in July, 1939. The memory remains vivid still.

Very English and Edwardian among the towers was that of the Cathedral of Saint George beyond the Mosque of Shaikh Jarrah, in the immediate foreground. Equally solid, but less conspicuous amid the roof-tops of the Old City, was the tower of the German Lutheran Church, hard by the Holy Sepulchre. Both were, of course, peripheral – in no way properly to divert the mind from the splendour of the Temple Mount, the Haram al-Sharif and the Aqsa Mosque. Even so, I was heading for the Hostel beside the former and there my ecclesiastical allegiance belonged, there the auspices to preside over my studies at the Newman School.

The two towers postdated by many decades the original 19th century presence of the two European disciplines, Anglican and Lutheran. The Jerusalem Bishopric had been inaugurated in 1841 as an imaginative, if controversial, venture of ecumenical 'compactness' – to use the psalmist's word. Erasmus and Luther had both dreamed of a comprehensive European Church. A friend of John Milton, a certain John Drurie, with Oliver Cromwell's blessing, had tried to achieve one. The German Van Bunsen, who was Prussian Minister to Britain two centuries later, and a friend of Thomas Arnold, mooted a scheme whereby the Church of England and the Prussian Lutheran Church would jointly establish the Jerusalem Bishopric with appointments alternating. The Lutherans in this way would bring 'Apostolic Succession,' as Bunsen saw it, into their Church by use of the English Ordinal, and recognition of Word and Sacrament would be mutual. Though Pusey spoke for the plan, J.H. Newman decried it as Protestant pretension and it served to prompt him Romewards. After three Bishops, the scheme foundered, Hence, years later, the two separate towers. The two Churches would separately negotiate the 'compactness' of Jerusalem.

Under the long tenure of the second of those Bishops, the Swiss Samuel Gobat, a considerable Arab allegiance to 'the Church of England' had come into being, not primarily by design but by dint of strained relations with Eastern Orthodoxy when lay people responded to 'the open Bible' and evangelical personal 'saving by grace alone,' and were ostracized or disowned by their ecclesiastical authorities. Gobat believed that pastoral and sacramental nurture should be provided for them. Though the Bishopric had been conceived as both provision for foreign Christians in Ottoman domain, and for the conversion of Muslims and Jews, it found itself contriving an authentic Palestinian dimension recruited from local Christian

Churches. That dimension was necessarily and properly continuous even when the reconstituting of the Bishopric in 1887, under Bishop G.P. Blyth, sought for ecumenical and positive relations with the Eastern Churches in a temper which, fully realized, would not have approved the *fait accompli* of the Gobat years. Also in the equation was the Jewish concern that had been present from the beginning, symbolized by the first Bishop, Samuel Alexander, a former Rabbi and learned in Judaica, and by the historic aura of Christ Church, in the Old City, which was the episcopal seat before the 1887 decision for a St George's Cathedral.

There are always things paradoxical and illogical in ecclesiastical story. Anglicans are no exception. There was a legacy of ambivalence in the Jerusalem Anglican presence, with the difficult vocation to be 'at unity in itself' as a community of English origin and a destiny to comprise both foreign and Palestinian in 'one fellowship in Christ,' and to do so in the ever more vexing setting of the Palestine Mandate and nascent Arab nationalism, embroiled inevitably with Zionist political decisions about the necessarily territorial and combative nature of Judaism as Zionism saw it to be.

These antecedents throw light on what obtained by 1939. There is no need for detail of the long story and its tensions.[3] I was soon made to realize, in my naivete, how taxing were the relationships, within a single episcopate, of Jewish-Christian concerns, ministry to an administering (occupying ?) power, with its High Commission, its officers of state, its police, and an Arab Palestinian church within a church, self-conscious, lively and increasingly restive for its centrality in the whole. The Bishop, or Archbishop, until 1975/76, need not be – though sometimes was – liturgically or more widely – an Arabist. I learned to decipher the letters P.N.C.C. as belonging to 'the Palestinian Native Church Council,' as a separate *Majma'* or 'synod.'

To represent these elements there were three centres – the original Christ Church, with its Hebrew adorned sanctuary and its implicit Zionist sympathies, St George's Cathedral where the Mandatory power was at home and

Liturgies were always English, and St Paul's where the Palestinians gathered. We students of their language often went there that summer for it helped the ear and memory in the mysteries of diction and of sense. Yet there was always a deeper yearning that our three 'tribes' might prosper in a common 'peace.' 'Ease in Zion,' as Amos saw it, would never be appropriate, but was our Anglican 'unease' no less to be deplored? The political disquiets of the Mandate and beyond, which we have shortly to explore, only sharpened what was domestic to a Christian presence in respect of love in Christ and ecclesiastical integrity.

ii.

The circumstances of World War 2 brought an unquiet respite to the region in that a more inclusive crisis was in agonizing progress in the western desert and from the beaches to the heartland of Europe. With the post-war recession of British power and the intensifying of the political confrontation, the Palestinian partners in the Jerusalem Bishopric sought more than the honorary Canonry held by the esteemed, Elias Marmura, of St Paul's Church. It seemed to them imperative that the principle of local leadership espoused increasingly (as we have seen in Chap. 5) by Archbishop Geoffrey Fisher in Africa, should be applied to them. The special circumstances of Jerusalem, however, were pleaded to dissuade him, though his old sister, Sitt Norah Fisher, a veteran of Palestiniana, gave the issue a warm place in his affections. How, it was asked, would the ecumenical 'embassy' role all churches somehow visualized for themselves in Jerusalem fare in Arab hands alone? And what of the Jewish dimension at Christ Church and elsewhere? Other participants in the debate resented what they saw, unsympathetically, as Arab pressure. In any event, Bishop Weston Stewart was still the seventh Bishop.

His retirement in 1957 gave Fisher the opportunity to move forward but he was still hesitant about an inclusive new order. Canterbury, he decided, would retain the final authority it had always preserved but the jurisdiction would be raised as an Archbishopric in Jerusalem, to which Campbell MacInnes, then Bishop of Bedford, but long experienced and nurtured in Palestine, was nominated. This, Fisher calculated, would admit of the creation within it of an Arab jurisdiction, a Diocese of Jordan, Syria and Lebanon, in which Canon Najib Qub'ain was appointed Bishop, overseen in some sense by the Archbishop, as would be the Bishopric in Iran, with the other parts of the area administered from Jerusalem.

This device lasted for almost two decades, from 1958 to 1975. It seemed to do well by the 'embassy' ideal among Patriarchates of the East and it cared for the tensions between the Arab and the Judaic Christian elements. However, it was deemed by many no more than interim, a structure partially granting and partially withholding the autonomy the Palestinian partners desired. Half a loaf was *not* better than no bread. Arab logic and emotion continued to press for what they held congruent with the Arabism they were urgent to express on every count of politics and integrity.

Though Campbell MacInnes had to weather many stresses as the external situation hardened, his tact and the esteem in which he was held kept the solution viable. It was more difficult when his retirement in 1968 renewed all the essential issues. After much consultation, Michael Ramsey decided to maintain the Archbishopric but with an inner agenda of study and decision within some five years by which a more ultimate solution could be contrived. To this end, Archbishop George Appleton was appointed. Though unfamiliar with the region and its languages, he already had archiepiscopal standing to smooth his path and a pre-retirement period suited to the agenda.[4] It was natural, therefore, that his tenure would undergo accentuating strains, given the trauma that followed 1967 and the birth of the P.L.O., and in view of lively anticipations about the future of the jurisdiction.

Lest the reader fears that I have lost the thread of my faith-with-life negotiation in this narrative of Anglican complexities in Palestine/Israel, let me now prove it not so. For they became part of my own story especially after

1968. Even a new and raw recruit to language study in 1939, trying to respond to all the *Fada'il*, as Arabic called them, the strange glories and 'virtues' of Jerusalem, could not fail to register things at odds as well as at one between St George's, Christ Church and St Paul's and their varied interests. There was little one could do except keep them in heart and hope, and think of any Arabic competence – if ever – as a future bridge. In its own sweet way later, the Study Programme intended some contribution to the unities of mind and spirit, as an exercise in Christian Arabism by its very concern for a Christian register of Islam. It was also in intention a harmonizing of all the elements involved. When the crunch of 1968/69 arrived I was in my post-Central College anxiety, not knowing what might be, but urged to stay available. I declined an academic post to which I was appointed, and tried usefully to redeem the time. In 1963, a plan put to me by Michael Ramsey, at the instigation of Campbell MacInnes, to become assistant Bishop in Jerusalem conflicted with the task in Canterbury, then so engrossing, and was allowed to lapse. On his own appointment in 1969, George Appleton renewed it – and urgently. He assured me he could not undertake his own task single-handed, but, given the agenda earlier noted, it was an invitation with a probable built-in redundancy. There would be no assistant Bishop within a terminated Archbishopric. Respected senior figures warned me of a potential *cul de sac*.

It was in this testing way that the long delayed Arabicization of the Jerusalem jurisdiction came painfully into my own story – and into an immediate negotiation with the logic of life. How was I to respond to George and, in turn, to Michael Ramsey? Ought Christian ministry, in any circumstances, to ask or expect some guarantee of continuity? Episcopal travels would give occasion to renew the vital ventures of the fifties, while the office might mark them as close to the centre of things and not, supposedly, an idiosyncrasy. Yet episcopal office would also complicate the task. I was in India in a six-week sojourn at Union Theological Seminary at Bangalore when the call became official. It might be, in the event, a short lease of opportunity and there were other misgivings. When I returned to England, Melita and I decided to accept. I was to be assistant Bishop across the whole Archbishopric, from Morocco to Iran, but from a home in Cairo, pending eventual changes by which Egypt might become itself again a diocese. Early in 1970 I was consecrated in Jerusalem.[5]

In due course, the Archbishop retired in 1974 and, after an interim period, the new Province of Jerusalem and the Middle East came into being, in complete independence from Canterbury and with its own duly constituted Central Synod. It was to be composed of the old Jerusalem jurisdiction of Palestine/Israel, Jordan, Syria and Lebanon under an Arab Diocesan; Egypt, with an Egyptian Diocesan; Iran which already had had its Persian Bishop since 1961; and the new Diocese of Cyprus and the Gulf. These would elect a Presiding Bishop from among their number to give an over-all unity to the new expression. It was a privilege to have been part of the development by which Anglicanism in the Middle East became almost the last unit to reach due, and long coveted, local autonomy. For my part, and for a third time, a loved structure was taken down around me, leaving us free to be 'bruised in another place.' This third time, however, it was not some tragic external calamity as with St Justin's House, nor unhappy acquiescence by authority as at Canterbury, but a welcome attempt to heal Anglican 'unease in Zion.'

It cannot be said to have succeeded. Perhaps 'unease' will never end. Jurisdictions, however vital, are only part of the equation and the perennial near-despair about peace in the region still lies heavily on the Churches. There was no legal room for me in the new set-up. If it was painful to be redundant we had always known that it might well so transpire. It was wise to see it as no more than a minor incidental matter in the perpetual struggle to weld into one all the disparate motives and concerns that belonged with Jerusalem and fulfill the vocation of a community in Christ suffering steady attrition by time and emigration and set where the 'prospering' that should go with 'loving' was so far to seek. It is time to turn from what was Anglican 'unease' expressly, to the enveloping unease those embattled

Teggart buildings told, strewn across the landscape that summer day in 1939, or the cemetery of British dead that lay across the bosom of Mount Scopus.[6] When for a time I served Bishop Graham-Brown as chaplain during my Arabic studies I became fondly familiar with the desk at which he worked. It was the centre-piece of his study. At that same desk the Turkish High Command had signed the surrender of Jerusalem to General Allenby in November, 1917. What followed through three decades was 'Britain's moment in the Middle East.'[7] What of the political story of that crowded brevity, the mandatory unease of the British in 'Pilate's seat.'?

iii.

What, in the tragic sequel, could ever have justified the ambivalence of the Balfour Declaration of November, 1917, by which the British Government announced that it 'viewed with favour the establishment of a national home for the Jewish people in Palestine.'? For, when written into the League of Nations Mandate to Britain over Palestine, it contrived a sorry bed of nails, a doom of costly futility, through a quarter century of enmities incorrigible. How could diplomacy and power have been so haplessly entrapped? There was, quite literally, a blot on the document Balfour sent to Lord Rothschild: there were blots a-many on its intentions – if these can ever be disentangled.[8]

It was a much debated text, subtly crafted, with portentous consequences and no legal status. How was it achieved? Partly by the negotiating skill of Chaim Weizmann. He, unlike other Zionists who favoured a German option, had decided that the British gave better hope of the cause. There were among them idealists in Bible lore having innate sympathy with Jewish aspiration. More importantly, the Declaration was calculated to sway American and Russian aid in the desperate throes of World War 1. There were imperial calculations – a potential client state athwart the route to India and the Suez Canal. There was even a kind of indirect Anti-Semitism on the part of British Jews who, though they feared the threat Zionism posed to diaspora Jewish citizen-loyalty, nevertheless saw the value of a far-away haven for east European emigré Jews, diverting them from seeking British sanctuary and so endangering the *status quo* of British Jews.

It was the deliberate deceptions of the Declaration that most discredited its makers. It connived against earlier assurances given to Arab allies. It ignored totally the 90% preponderance of Palestinians in Palestine, whom it never mentioned by name. When it purported to 'safeguard' their 'civil and religious rights,' the clause, though vaguely reassuring, could be interpreted as meaning that 'political rights' would not exist, for – if they did – the assurance would be unnecessary. Most of all, there was the hidden 'agenda' of 'a state of' behind the nebulous language of 'a home in.' What did the latter mean if not, by implication, the former? The very subtlety and prevarication generated lasting, and crippling, suspicion when Britain found itself administering a Mandate commissioned to fulfill what it had so evasively defined.

It is necessary to summarize the iniquities of the Balfour Declaration as a prescript set to stultify the entire sequel, laying an impossible burden of futility on an administration caught in irreconcilable, and ever more accusatory, partisan interpretations of what its Mandate meant. Chicanery can never implement truth, for it only lives by defiling it. British 'unease' in Palestine was the more distressful for its origins in British prevarication. British power became inevitably oppressive, trying to hold a ring that had no ring of truth, and was itself increasingly oppressed by the toll in lives and the misery that waits upon the atrophy of hope.

How intractable the Mandatory's imbroglio was is the more evident from how it has remained so when passed to the United Nations and retold – 'with advantages' –[9] through partitions, voted or violent, through wars, resolutions unresolved in fact, and decades of missed chances and fatal obduracy. 'Unease in Zion,' and about it, persists internationally far beyond what British Mandate knew and yet that power's bitter legacy. It is, perhaps, some consolation to remember that British and allied forces, in the

Western Desert and North Africa, physically ensured the feasibility of Israeli statehood. Had Rommel broken through at Alamein, what might there have been of Herzl's 'dream' and Ben Gurion's 'reality.'? How odd on the part of Elie Wiesel to insist that survivors of the Holocaust had no debts except to non-survivors.[10] Gratitude, however, is rare in politics – or religion.

It was in Jerusalem in 1945 that we heard about Hiroshima. What could the juncture mean? What sense could such an enormity make of 'chosen people,' unless, as duly happened within thirty years, they acquired the nuclear thing themselves? More and more, the Judaic panacea of statehood and its military backing was in danger of making of Israel an increasingly 'Gentile' thing, in the sense that even 'chosen-ness' could not escape the lower common denominators of deception, subterfuge, realism, espionage, and power-reliance to which all politicization leads. Had the champions of Jewry and all things Judaic been right to go down that road?

At least the ignominious, but ineluctable, end of the Mandate relieved the British conscience of the present burden of presiding over the tragic issue of events, but never of the retrospect of liability for what would make 1921–1947 seem no more than an episode in a saga set in train by its sanguine 'favouring' in 1917. 'Unease' persists in historical memory and is not allayed by the realization, as the decades pass of conspiracy against peace, that history can neither exonerate nor console. Being the novice I was in the forties to all that was at stake in Zionism and its British 'connexion,' I could be no more than puzzled and confused. Later, in more responsible role, around the Suez crisis and post-67, if only via the Study Programme, I could try to identify what properly lay upon an English Christian conscience from the history one had inherited and its ambivalence about the legitimacy of Zionism, though not of 'Zion,' and about the travail of Palestinianism. One result, after long retrospect, was *This Year in Jerusalem*, the hardest book of all to bring to print.[11] It had to do with four dimensions, as they seemed to me, of the 'unease' in Zion which haunted Zionism itself, this being the ultimate predicament of all. The Balfour Declaration, at its point in time, may have been re-assuringly British but it could equally have been labelled 'Weizmann's Instigation,' – an instigation traceable to factors far beyond the purview or the motives of Lloyd George's Cabinet and Balfour's philosophy.

iv.

It is always hazardous for non-Jews to think aloud, still more to write, about things Judaic. For there is always present the suspicion of anti-Jewish prejudice which can, therefore, always be invoked to disqualify even thoughts that have honestly repudiated it. For it can be Judaically assumed that there is no such honesty. Anti-Jewishness is inherent in all other human beings and is the more suspect precisely in being (only ostensibly) disavowed. It follows, further, that in this paradoxical way, things Jewish, being rarely honestly criticized, possess a kind of immunity to invade which is always 'anti-Semitic.' Aspects of this anomaly will come more properly in Chapter 7. Many in Jewry are, of course, aware of it, want to be accountable to genuine criteria other than their own, and deplore the kind of escape from liability for truth and candour which the negative alibi of anti-Semitic motive affords. Nevertheless, in subtle ways it persists. When one's identity in the world is theologically defined in 'otherness' it must follow that all 'other otherness' – singularly characterized as 'Gentile' – should be suspected as inimical. Jewish self-awareness has been entailed for centuries in this perception of 'the Gentiles,' and urgently needs to know 'belonging with mankind' for what it is. Political Zionism was, and is, at once a bid to do so. It is, however, by the form adopted in statehood, a deep accentuation of the dilemma. What Zionism does to Zion is the greatest 'unease' of all. Is it ever feasible to explore it and truly keep anti-Semitism at bay? The hazards are many but if the hope to do so is doomed then anti-Semitism wins, if only by default.

Through all the long story of political Zionism since its

'base-camp' in the Balfour Declaration there has run the question: On whose side is time? It still presses. Thanks to the Jewish lobby in the U.S.A. the assumed dependability of super-power sympathy suggests an answer satisfactory to Israel, even though acute worries about demography stretch into the coming century. With whom time may side is not, of course, the only question, if we care about where justice sides, or truth. Yet astute partnership with time, with times, has throughout been the hallmark of Zionist realism and policy. Thus it has been drawn steadily down a path and gathered a momentum which only some have had the conscience and the clarity to call in question. Finding succeeding successes and success succeeding, the majority – however diverse their Zionisms – have compromisingly acquiesced, or heartily approved. But for any 'love of Zion' in truth and holiness, the consequences have been dire and grim.

Dire and grim because there is a clear parallel – of deep irony – with the symbol of Masada and the Zealots. As every tourist discovers, the massive ruins of Herod's fortress in the wilderness have become the shrine of Israeli militant prowess, the temple of initiation into the 'Defence Forces.' The events of 66–73 under the command of Eleazar were – in their different idiom – a sequence courageously pursued in confidence about God's partnering approval and a logical impetus of their own which the participants had no mind to call in question until it was too late. When disaster overtook them, their leader had to confess –. according to the historian, Josephus – 'We weakly (?) hoped to have preserved ourselves, and *ourselves alone* . . . It had been proper . . . for us to have conjectured at the purpose of God much sooner, and at the very first.'[12]

Disaster, to be sure, has not overtaken contemporary Israel. Hopefully, it never will, but compromise has, and power-politics, cruelty, aggression, harsh enmity and brutal violence. The many anguished consciences that deplore it being so are the most eloquent testimony to the reality, if callousness, or alibis of 'holiness,' are differently so. Are there not dark aspects in what political Zionism has become, and has entailed, about which 'it had been proper to have conjectured the purpose of God . . . at the very first.'? Its story is now more than a century old. Time, broadly, thanks to tenacity and ingenuity employing it, has, for the most part, proved to be on its side, but at what a price measured by where it started.

It is possible to plead that all that sullies the history stems from the Palestinian resistance it has encountered. There has always been this will to 'innocence' and a failure to see that Palestine, demography, justice, reality, could never admit of it. For what due conscience in Israel must acknowledge as guilt belongs essentially with the dispossession, the occupancy, the territorial and political requisites it intended and demanded in being the sort of Zionism it was. It is true that the ends, thus far, were still hidden in the beginnings and only the twists and turns of an evolving story would disclose what the progress towards them might involve. It is, however, the actual happenings, policies, opportunisms, of that progress which have defined what Zionism is and, so doing, kindled tragic 'unease in Zion.' Many of the early dreamers would surely be appalled by the fruit of their hopes.

What can, or should, be the relation of the outsider to the bitter/sweet history of Zionism *qua* Israeli statehood? Remitting the question for theology to the following Chapter, it is fair to see the story as a series in impasse hardening as it went, and to ask about Zionist capacity to redeem itself from where the present leaves it. My recollection of 1939 is only of something vague and pending, of a tension hardly contained and a back-drop already of Jewish Agency pressures, Arab uprising and a foreboding of things insoluble. When Bishop Graham-Brown first talked with me in 1938 about the plan for Beirut, I knew that the reason why he was detained in London had to do with 'peace negotiations.' He was a close friend of figures like Judah Magnes, first President of the Hebrew University, and the eminent Jewish lawyer, Norman Bentwich. Why not a single, bi-federal Arab-Jewish state, a shared polity in an indivisible land? Set up a framework in which two communities could grow together and let the young of coming generations learn together, subdue their competition and become one people.[13]

It was, and could only prove, a fond dream. Judah Magnes was anathema to the state-visionaries. The whole logic of political Zionism was at stake. Its urgent objective was not a 'host-nation' in Palestine: it was salvation from 'host-nation' situations once and for all. Arab sojourn would be, at best, no better than German or Russian. Persecution, and/or assimilation would always be lurking ominously around the Jewish will to be unfettered as Jewish. This could only be achieved by statehood in which there could be no partners – a philosophy matched by a Palestinian nationalism pleading territory and state by an identical logic. These were the odds. One or other would have to be denied. Bi-federalism betrayed Zion. There was even treason in the likes of Magnes. For Graham-Brown death supervened as he rode in his car with men of both nationalities both of whom escaped.[14]

Prior to the war years, the notion of partition had arisen, only to wait on post-war circumstance. It quickly ripened into a United Nations issue around which Zionist pragmatists scented diplomatic prospects of victory. The idealists were scandalized. For 'the Holy Land' was a single whole, with the holy duty of possessing it to the exclusion of those who had no 'holy' right there. Take what is presently feasible, said the realists, marshalling the case, the tactics, and the international diplomacy and image-making to achieve it.

In contrast, the Arab world, disputing any international or legal right to partition one inch of Palestine, adopted a policy which has repeatedly disserved them, the policy of a 'justice' that is non-negotiable. Palestine, nevertheless, was duly partitioned. Palestinians were a notch further down into the enmity of an outrage done to them, Zionism a notch further down into self-righteous fulfilment and pragmatic vindication. The ensuing trial of strength in the conflicts of 1948/49 took the parties further down into an irreconcilability now sanctioned, on the one part, by success at arms, and on the other by defeat and humiliation that made the partition both more ruinous and more agonizing, accompanied as it was by a massive exodus into refugeedom and privation. At this point, significantly, the decision to name the new state 'Israel' focussed darkly the overtones of divine sanction which were more and more to plague the confrontation.[15]

'Zion' was, indeed, 'prospering,' but not as the psalmist would have had it with 'peace enveloping its walls.' What, by another psalm, were these 'bulwarks' the faithful were invited to 'tell with pride' as guarding 'the city of God.'? (Psalm 48). 'Telling the towers' was good, but what were the towers telling, and what of 'them that come after'? Injuries were festering on the other side in camps and tents of non-repatriation. Palestine, still an identity if no longer a territory, struggled out of mere international pity into a cause for international recognition. As it did so, Israel faced new occasion for such self-interrogation, as its several Zionisms might admit.

Self-congratulation became the order of the day in the amazing summer of 1967. Bidding for some pan-Arab leadership, and espousing the long simmering passions of almost two decades, Jamal 'Abd al-Nasir provoked Israel into pre-emptive strike and released for the Palestinians an avalanche of disaster. The June War had a traumatic sequel for both parties. Zionists believed they had ever less reason to 'conjecture the purpose of God.' It had been miraculously, infallibly, vindicated. Many half-reluctant Jews, especially among the Reform communities, withdrew their hesitancy and surrendered to the legitimacy of a political Zion, thus enjoying the obvious imprint of the divine.

For Palestinians there ensued a deeper, more oppressive, form of 1949, with renewed refugeedom and total, physical forfeiture of territory. Jerusalem, enlarged, was wholly annexed. What came to be known as 'the West Bank' was occupied in a juridical limbo. All that was at stake went angry notches further down in the tally of enmity, suspicion, hatred and obduracy.

Or did it? There was, to be sure, for a few years, the suggestion that post-1967 could paradoxically contrive some liberation. Let the victors be magnanimous and trade surprisingly acquired territory for genuine peace. Was not the ideal of Zion a truly Jewish society which would be elusive or impossible if the state enclosed a large non-Jewish population, the more so if that population had legitimate grievances the surge of which would require the state to connive with repressive measures that would belie its whole mission? As a potentially brutal police state how could Zion be Zion any more? The will to homogeneity, or Jewishness, dictated a foregoing of some territory as the price of hopeful co-existence. The logic was sound but the will wanting. The chance departed. What could be duly partitioned in 1947 and could have been negotiable after 1967, became, at least for the Likud, essentially indivisible by the mid-seventies. The U.N.O. Resolution 242 about 'territories occupied' left a loophole of ambiguity that made it only a rubric for contention.

Palestinians, for their part, could not emerge from the trauma of humiliation in 1967 in any posture to recognize or clinch the case made in Israel for a peace policy. It was only late in 1988 that they came to play their final card – namely recognition of the State of Israel, given ultimate and binding agreement of its legal boundaries. By that date the Israeli advocates of total territory west of the Jordan seemed to have won the day. If Palestinians were at length reconciled to getting what they could, not what justice sought, the die appeared cast against them as long as Likud logic held. As for Israel, questions about demography could be deferred or otherwise resolved. Let defensibility remain the first criterion. Given the loaded legacies of distrust and antagonism, security brooked no risk-taking.

Nearly five years passed. The Likud reading of the Israeli future remained in power, its mentors being only reluctantly cajoled into participation in negotiations formally opened in Madrid in 1991 to give a semblance of life to the ever-languishing 'peace-process.' With the advent of a Labour Government in 1992 hope could be forgiven for raising its querying head. The immediate portents, however, were not encouraging. Prime Minister Yitzhak Rabin seemed eager to establish no-nonsense credentials and made them evident in harsh measures and sharp rhetoric culminating in the exile to limbo on Lebanon's border of actual or alleged terrorists of the Hamas movement.

The ambiguity of these portents is not wholly dispelled in the September 1993 'accord' between the Israeli Government and the P.L.O., hailed as it rightly was by the wondering world as a benison if not yet a viable formula. Numerous caveats, issues and suspicions attend on the sequel.

Was it perhaps the increasing appeal of militant Palestinianism that persuaded Israeli policy-makers to decide on barter with the moderates while they were available? Does a Palestinian administration in Gaza and Jericho imply an ultimate Palestinian state across the West Bank, including some prescript for a shared Jerusalem? Or are unreconciled Palestinians justified in seeing the 'accord' as a subtle formula for a mitigated but still effective Israeli control?

Ambiguity a century long has bedevilled this history and the old irony persists of double meanings waiting on elusive purposes, with suspicion besetting all. Is a Palestinian entity feasible and sustainable? Can the P.L.O. deliver what Israel requires of it – protect alleged Palestinian collaborators in exchange for the liberation of Palestinian prisoners? Can Yasser Arafat move rapidly and decisively from secretive, dominant personalism within the P.L.O. to the collective, managerial skills now urgently to be brought into play by and for his people?

Has Israel done well for itself in opting to be rid of the incubus of Gaza? Despite the settlers there it offers little of vital relevance of Israel. What of the Jewish settlers on the West Bank whose numbers, opportunism and tenacity were seen by the previous Likud régime as effectuating an irreversible *fait accompli*? Can they ever accommodate to Palestinian administration assumed, by Palestinians, to be a prelude to statehood? Are the negotiators caught in a web of contradictions of intent? And where does the whole long legacy of injustice and alienation come to its term in forgiveness and mutuality?

Handshakes on the White House lawn gave promise about prejudice but prejudice more adamant than gestures can resolve attends ominously on the promise. There still remains a Palestinian obduracy urging a complete dismantling of Zionism – an obduracy whose futility only hardens it the more. There is an abiding demand in Israel for a total repudiation of Palestinian autonomy, if not of Palestinian identity, in any political, territorial expression. Only negotiation is proceeding while hope waits precariously upon it. The years ahead, which negotiation anticipates, not only for its own complexity, but as a contrasted 'probation' for both parties, could creep towards compatibility or stumble towards frustrating impasse. In the latter event the ensuing reactions will be unpredictable whether in the counsels of Israel or the desperation of 'Palestine.'

v.

The tribulations, as history has brought them, of Zionist self-definition by dint of confrontation and conflict was implicit from the beginning in the very nature of Zionism, as politics and territory defined it. In keeping any conscience it had always to be at odds with itself. An honest will to innocence, however naive, early characterized some of its ideologues. When it proved illusory, more worthy of note are the protests, the disavowals and the reproaches that have accompanied from within the steady connivance with compromise and deviance incurred by being Zionist this way. The verdict of history is not only that Zionism has been grimly pragmatic, forcible, opportunist and violent: it is also that these features have been the burden of consciences knowing them for what they are and striving to have them otherwise. Cynics may say that all these sensitive souls achieved was to improve the image, failing as they did to alter it. Yet caring for the image, however prey to the sceptical, is nevertheless at the heart of the story. As the atrocities accumulated – the King David slaughter, the massacre of Dair Yasin, the hanging of the two sergeants,[16] the murder of the U.N.O. Envoy, Count Bernadotte, on the verge of a potential solution, the sundry outrages of the Irgun and the Stern Gang, the subterfuge and aggression of 1956, the devastation of southern Lebanon and the onslaught on Beirut, the catalogue of procrastination over U.N.O. and the flouting of U.S. friendship as if it were captive to Israeli interests – the vocation of the Israeli conscience was incessantly tested. That it found voice at all is a measure of its resilience in disowning, if not often in transforming, policy.

Whether politics and statecraft can afford a conscience at all concerns history everywhere. There is, however, a unique form of it in respect of Jewry and Israel. Having 'conjectured,' via the logic of bitter experience, that political Zionism was 'the divine purpose' for Judaism, Israel came into perpetual debate with itself about how 'holiness,' 'divine warrant,' 'covenant' and 'election' aligned with the political enterprise. However secular in their orientation, leaders like Ben Gurion, Golda Meir, and Menahem Begin – not to say Vladimir Jabotinski – could readily see divine sanction as a useful, if not a sublime, partner in the enterprise. Others saw it not merely as a useful asset but as an outright 'mandate' justifying whatever proved necessary. The most subtle guilt of all was to let the sanction of the holy override the claim of the ethical. For the premise denied there was any guilt at all. 'Holiness' could then become quite other than moral. 'In the beginning,' wrote Jabotinsky, 'God created the nation: whatever assists its rebirth is holy, whatever disturbs it is impure.'[17] The Torah entitled the people of Israel to set aside all accusation of usurpation. By *mitzvah asseh* conquest was no-conquest. By settlement, according to its zealot ideologues, people-and-land possession realized 'holiness,' and neutralized any moral reservation about the parallel dis-possession of the unhallowed. Such theology left the Palestinian no case. The fact, thought these custodians of 'the holy,' should be brought home to them so that, though by their own ethic – and patriotism – they might resist, they must know that, by divine decree, they were not 'natives' of 'the land' at all, only 'the people of God' were.[18]

The surest corrective to this distortion of 'the holy' in the sacrifice of the ethical was already there in the moral passion of the greatest Hebrew prophets, of Isaiah demanding 'righteousness like a mighty stream,' rather than 'vain oblations' and damnable incense, of Jeremiah reproving the purveyors of 'holiness' and deriding their invocation of 'the temple of the Lord.' Yet such conditionality of 'the covenant' was hard to square with the exigencies of Zionist politique. 'Except the Lord build the house . . .' was a hard precept when men of violence, of astute diplomacy and no-nonsense purpose, were building it anyway with little mind for the reminder. Even so, there was always the Torah warning about 'taking the Name of the Lord in vain,' if only those invoking it politically could realize that they, as much as any verbal swearers, were patently doing so at many a devious turn.

If Jewish self-understanding in political Zionist form tended to neutralize a moral awareness of the Palestinians, there were always the resisters who stood for the practice of righteousness. These did not avail – thus far – through the long story, to bring an equal humanity to all that was contentious. The human mind is less likely to take responsible moral judgements if law, or Torah, or code, have the role of doing so for us. Hence the rarity, in the Hebrew Bible, of language akin to the Greek, and New Testament, term, *suneidesis*, meaning 'seeing for oneself in whole-view.' That wise woman, Abigail, in 1 Samuel 25.31, seems to be speaking of 'pangs of conscience' around some personal discrimination against given law. Such instances are rare. When the prophets appeal, for example, against the law as ritual, they do so in the name of the Torah as the moral norm. It was precisely their inclusive *suneidesis* that political Zionism made at once more urgent and liable, yet also more difficult and controversial, for the reason that state and nation, war and power, fear and enemies were the arena. Just as the Zealots of the first century who defied the Empire had their fixation about Rome, so Zionism had its fixation about the Arab adjacency to its uneasy frontier.

The Israeli appeal to 'holy' sanction, pragmatic or passionate, had a paradoxical effect upon Palestinian politics. Sensing how elusive was this asset of 'the people of God,' it did not opt to be 'the party of God' in return as Islam might have argued. Rather, its National Charter stressed the 'secular' state in which it proposed the conditional inclusion, indifferently, of Muslim, Jew and Christian. Though the Charter had ever diminishing hope of being implemented, the secular principle was seen as significant by the P.L.O. They could hardly de-mystify Zion – which it was urgent for them to do – and at the same time mystify themselves by God-sponsoring nexus. The lurking danger for Israel is that this stance may give way to a more forthright Islamic 'divination' of the Palestinian cause, if only for the limping fitfulness of the 'peace process.' It would seem right to conclude that Israel has no less sound reason for closing with a viable peace formula, than does the P.L.O. Perhaps that would also help dispel the haunting suspicion that political Zionism has throughout been a sad treason to Judaism.

vi.

How, it may be asked, could that last dark conjecture arise? Only rank ill-will could ever harbour it. It could be no part of honest history, still less occur in any properly Christian Judaica. Yet, to reach one, we must not suppress it. Clearly, political Zionism has been a prolonged and passionate Jewish negotiation of faith with life, of destiny with experience. In all the foregoing, have we – or have we not – been right in seeing an intention more and more determined by the politics in which it was embroiled and, therefore, the more distanced from its original 'conjectures'? If so, it cannot be argued that such distancing was the fault of resisting factors with which it was obliged to contend. For those factors were present, evident, legitimate and broadly predictable, in the form and setting political Zionism had chosen to take. Here we encounter the deep irony implicit in the drama of what was 'conjectured' and what eventuated. The form seemed demanded by the logic of long exposure to 'Gentile' insecurity, the dark options of either persecution or assimilation, the non-Jewish 'jury' always having Jewry embarrassed about its Judaism. The setting 'from Dan to Beersheba' was imperative by every reckoning of Jewish soul and sense.[19]

Thus the other irony follows. It would seem that political Zionism, never – of course – blaming itself for succeeding, whether fortuitously or by bold design, has incurred yet another experience of rejection, of resistance and unwantedness. It is not, this time, anti-Semitic, for its operators are Semites, and Zionism has girded itself with sinews, alliances and forces to confront it. It no longer spells the same ghetto-hazards or the old search for inoffensiveness. Even so, this time, the rejection, the antipathy, the ostracism, have – out of injustice, homelessness, and tragedy – a legitimacy political Zionism has itself bestowed on them by the history in which its intentions have embroiled it. Yet, given all the factors, could it have been otherwise?

Reflection needs to pursue the tragic irony further. Did political Zionism mislead the Jewish mind or – more exactly – those counsels in it which adopted it? Judaism has amply proved how spiritually viable it was and remains, whatever the pains of the diaspora condition. Did it need, at such far cost, to commit itself to statehood? There were those who said it did, and that urgently. Jacob Klatzkin, eminent lexicographer of Hebrew philosophy, wrote:

> 'Either the Jewish people shall redeem the land and thereby continue to live, even if the spiritual content of Judaism changes radically, or we shall remain in exile and rot away, even if the spiritual tradition continues to exist.'[20]

He seemed to suggest that 'spiritual' Judaism was doomed[20] without nationalist expression. Yet he did not wish to 'redeem the land to create a base for the spiritual values of Judaism.' On the contrary, land, for nationalism, was an end in itself.[21] 'Zion,' effectively politicized, was on behalf of nothing but itself, Jewish nationalism for its own sake. Given what this entailed ethically, what becomes of the Judaism, and with it the Jewishness, with which nationalism can so easily dispense?

For some, there might be a sort of double insurance, a Judaic 'both-and.' Diaspora spiritually, with all its risks, would remain authentic. Manifestly, all Jewry would never 'Zionize' – as Ben Gurion saw it their duty to do – by leaving diaspora and settling in Israel. Yet diaspora authenticity could take comfort and pride in the symbol, the prowess, the energies, of political Zion without conceding that it either monopolized things Judaic or forfeited the spiritual finality of Torah and 'election.'

Not so Jacob Neusner, prolific scholar of Jewish self-interpretation. On the one hand, he saw Zionism offering 'world Jewry the *sole* meaningful explanation of how to endure'. As a system, 'it bore self-evident truth, placing the State at the centre of Jewish existence' and 'accurately assessing the power of anti-Semitism.' 'It had selected the right problem and given it the right solution.' On the other hand, by using what he frankly acknowledged as 'ethnic identity,' in form of 'the nation-state,' 'it denied any conception of Jewish identity based on spiritual criteria.' He added, cryptically:

> 'It is not Judaism insofar as Judaism is a religion. With that it is entirely incongruent, but it is in conformity to Judaism as a world-view and as a way of life.'[22]

Granting that Israel was 'exclusionary racial,' he seemed to be divorcing 'spiritual criteria' from the very processes of state-creation, thus returning us to the problem earlier noted concerning the moral responsibilities of a political ethno-fulfilment. This is the reason why, throughout these paragraphs, 'political' has preceded the word 'Zionism.' For passive Zionism, which Arab hospitality might have accommodated – settlement, agriculture, *Hibbat Zion* in its pre-Herzl form – was the first ambition. Herzl and Weizmann dismissed it as toothless, simply a more romantic version of the old jeopardy. Land via power, power over land, statehood – these were indispensable, the *sine qua non.* Tragically, from the other side, there was a *sine qua non* of incompatibility, namely the priority of Arab statehood. Events, by Palestinian as well as Zionist contrivance, have negated any such priority on the ground, but the emotions and passions around it, continue to interrogate Zionist politics, the soul of Jewry, and the enigma of their relationship.

The fact of 'unease in Zion,' in Israel, can mean hope as well as reproach. Either way, it leads all who, in any sense, are parties to it by suffering, sympathy, study or personal story into reckoning, by its light, with the faith, practice and vision that together define Jewishness. For me, as the years passed, it meant the effort to reach a Christian Judaica. It remains, perhaps, the most difficult inner 'negotiation' of all.

Chapter 7

A Christian Judaica

i.

It seems clear that to believe in God is, in some sense, to believe also in ourselves. In what sense? will be the crucial question. From Moses, perhaps from Abraham, the Jewish people have had a sharply distinctive fusion, or amalgam, of faith in God and in themselves, a faith which wedded the divine reality to the necessity of them. What obtained between 'God and His people' was strictly covenantal in a relationship unique in the divine economy and – being unique in the divine economy – somehow also integral to the divine nature.

This covenantality, however sublime in its inward significance for both parties, God and people, has generated in history a tragic antipathy, known as anti-Semitism, which has engulfed Jewish existence in intense anxiety and tribulation, making 'sufferance the badge of all their tribe.' It has also entailed upon the persecuting 'Gentile' world a fearful burden of guilt and moral shame. The resulting, double, human anguish might well make some initiated observer from another planet cry out: 'If only Jewry could become unchosen!' Or better, if only that 'chosen-ness' could be a private secret, cherished only in inwardness like a true 'mystery,' without requiring the recognition of the world. Yet, having to do essentially with God and history, it was – for its own heart-ache – a secret that 'could not be hidden.'

Here, in this tangle, is the first distress of any Christian reckoning with 'the mystery of Israel.' It is the more compounded by the fact that, in its very genesis in sequel to Jesus and his Cross, the Christian faith – by Jewish minds and hands – proposed an opening out of covenanted people-hood to all and sundry, on the sole condition of penitence and faith, without prior distinction of birth, or place, or culture. That initiative, Jewish-made and 'Gentile' greeted, gave promise of an end to the trauma – in both directions – of essential differentia before God. Sadly, the vision faltered. Jewishness turned back into its ancient separatism in new guise and the Church was steadily resolved – almost – into a 'Gentile' community where only in defeated intention were 'Jew and Greek' one in Christ.

The story of that forfeited vision, and its causes, we must examine later. So critical was it that the very narrative becomes a quarrel, but with or without narration, its legacy is clear. The ongoing, unremitting peoplehood of Jewry could not fail to be antithetical to the new interpretation of their destiny to belong, finally, with all mankind. What might have excluded anti-Semitism for ever came to be seen as a prime source of it. The Church, in loyalty to its own birthright, seemed to proceed upon some mandate of 'supersession.' It took over the Hebrew Scriptures, called them 'the Old Testament' and sang the Psalms of David as their own. How confidently it did so can be gauged in the tone of innumerable Christian expositions of the 'fulfilment' concept of history by which the Judaic was esteemed only for its preparatory role in what was meant for due completion – a completion which ongoing Jewry saw bitterly as an abrogation.

One example among scores is the admired exponent of 'Christendom,' Christopher Dawson who wrote:

> 'The Word of God was first revealed to the people of Israel and became embodied in a law and a society. Secondly the Word of God became incarnate in a particular person at a particular moment of history, and thirdly, this process of human redemption was carried on in the life of the Church which was the new Israel – the universal community, the bearer of divine revelation and the organ by which man participated in the new life of the Incarnate Word.'[1]

'The divine intervention in history,' in Judaic story from Abraham to the first century of the Christian era did not provide for that story to go on otherwise than in terms of its proper, universal climax.

Jewry did not agree. It found its own ongoing reality precisely in not agreeing. Thus it called into radical question the whole *raison d'être* of the Church compelled, as it saw it, by the *raison d'être* it had always cherished and could not betray, namely its abiding privacy with God in unchanging covenant.

What, then, of the Christian mind today, conscious of the tenacity of Judaism, the vigour of its contemporary spirituality, and the ardour of its disqualification of what disqualified it? How ought we to respond? The question ramifies into a bewildering complex of other issues about Messiah, law, grace, the Sabbath, historical enmity and the bitterness of its desperate legacies. Add to the equation all the promise and the prejudice of Zionism, its chronic, crippling ambivalence about the very meaning of Judaism, and what was an ordinary Christian to think, finding himself in life-long connection with Judaica in the triangle of 'the Semites,' as Islam also comprised it? Had not my examining Chaplain in Chester told me to understand Abraham and all the patriarchs as 'domestic' to us Christians? Jews whom I was keen to heed would have no truck with the idea and found it offensive and pretentious. The search for 'a Christian Judaica' became central to my groping mind as early as my first sight of Jerusalem. Years later in New York, the acquaintance of Rabbi Abraham Heschel gave it new impetus and direction.[2]

ii.

The first necessity was to let the issue stand, with no evasion and without palliative. It is unworthy, on either part, to dream it or to argue it away. Let it be as clear as Ignatius of Antioch had stated it early in the second century:

> 'To profess Jesus Christ while continuing to follow Jewish customs is an absurdity. The Christian faith does not look to Judaism, but Judaism looks to Christianity, in which every other race and tongue that confesses a belief in God has now been comprehended.'[3]

Judaism, however, did *not* 'look to Christianity,' nor could it admit that universally inclusive theism for, if doing so, it would impugn its own definitive status before God.

The second necessity I came to realize was not to rest in solutions that purported to decide the issue but, in fact, avoided it. This happened on the part of Christians who decided to affirm a purely 'Gentile' Christianity for which Jews were never intended. The Gospel on this view was a sort of 'second covenant' taking care of 'Gentile' inclusion in the mercy of God but only mistakenly first perceived as incorporating 'all one in Christ,' Jew and Greek alike.

Or it was possible, from the Jewish side, to argue that, in fact, there never had been any common Judeo-Christian tradition. That notion was a myth. Christianity was a wholly 'Gentile' entity, properly to be seen as a new religion, coined in Greek or Roman idiom and in no genuine connection whatsoever with Jewry and Judaism.

Both these 'solutions' constituted a treachery. They had to be rejected precisely for the sake of an integrity ready to register and undertake the burden of estrangement as it really was. The old prophets had inveighed against those who 'healed hurts slightly.' Theologians ought to do the same. We end discord if we unstring the instrument but we also forfeit all that music, and musing, should explore.

To have fully present what is at stake, it is well to review these two ways of opting out. On the Christian side, especially since the Holocaust, the urge to atone for long centuries of Jewish persecution or to sustain the enterprise of Zionism, has prompted the 'two covenant' theory. It seems a way of theological co-existence, of mutual recognition and approval. It absolves Christianity of any taint of displacing, any opprobrium of superseding, things Judaic. These persist in full authenticity and, so doing, in no way imply or require the invalidity of the Christian faith. The solution seems ideal and, for better pleading, it elides all those real, or alleged, Christian factors in anti-Semitism.

Given what may seem admirable in its postures and

effects, it is hard to resist and, indeed, many in Jewish-Christian dialogue have lately opted for it. However, the crucial problem on the Christian side is its complete betrayal of the New Testament or – avoiding that loaded term – the Gospel and the being of the Church. It may even be unwittingly guilty of another form of anti-Semitism, or at least of Jewish 'unwantedness' within a society meant for all but them. It cannot be Christian to hold that any are excluded from Christ. We may not, and cannot, re-write the evangelist and have him say: 'God so loved non-Jews that He gave . . .' or have the old Creed re-phrased to run: 'Who for us "Gentiles" and for *our* salvation came . . .' It has long seemed to me strange that Christian minds have failed to realize their treason here. If we are to find a rationale for ongoing Judaism in all its authenticity we must do the 'new' covenant better justice. We must find a livelier reckoning with the 'old' than this one which leaves it in splendid isolation from the mutual world and from all that transpired when Jews themselves first wrestled with what 'Christ-Jesus' signified for all that they had been and were meant yet to be.

The treason is not only in the re-writing of faith: it is also in the undoing of history. The sense of the 'new' did not emerge as merely an 'alternate,' in sequel to Jesus' ministry. Had that been the case, how should we explain the vehement debate it kindled, the exuberant joy at long last in liberation into the human whole, the anxious and, later, combative, apprehension about the forfeiture of Jewishness? Was it only the 20th century, burdened with long cycles of guilt and intent on any reparation in the wake of Zionism, conceiving a way to do justice to neither while conceding both?[4]

We need to realize how it was Jewish vision and venture which conceived the open Church. Prior to the Fall of Jerusalem, there was indeed, tension – as the New Testament reveals – between the ardent and the reluctant in that action. With the loss of the Temple and the hard dispersion, fears accentuated and ranks began to close. The story is tangled and deserves some further thoughts below. Our duty here is simply to see that the emergence of faith in

Messiah Jesus reached back into Hebraic faith in God as Creator, purposing in history and faithful to covenant. The Gospel could never have been the thing it was without Jewish minds, Jewish labours and Jewish love to God and men. Paul may have had the idiosyncrasies of genius but he was 'a Hebrew of the Hebrews' in his inclusion of the 'Gentiles' in Christ. He wrestled long with the puzzle of continuity and fulfilment. He would have been saved both his ardour and his anguish if he had seen the inclusion of the 'Gentiles' as the exclusion of the Jews. The two-covenant theory parts Christians who hold it from the mind of their own Scripture and the ground of their own genesis in Christ.

iii.

What of the other solution of tension by pronouncing Christianity a thoroughly pagan, Graeco-Roman, Hellenistic, non-Semitic creation fit to be severed from any alleged roots in the Judaic tradition? The thesis has been attractive to some Jewish thinkers. It frees the mind from unwanted connections. It chimes with moods of Jewish assertion. It cuts the Gordian knot of uneasy relationships and leaves Christendom to its unworthy self. It also penetrates into scholarship about Christian origins and the allegedly complete 'Hellenism' of Paul.[5]

Rabbi Leibowitz, Zionist and yet a thorn in the flesh of the Israeli State, is a strong representative of this position. Christianity is wholly antithetical to Judaism and by its 'saviourism' overthrows the halakhic life under law which is its essence.[6] Again, David Hartman, in *Conflicting Visions*, sets a vast distance between Christian redemption and Judaic covenant. There is for him a fond triumphalism in any perceived Messiahship. Jews stay with Torah, concede their human finitude, abate the longing for certainty via some 'given' in history which can attain what is, in fact, left to us as loyal halakhic Jews. Were it valid, Christian 'saving-event' would, indeed, abrogate things Judaic but God, in command and covenant, via Jewish exceptionality, is of another mind. The diaspora proves that Jewry has not lingered these two thousand years in a limbo of undoing nor – he adds – have they waited concurrently for Zionism to gratify their patience. Israel's 'golden calf' in wanderings did not rescind the Exodus. God stays in their particularity.[7]

The degree to which the 'common bond' has to be excluded or strictly delimited varies from writer to writer among Jewish verdicts about Christianity and its origins. Thus the prolific scholar, Jacob Neusner, sees 'the Jewish-Christian argument in the 1st century' as 'different people talking about different things to different people.' Yet it remains 'a family quarrel,' since 'only brothers can hate so deeply.' Where he concludes that

> '. . . Christianity, through its Messiah (is) for the gentile, Judaism, through its definition of the two Torahs of Sinai and its embodiment in the figure of the sage, for Israel . . .'

the incompatibility seems complete, the more so when he states his view of the Church, by remarking: 'The authors of the Gospels chose a broad range of enemies for Jesus, hence the church.'[8]

In his *The Myth of the Judeo-Christian Tradition*, Arthur A. Cohen, writes:

> 'Christianity affirmed that a redeemer had come out of Zion, but that he had not come alone for Israel but for all mankind. Judaism denied that claim, calling it presumption and supererogation, denying his mission to them.'

Christians had 'historicized an ancient misuse of power' and were mad enough to imagine that the death of a single man could save all mankind. Further, 'to the born Jew God allows no option. To disavow the covenant would be saying No! to God . . . nullifying God as well as one's self.' Thus, there is no possible parley of Judaism with the Church. Judaism keeps the future 'as empty of finality as possible' and 'has never had to explain, (as Christians have) a failed eschatology.' The two, on every count, are poles apart. Eliezer Berkowits writes bitterly:

> 'Judaism is Judaism because it rejects Christianity, and Christianity is Christianity because it rejects Judaism . . . (It) does not have the ambition to save mankind because it never maintained that mankind was lost without it.'

Jews who 'go in for dialogue' are 'Jews without memory.'[9]

iv.

If, as is our case here, we are not falling back on the reprieve from travail which the two-covenant thesis affords, nor yet reconciling to total disparity, how ought we to proceed? To be left face to face with how we relate without treason, in our joined and separate identities, is precisely the reason for rejecting the alternatives. Where we most differ we have still to belong. Tension and loyalty come together – as it must seem to me.

The first duty of a Christian Judaica must be to appreciate what made Jewry withdraw and withhold itself from the Christian faith in the Christ-event and from the open grace that duly followed from it. A whole complex of issues confronts us made the more taxing because the very history of them is controversy. Some aspects of that faith, event and grace had better come in the *confessio fidei* belonging to Chapter 9 below. Here perhaps it will be safe to formulate the matter in terms of the Christian sequence from a realizable Messiahship, actually realized in Jesus through ministry and suffering, and – by help of both Hebraic and Greek norms of thought – acknowledged in Christology.

Each clause in the foregoing is vital. On each count there was a Jewish instinct – some would say a necessity – to dissent. On the first count, there seems a certain consensus in Jewry that if there is to be Messianic hope there cannot ever be Messianic fact. The world, as they bitterly know it and as we should recognize, is plainly unredeemed.[10] Secondly, it follows that 'Jesus-Messiah, crucified' embodies on every score an impossible contradiction. On the third count, the elaboration of the assumed Christ-event into Christological faith carried the Jewish, and other, Christians, so elaborating, into realms of 'Gentile,' gnostic, even pagan, speculation quite foreign to the habits and heritage of the Hebrew soul.

In developing here – as far as space allows – the items of this summary, we must keep in mind deep, parallel motifs around the understanding of humanity and the cherished destiny of Judaic exceptionality. Throw into that hard equation the rival claims to Scripture, typology and 'the rock whence both were hewn' and scholarship, without patience, could be near to despair.

On the first count, there seems to have been a strong tendency, at least of late, in Jewry to discount the Messianic theme, to see it as the dimension of hope to which Jewish fidelity is called without ever enjoying the false luxury of its actuality in history. For evil will always post-date the Messianic thing alleged to have defeated it. If we want to hope a future we must disavow a past – although the Jewish mind did not do so about the Exodus, which remained through all time their 'Ebenezer.' The enormity of the Shoah, or Holocaust, has massively reinforced that stance, calling into radical doubt not only God's Messiah, but God Himself as ever, credibly, 'jealous' over Israel. If there were to be Messianic faith at all it must be, in Gershom Scholem's words, 'perpetual futurism.'[11]

Christian faith in 'Messiah realized' in 'Jesus crucified' has then to show how it can 'hold that faith against the unredeemedness of the world.'[12] It can best do so by explaining how a Messiah of the Cross and the Cross of Messiah purport to do so. This entails our thinking on Messianic alternatives and the limits – or otherwise – of their bearing on a world redemption. A recent array of them can serve.

> 'Assumptions of the community (are) always reflected in the image of the redemptive agent. If the communal goal is political independence, then the rhetoric is that of . . . dominion, of triumph over foes. But if the chief concern is for purity, the agent is seen as priestly in function, reconstituting the cultic system and purging God's chosen people. If the group is in despair of the present order of things the agent is seen as one who radically transforms the present

> epoch, replacing it with a new age in which the helpless are vindicated and the evil powers routed. If the ethos is more intellectual in nature then the agent is expected to effect, through wisdom, the triumph of order and rationality.'

An apocalyptic Messiah should be added to this analysis, intervening from heaven to rescue the remnant.[13]

All these Messiahships, however, are restrictive – to the nation, to the holy, or the élite, or the worthy. They are inconclusive because they do not provide for forgiveness or the release of wrong-doers from their wrong. They are not at grips with 'the sin of the world' but only with some of its effects in political oppression or social disease. There is about them no travail of love, no remaking of the self within.

Christian faith was born as the conviction that in the acceptance to suffer Jesus had recognized and fulfilled the inclusively Messianic role. The conviction came with extraordinary rapidity via the confidence that, having done so, he had been divinely vindicated in resurrection. In one sense, the resurrection and the conviction were one and the same. 'Father, forgive them' – interpreting the Cross from within – was heard, in the faith that gave birth to the Church, as the clue to love overcoming evil. If the context of the words could be understood as a drama in which the evil of our world was inclusively expressed in the will to crucify then this Cross could be understood as where 'the Messianic' had happened, namely in the love that, 'not being overcome of evil, overcomes evil with good.'

So the faith in Messianic actuality was born and, with it, by virtue of its impartial reach, the open community of its recognition which was the Church. To be sure, this reading of Jesus crucified only fulfilled Messiahship by radically transforming Messianic expectation. By its nature it gave rise not only to an open peoplehood of forgiveness, but to the vocation of that community to conform itself to the same redemptive love in its own encounter with suffering and wrong. This must be the answer to the Judaic fear of every 'Messiah' being 'premature' inasmuch as evil will always post-date the 'fact.' Before we worry about *whether* time disproves it we must know *what* fulfills the Messianic role. To find it in the Cross sets the worry at an end. For 'the suffering and the glory' are never post-dated, their principle is eminently reproducible and 'Messiah' can then be 'all of us,' but only because He once has been who and how He was.[14]

Here we need to consider the historical aspects of this core of Christian meaning and some of its Judaic antecedents in prophethood and 'wisdom.' We have reached the third of our listed concerns, namely the elaboration of this faith in Messiah-Jesus crucified into Christology. For 'Jews have seen in these claims Christological the great non-negotiable refutation of Christianity's continuity with Judaism.'[15]

Need they have seen them that way? I have long believed that Christian Christology is eminently 'negotiable' in the Judaic context. In the first place, it had its inauguration in Jewish hands. Paul will always be the trysting-place here and no doubt the issues around his Jewishness will be perpetual. But he was not alone and, in all his Letters, he coveted what he called 'the mind of Christ.' So it was a Jewish initiative that set Christology on its way. Christology aside, it seems now agreed by scholars that 1st century Jewry, both Palestinian and diaspora, was deeply responsive to Greek thinking and eager to align its own identity with a secular ontology. There is no viable case for the view that when Christians, Jewish and Gentile, began to express the divine significance of what they had experienced of grace in Christ, they were indulging in un-Jewish aberration or defiling themselves with pagan notions.

On the contrary, they were requiring themselves to 'believe with all their mind' concerning the bearing on their monotheism of the divine action they had experienced in all that Jesus was to them. It is not credible to attribute Christology, whether in Pauline, Johannine or other, form, to the malign blandishments of gnostic speculation. It 'was not,' remarks Martin Hengel

> 'a gnostic, syncretistic falsification but a necessary last consequence of primitive Christian thinking . . . How could "the beloved Son" not become "the first begotten before all creation" (Col. 1.15)'

Commenting on the role of hymns in theology, Hengel goes on to link the great poem of Philippians 2.5–11 about the divine self-giving (*kenosis*) in Christ with 'the Messianic psalms' and finds it culminating 'in the Prologue of St John.'[16]

Need any Judaic thinking, mindful of the profound sense of divine pathos, of eternal compassion seeking out temporal charge, even if limited to Israel, fail to find it in the enterprise of 'God in Christ'? Or need it fear some compromise of the divine glory in the faith about Christ, given the divine co-partnership with the suffering prophets from which, we may conjecture, Jesus himself had drawn his Messianic clue?[17]

So then we falsify both history and theology if we say that there was a de-Judaizing in Christianity resulting from non-Jewish influences or anti-Jewish prejudices entering in via 'Gentiles' with pagan backgrounds, as if they consciously defined themselves as being 'against the Jews.' On the contrary, their deepest origins and instincts were from, and with, Judaica in all sincerity. Does it follow as a corollary that Judaism still has to come to terms with Jesus theologically, not merely to 'appreciate' Christianity but also to do right by its own Hebraic self?[18]

The central Biblical theme (both Testaments) of divine suffering apart, there was ample incentive from Jewish Wisdom literature to perceive divine-human association, of 'light' here from 'light' there, of pre-existing 'Word' dwelling with 'the Most High' authentically with God yet coming from God as 'equal subsidiary.' Divine 'agency' is personified, for example, in Isaiah 55.10–11, Wisdom 9.1 and 18.15. Philo could think Moses to be in some sense embodying divine authority in dealing as 'a god unto Pharaoh' (Exodus 7.1.) With such stimuli, Judaic thinking, contemporary with the early Church, knew the need to comprehend distinction within transcendence, to re-think what would otherwise be the desolating solitariness of the Almighty.[19] Was I wrong myself in thinking, from an early date in my love of Jerusalem, that Christology had strong Jewish credentials and that there was no spiritual need for the synagogue either to deplore or decry it out of right concern for 'the Lord God of Israel,' 'holy His Name,' ever 'mighty and wise?'

V.

If so, then the crux must have been about 'peoplehood,' or, about God only in the bond with peoplehood. That there should have been tensions in its opening out to all and sundry, as the clear corollary of the sort of Messiahship perceived to be in Jesus and the Cross, was inevitable. We cannot hope to do them justice here. It needs to be acknowledged that they were mutual. We should not sanction them again by misconstruing them now.[20] The sages of Yavneh, after the tragic Jewish War of 66–72, were properly bent on survival round the Torah and the synagogue. They could ill afford the ambiguities and diversionary freedoms of a new sect. Any abeyance of circumcision threatened identity and loyalty even while it greatly facilitated the incoming of those 'Godfearers' who – repelled by its barbarity as a religious necessity – welcomed access without it into 'the fear and love of God.' 'Bread and wine' jeopardized dietary laws and eating with non-Jews broke faith with ethnic Israel. The incorporation of 'Gentiles' endangered corporate holiness, incapable as such strangers must be of Torah purity. Antinomianism, however roundly excluded by the Christian principle of love, lurked around 'the ark of God.'

There is a certain irony in the fact that it was the very urgency of Judaic misgivings about 'God in Christ' which fostered the Christian apologetic pre-occupation with the Hebrew Scriptures which the sages of the synagogues resented and controverted. Only in those Scriptures were the *argumenta ad homines* the Church needed in heeding Jewish objections. Controversy was only the more entailed by the means invoked to end it. The Christian refrain 'that it might be fulfilled . . .' was at least proof of a will to good faith about a single heritage, even if it served only to widen a schism. The great divide was about the possession of a past in being over the course of a future.

Where there are strains attaching to deep loyalties,

whether old ones or new, there are always tense local and social situations that human nature turns to enmity and prejudice. Suspicions breed in sharp encounter. Over issues like the Sabbath, common Eucharist, the oral law, liberty and conduct, there were Jewish Christians hesitant about full-throated welcome to the 'Gentiles' as fellows. There were ardent 'Gentiles' requiring uninhibited commitment. Hence came impatient notions of 'crypto-Jews' or 'crypto-Christians' – either way. These, in turn, might be supposed 'spies,' hidden enemies in the camp, reporting back on deviants and hesitants.

There is ample evidence of this scenario in the New Testament. It is important to know that it was reciprocal. Where there is Christian 'anti-Jewishness' there is Jewish 'anti-Christian-ness,' varying no doubt from place to place and time to time. What we can conjecture about 'the Johannine circle' is a case in point.[21] Christian abstention from 'the Jewish War' against Rome and the differing legal situations in which the two faith-communities stood, shifting as their boundaries were, all contributed to the stresses of their co-existence and the love-hate in their loyalties.

It is well to understand how it was and how it could not escape so being. There is no need, or warrant, for us to see ourselves now as then. Centuries of history have rolled between. It is of those we have to take stock. Things Christian have stained and defiled them: things Judaic have surmounted and survived them. They all return us to the present task, namely a positive Christian relation to the covenant which was 'already there,' before 'God was in Christ,' and abides beyond and despite that disclosure which is, for Christians, the covenanting fulness of altogether open grace. We cannot exclude Jews from that significance: they believe they should not accede to it. Where can our respective loyalties lead us except to peaceful acquiescence that it is so? But then how loyal are they?

vi.

With these questions, we pass from our theisms and

their transactions of mind around God and Messiah to our communities and their perceptions of each other. Here it is often assumed that there is onus only on the Christian side. Jewry, for its part, pleads only to be left in peace. That was the age-long posture of the ghetto. Even militant Zionism, with its 'defence forces,'[22] protests the same. Jewry is well content for Christianity to persist as a 'Gentile' identity, a faith it only intermittently considered pagan, of which it has long been agonizingly apprehensive, and from which it sees no pressing obligation to recruit into its own fold. Indeed, with rare exceptions, it hedged such recruitment with formidable dissuasives.

By contrast, it seems, Christianity may not loyally relinquish the 'ever-open-ness' of its first genesis, nor may it ever consider anyone unwanted. Grace itself is not that way and we should be 'conformed to the divine image.' There is no Christianity anywhere that did not first come as invitation.[23] This vocation obviously collides with the Judaic conviction that Jews, being 'already there,' have no need of conversion, and every reason to reject as futile, if not scandalous – as history must have it – the 'invitation-stance' of Christians. This will always be so, irrespective of how patient and sensitive – or otherwise – are 'inviters' to their invitees. Jewish exceptionality prevails here also in demanding to be spared such embarrassing hospitality. Contemporary Christians, in part, have shown they are ready thus to disembarrass both themselves and Jewry. As we have seen, the onus of the situation remains for those who do not.

However, though less readily evident, but no less oppressive, there is an onus the other way. It has to do with the Judaic incidence of 'chosen-ness,' of 'holy' status in land and people. Has the Judaic mind ever really resolved the dilemma of the 'Gentiles.'? If there is tension deriving from Christian 'open-ness,' there is tension arising from that which resents it, namely Judaic 'closed-ness.' Anti-Semitism is in no way exonerated in being reciprocal to 'Semitism' and must always be disowned and condemned for the heinous sin and crime it is. Yet it lives in history as a strange fixation, a neurosis, a perversity which damnably 'scape-goats' the victim on which it seizes and feeds.

That victim is only 'Semitism' as the word that has the 'anti-' prefix. 'Semitism' – insofar as it has currency – must include races more than 'the tribes of Israel.' But them it does include and, when negatived by 'anti-,' them alone. Is there no escape, we must ask, from this tragic, incessant double bind of a people caught in perpetual unease under the desperate burden of exceptionality, and other peoples variously tempted into the degradation and criminal perversity of rejection of them and succumbing abysmally to fill history with their obscenity and guilt.? Is it coincidence that the world's most insistently persecuted people are the world's most insistently 'chosen' – living perennially with the tragedy that waits so cruelly upon the dignity?

Would that the story of Joseph and his brothers offered any hopeful clue. His 'advantage' over them, his privileged status, his father's ill-judged fondness, his pretentious dreams, their inferior mothers, their jealous conspiracy – all find parallel in Judaic/'Gentile' history. 'God,' however, 'meant it unto good,' and so contrived it by means of Joseph's skill and tribulation. There *was* a truth in his dreams. As the Qur'an's account has it, 'God was mastering what He had in hand.' (Surah 12.21) It is impossible to discern any parallel retrieval of tragedy in the long saga of Jewish anguish at the hands of anti-Semitism, no comparable reversal of wrong. Jewry has paid too dearly for the mystery of 'election.' The saga has spelled catastrophe on every side. It is a wretched irony that the people whose care for corporate penitence devised the ritual of the scape-goat should have been made so grimly to fill the role. What, 'to these things,' has the Christian to say? Or can we only clutch at straws?

vii.

Very early in my sense of the 'mystique' of Jewishness, as Jerusalem presented it, I came to realize that the basics on which Jewish exceptionality was understood to rest were, in fact, common to all humanity in tenancy of territory, retention of memory and heredity through time. These were shared denominators of every corporate identity. In some sense the same triangle of place, story and birth belonged to every race and kind. The elements might vary by accidents of geography and culture but the experience made them all kin. There was, therefore, no natural ground for believing that the rain on Canaan was different when earlier it had fallen across Crete and would later refresh the eastern desert. Other peoples also had their migrations under God, as Amos knew (9.7). They also guarded their fathers' sepulchres and celebrated their harvests. Nature partnered native genius in measure everywhere yet, so doing, made them all one human kind.

It seemed right to me to note such 'Canaans' on all sides and to surmise that all things shaping diversity were doing so in common, in ways that were relative and never absolute.[24] In that way, should any land be 'holy' if not all, any people somehow uniquely human? I responded eagerly to Rabbi Heschel's often lyrical writings about 'the glory of man,' but found that, while the theme was universal, the case made was Hebraic.[25] Was he meaning 'humanity' or 'Jewishness'? Should our theology require us to exceptionalize ourselves?

The reason had to be sought in history and here the Christian instinct was trained to agree. God chose a hero, Abraham, to call a people, Israel, to send a Saviour, Jesus. That I heard from Sunday School. Judaism believed the first two clauses but repudiated the third. The 'calling' had no finale but itself. It had entailed all this tragedy, assigning its possessors to perpetual anxiety and its non-possessors to subtle umbrage and, through long centuries, the rage of Simeons, the troubled consciences of Reubens, wherever 'this dreamer' came.

The price was paid in the depth of the corporate psyche. In my youth I had learned to love the Psalter. It passed into the blood-stream. In my curacy I acquired all six volumes of C.H. Spurgeon's *Treasury of David*. In later years, however, I have come to feel ill at ease in much psalmody. It gives such prominence to 'the hand of our enemies' and 'them that hate us.' There are far fewer psalms that do not mention 'foes' and 'fears' than there are those that do. The sublime reaches of Psalm 139 are rarer than the dark enmities of 58 or the bitterness of 137. No doubt, devotion can allegorize, but allegory what not what the authors meant. They meant a wearing, worrying sense of what one recent writer called 'the jury of the Gentile world,' the sinister, threatening presence of the adversary of their status if not also of their security.

One had to ask what all this meant for the validity of that which made it so. Should they, or God, ever have 'Gentilized' the rest of the world in order to have them be 'His people'? I have found no answer, but I cannot suppress the question. Was the Lord Himself a strange ironist, allowing a world that would always find, or imagine, offence in the very terms on which Jewry sought to be accepted? For there is that about 'chosen-ness' which requires to be acknowledged. Otherwise it may fall into abeyance. 'Its being is to be perceived,' and the anxiety is perennial.

It seems clear from many passages in the Hebrew Scriptures themselves that Hebraic faith in God and themselves began in tribal and territorial terms and that these persisted when *their* Lord came to be known as 'the God of all the kindreds of the earth.' That sublime monotheism, however, retained the tribal, territorial dimension that, properly understood, was at odds with it. The all-inclusive sovereignty still had a people-selective quality despite those magnificent strains of the greatest prophets proclaiming that it could not be so.

There was no irony, some Jewish apologist may say, neither was the exclusive status incompatible with the divinely inclusive sovereignty. Your anxiety, he says reassuringly, is relieved if you only appreciate history. Judaic particularity is purposive. It may be privilege, but it is not divine favouritism. In no sense has it been a sinecure. Jews are divinely differentiated from the 'Gentiles' for the 'Gentiles'' sake. We Jews cannot have God abrogate *our* 'covenant' without putting at risk *their* benediction. We read our Torah and live it on their behalf in a way that could not happen unless it was ours alone. You do us wrong to think us advantaged seeing that we are so for your sakes. We are proxies under God for the benefit of all and surely you can read this in all you owe to us.

There is much Christian logic here but as identified in the 'preparation of the Gospel' and the coming of the world's redeemer. Jews, having first and in part read their fulfilment that way, and having largely withdrawn from that conviction, the old rationale of necessary particularity returns – and returns to be the continuing burden both of Jewry and of Christian Judaica.

viii.

That common burden leads on to another question. Accepting that divine agencies have to be particular and thus, so to speak, 'vocational,' can vocations not be multilateral? And do they require the sort of continuing theological imprint which makes the human agency a different human category on that account.? Need it exceptionalize its births, its land, its language, its *Halakhah*, save in the way that all nurture-culture is relatively distinct? In a word, may not 'chosen-ness' be shared, shared in a way that neither makes the holders solitary nor inferiorizes others.? The ethics of Torah have, in fact, entered far into the moral marrow of the human frame irrespective of the 'covenant' conviction about Jewishness on which Torah itself proceeds, and despite the trauma that 'covenant' has meant.

There was in that first Christian vision precisely such an equal place for 'all nations (to) bring their glory and honour into the kingdom of God.' But schism overtook it and the fact, though not the vision, faded. It follows that the vision of multilateral divine-human partnering must always remain part of a Christian's concern with Judaica. The Church was, is, called to something beyond the old prophet's hope: 'Ten men out of all the languages of the nations shall grasp the skirt of him who is a Jew, and say: "We will go with you. For we have heard that God is with you."'[26] Why the skirt and not the hand? Why not the shared confession: 'God is with us,' as it is in 'Emmanuel,' using 'us' in no restrictive sense.? After the Christ-event we find the direction reversed from a centripetal errand to a centrifugal mission. Instead of the nations 'seeking the Lord in Jerusalem' (v.22), Jerusalem goes 'round about to Illyricum' and beyond seeking out the nations. Then the 'Gentile' offering comes back to the mother city and its poor as the sacrament of that reconciliation Zechariah's pilgrims were seeking so eagerly. In doing so, they were like the 'proselytes,' 'the askers-to-belong,' who were so numerous among the Jewish dispersion in the first Christian century. It is odd that 'proselytism' has now become such a word of reproach, since it means simply 'that which creates a seeking,' as Jewry everywhere did and which the Gospel could satisfy on the sole condition of penitence and faith and 'all God's people gotta home.'

ix.

It is easier thus to explore what is at issue for a Christian in Judaica than to resolve it. It is loaded, if not overwhelmed, by two other factors to which we must pass, namely political Zionism and anti-Semitism, as the Shoah programmed it towards 'a world without Jews.'

It might seem that the logic at which we have arrived – though, logic apart, quite inconceivable – would be for Jewry somehow to 'depeculiarize' itself, and simply to belong with mankind without any special privacy with God. This is precisely what political Zionism contrived, if it did not aim, to do. As necessitated by statecraft and geopolitics, Israel is like any other nation, served by the same diplomacy, subject to the same intrigues, beset by the same fears, vexed by the same hopes. Its 'choosing' energies are the form now of its 'chosen' self-awareness. Some Israelis may contest this, deplore it, deny it, but it remains the reality of a politicizing of Jewish identity.

The urge to incur what statehood means stems directly from the pains of the diaspora condition and so in turn from the enormous wronging which is anti-Semitism.

Political Zionism did not surmount Jewish reluctance nor galvanize the Jewish will without the inhibiting or hating world around. We have seen in Chapter 6 what remains deeply at issue, namely how diaspora 'Israel' 'functions much as "the Church" or "the body of Christ" in Christianity,'[27] but what when 'Israel' – by its own deliberate naming – is the nation-state enmeshed in the political and moral toils of its establishment in erstwhile Palestine?

My conviction is that Christians, in Judaica – whether as scholars, analysts or simply friends – need to show every understanding of why Jews became Zionist. For the reasons contain our Christian guilt. Further, we need to have every compassion for the adversity, psychic as well as political, in which the contradictions of Zionism have involved them. Most of all, if it is ever within our power, we need to enable Jews to interiorize the mystery of their self-understanding. They cannot be asked somehow to undo themselves as if to give anti-Semitism the last word. Disavowal of it must be insistent, perpetual and unrelenting, which means in turn the abiding legitimacy of Judaic identity as Jews believe it to be and choose to fulfill it. Can such believing and choosing, uninhibited as they must be, nevertheless de-singularize what is Jewish so that the category of 'the Gentiles' is no longer necessary to give them authenticity? To some degree secularity achieves this already but only by compromise of the spiritual truth. Politicization, in Israeli form and context, makes it almost impossible. For statehood intensifies otherness, sharpens enmity, confounds the ethical and gives 'anti-' its old and tragic hyphen. A world without Jews? blessedly, Never! a world without 'Gentiles'? hopefully Yes! If the distinction is not to be transcended, as once it was, in the reconciliation of grace, then let it be obsolete in the common-ness of humanity – as it may well be while retaining all, in that common-ness, Jewry and Judaism bring to it.

'Gentiles,' after all is a curious word, meaning in its true Latin, simply 'peoples,' but acquiring the further sense of 'non-Jews,' *goyim*. The idea of characterizing all others *en bloc* by distinction from ourselves has had tragic reproduction in history. We can have 'Aryans and the rest,' 'British and the rest,' 'Mother Russia and the rest,' with varying implications about the role of 'the rest' outside the prime dignity, the one destiny. The theme of 'chosen-ness' is eminently imitable with the Bible recruited to that end. This has happened darkly to argue anti-Semitism itself. It has spawned apartheids in many parts. 'Let God arise and let His enemies be scattered' can be invoked in Drogheda, or Kiev, or Khartoum, no less than in Jerusalem and make an irony of *terra sancta* anywhere. Was it not an early President of Yale, one Ezra Stiles, of Biblical name and Biblical mind, who spoke of 'God's American Israel,' wondrously emerged from colonialism, with land-tenure and divine favour, entering 'a sacred history'. Such 'rhetoric of Biblical analogy would characterize American political discourse for centuries.'[28]

Is there not then a certain sense in which those who take the brunt of such illusions are a sort of 'non-Jewish Jews.'? They have to tell their over-riders

> 'You have mistook me all this while.
> I live with bread like you, feel want,
> Taste grief, need friends.'[29]

Then, further, perhaps they learn also to say with Arnold Zweig's Shylock:

> '. . . All whom you have robbed shall be my people:
> Whom you denied the law shall be my brothers,
> Whom you have disinherited my heirs,
> And those you mock and spit upon (and I
> Once mocked and spat upon) shall be my army . . .
> Sends up the self-same cry for justice . . .'[30]

This is why it is urgent there should be 'no more Gentiles,' no more 'only peoples' other people.'

x.

This has brought us finally, in all honesty, to the dark role Christians in Christendom have played in the anguish of the Jews. The confession of the guilt of it has to be unequivocal and deep. Nor can we plead the alibi of what we may have taken from the Hebrew Scriptures, from Joshua or Samuel, once we shifted the mandate to ourselves 'in the Name of the Lord.' There is no relief from wrong done, in pleas of ignorance or casual connivance. The Shoah and all that preceded it is starkly there in history and will accuse the time and place for ever. Yet this very fact has led some to misconstruction of the arraignment of anti-Semitism, particularly in relation to the New Testament. We distort truth utterly if we claim to trace a straight line from Good Friday to Auschwitz, as some have wildly done.

There is no equation that 'requires' the Christian to be anti-Semite. As we have seen at the outset, there was a will to complete embrace of Jewishness within the new community of faith, to which early 'Gentiles' gladly acceded. How could they do otherwise when they were themselves the welcome guests of Jewish invitation.? The subsequent 'Gentilizing' of the Church resulted, against the grain of the Gospel, from the bitter circumstances around the loss of the Temple and the sages' refuge in Torah community. The tensions were sometimes acrimonious, as the New Testament makes no pretence to hide, because of the depth of feeling the issues raised. The Church was not in the business of excluding Jews, nor did it readily reconcile to their opting-out.

The adoption of the ancient Scriptures by the Church was itself a signal of how deep it felt the bonds to be and how crucial the precedents they thought to have been fulfilled. As a thing of freedom and uncompulsive grace, the Gospel had no reason to apply duress or turn the non-acceders into criminals. That 'whosoever will may come' did not translate into 'whosoever won't must be compelled.' The faith did indeed see enormous reproach in the crucifixion but its classic formula was 'Behold, the sin of the world:' there was nothing exclusively 'the sin of Jews and Romans.' The Cross only mirrored human wrong. When later, medieval generations chose to see it differently, they betrayed their apostles and the Lord Himself, He who prayed 'Father, forgive them . . . they do not know . . .'

His words can never well be twisted into calumny or hatred and they remain the inner clue to all the Gospel is.

That travesty developed no sincerity will, or can, deny. It must be known for the travesty it was. We shall not know it so if we allege that it is all there ever was.

Travesty, in all its foulness, was born of the claim to 'new peoplehood' with the old mandate to possess God's Christian 'Canaan' and deny it to those who had not acknowledged the new inheritors. Joshua, or perhaps only his chroniclers, could show them how.[31] The travesty lay, further, in the merging of that new peoplehood with nationalisms, tribalisms, power-structures to the like of which in its genesis it had never belonged. To be conscious of 'peoplehood under grace,' inclusively of all on the sole principle of faith, without relevance of birth, or sex, or clan, or tribe, or language, was one thing. It was quite another for this 'peoplehood' to be purloined by the politics of empire and of state.

There are those in modern Judaism who see such purloining as inevitable, indeed as the tutor of political Zionism. They would claim, further, that the universality was always phoney and unreal, hardly ever viable and, therefore, evermore illusory. The reply here must be the gentle witness that believes its primal reality and its present ecumenical will-to-be, despite all odds, a 'peoplehood' ready to relegate what it is *qua* speech, or state, or local soul to the margin of its primary identity in faith and love. As such, it is entirely ready to live in parallel with a Jewry struggling, despite the politics of Zionism, with a similar ambition having Torah where we have Christ.

That the two differ sharply need be no impediment to their continuing mutuality so long as the Christ-bearers do not exclude Jews from His reach or the Torah-bearers Christians from their forgiveness or from the mind of their Judaism now. In that way, each may be worthy of a convergence of their worlds.

I have in the foregoing left many themes to silence. The concern has been a personal reckoning with what a Christian Judaica requires. Points which might have been expected on the Shoah may be gauged from a study of Elie

Wiesel in *Troubled by Truth.*[32] To think, as just now, of Torah as the Christ of Jewry and Christ as the Christians' Torah raises large questions about law, evil, grace and human amenability/perversity in respect of any revelation of divine will, short of redemption. Some aspects here may better come in the next Chapter. For Islam is equally concerned in them.

This Chapter began with the subtle bearing of faith in God on estimation of ourselves. Nowhere has that bearing been more crucial or more compelling than between Hebraic faith and Jewish people. Outsiders do well to take in, as far as outsiders can, how tenacious, how anxious, is the mystery for those within. This Chapter was in hope to do so. For no people can be externally defined. All are as they will to believe themselves to be. So believing, they are part of the world of all of us in this mortal, human scene. As such, 'their being is to be received.' For none – less so now than ever – are in some vacuum of nature or of time. The self-awareness of every nation, folk or corporate identity, is part of the *conspiratio*, as the Latins called it, 'the breathing together' of humanity. It can also so readily become a conspiracy, an enmity of apprehension, pitting each against all and so, finally, against humanity itself.

The Sioux author, Vine De Loria, of the Dakotas, wrote:

> 'Before the white man can relate to others he must forego the pleasure of defining them. The white man must learn to stop viewing history as a plot against himself.'[33]

He had in mind the white arrogance that saw all things, a whole continent, its people and its lore, through the lens of its own uneasy ambition. The long tragedy of Jewry has been that the world scarcely left them any option but to 'view history as a plot' against them. Christians, though not the faith of Christ, have been darkly part of that 'conspiracy.' Political Zionism aims and hopes to foil it. Ambiguously in, and yet beyond, that aim and hope, Judaism abides in the self-awareness of the covenant, of Torah and its trust. Can it not forego the need of defining others as parties to a plot against itself? Let there be now a single quest of common human meaning that covenants shall not exclusify nor plots deface.

Chapter 8

The Tribunal of Islam

i.

That Islam, with its imperative – not to say imperious – finality, constitutes a tribunal before which all other faiths, and Christianity in particular, must be brought to the bar is familiar enough. A Christian and contemporary honesty of mind has to be ready to submit to such interrogation and open to whatever indictment it has to bring. That has been ever the way since the incidence of the Qur'an, made all the more crucial because sacred writ in Islam is its fount and origin. An insistent rejection of convictions central to Christian faith is built into the very text of Islam. Tribunal, therefore, it has to be seen to be, since to bring its judgements is the obligation of its own loyalty.

It follows from this quality in Islam that the roles require to be reversed in the sense that if incompatibles dominate they are, by the same token, mutual. Where adverse judgement is made there judgements adverse are directed. A tribunal's verdict invites a verdict on the tribunal.

This situation has been the blight and bane of Muslim/Christian history through fourteen centuries, burdened with physical, military and political factors as well as those that belong with faith and theology. It has, therefore, long been urgent to try and circumvent what is trapped in confrontation and controversy and to break free from attitude and authority that live only for the incompatibles, in order to gain the perspectives that de-alienate and mediate. This will in no way ignore the traditional issues. We can aim to discover a way through them if the themes of contrary judgements are themselves acknowledged to have positive and significant relevance for each other.

This is what will be meant here, in a vital negotiation of

faith and life, by 'the tribunal of Islam' in both kinds of genitive – the tribunal it constitutes and the one it undergoes. In that sense 'the tribunal of Christianity' would be equally appropriate except that Islam, in the 7th century is the later arrival.[1]

This reckoning of the one with the other, both ways, has been expressed in a wide variety of formulae. An unusual one, with which we may well begin, is suggested by Frithjof Schuon in terms of the Meccan Ka'bah and the Cross. He writes:

> 'The cubic Ka'bah contrasts with the Cross whose arms branch off indefinitely from the centre, while remaining connected with it, whereas the Ka'bah is reflected as a whole in the least of its parts, each one of which by its substance and internal cohesion is identical with the other parts and with the Ka'bah itself.'[2]

Analogies from symmetry have long been favoured by Muslim philosophy and are seen as implicit in the loved geometric forms of Islamic art.[3] Certainly the 'cube' structure at the centre of the great *Haram*, or sacred enclosure, in Mecca may be interpreted as a symbol of something coherent, consistent in length, width and height, with nothing obtruding to perplex and dimensions only to admire, an edifice arguably embodying proportion, finality and unity. The contrast with the Cross is certainly complete.

Yet two reflections give pause to this conclusion. From earliest Christian devotion the arms of the Cross were not seen as 'branching off indefinitely:' rather they were seen 'reaching round definitively' in a costly embrace, which the early Church called, in the Greek, *ekpetasis*, 'taking in the human world,' as love does when arms enfold. They did so 'to the ends of the earth,' indifferently as to race and sex and place, but only by worth of love's self-giving. Does not the gesture of 'embrace' – reaching out to clasp the other – make the human shape itself cruciform when so employed? Could this then be the shape also of a costly divine love?

Being taken to the heart, in this way, as the Cross

defines what is between God and ourselves, would seem to be impossible when a cube is the sign of the divine to the human, of the human at rendezvous with the divine. Not so, for after crying: *Labbaika, labbaika*, 'Here, here in truth, in Thy presence,' the pilgrim on entering and circumambulating the shrine of the Ka'bah tries hard, as the throng allows, to perform the *Iltizam*, the 'embrace.' At the place called the *multazam*, the pilgrim presses his breast against the stone and stretches out his arms along it. The rite has no mention in the Qur'an and seems to have been maintained in Islam from pre-Islamic usage. However, *Iltizam* and *multazam* have a poignant significance, deriving from the verb *iltazama* which occurs in Surah 17.13.[4] 'To cause to cleave,' or 'to necessitate' bring together the twin ideas of an urge to living contact, i.e. precisely the concept of 'embrace' as crucial to the believer's conviction and a concept of need and its satisfaction where, in some sense, the divine and the human are at rendezvous, as *Labbaika*, the pilgrim's cry of greeting, so ardently declares. What *Labbaika* says orally *Iltizam* transacts physically, if individual access to the crucial spot can be gained. Negotiating it amid the crowd, holding back while others accede, drawing away as others follow in the endless press – all these are dramatic items of a rapid sequence in pilgrim experience.

'Embrace,' then, whether *ekpetasis* or *Iltizam*, belongs, of necessity to both faiths, however far the contrasts. Indeed, the urge and yearning, finding and being found, which it enshrines may be said to be at the heart of all religious quest. Perhaps, then, it need not seem a strange place to begin in an effort to trace – as it were – the biography of my Christian story-study vis-à-vis Islam in the explorations of this Chapter. Before, and inclusively after, *The Call of the Minaret*, I found myself wondering more and more what converse with the minaret (or, rather, with its people) there might conceivably be. The fact that many thought it non-existent, impossible, futile or romantic, seemed only to make it more proper to seek, more urgent to find, unless we were also to repudiate vast areas of vital conviction which were obviously common, and unless we were to ignore the sorry legacies of a long embroilment it was becoming more and more imperative to end. We had, indeed, tribunals of judgement on each other, the onus of them deep in traditional loyalties. Could their verdicts *first* undertake some sincere mutual reckoning with what – in the unitary predicament of being human – we truly had in common? The hope that it might be so became the motive of my work and writing before and after the demise in Canterbury and through the sundry vicissitudes that followed it as Bishop in the Jerusalem Archbishopric. As in previous Chapters there was the same interaction between story and study, between thoughts and situations.

ii.

We could at least agree on our humanity if not on how to read it. Any reading, however, would necessarily be about divine reference of our human-ness. On that we were at one. There have always been two ways of comprehending theology. The one is 'the being of God as posited by man,' the other 'the being of man as determined by God.'[5] The former derives from human subjectivity projecting need, hope, prayer, faith, upon what is no more than a shape of human thinking, having no real referent other than the notion that believes it. Clearly no Muslim, Jew or Christian, unless secularized and inwardly compromised, could accept 'theology' in that guise. 'The being of man as determined by God' affirms reality reciprocal to all those human awarenesses of dependence, creaturehood, obligation and objective love for which the other view allows no substance other than empty human credence.

It is worth noting that either 'theology' is one for which we opt. Neither can underwrite itself with guarantee. We can read hunger as that which exists by the absence of what it seeks. Or we can read hunger as inexplicable except in a situation of food-reality. Theologies will never be like geologies, where evidence, research, data, are readily accessible to pick-axe, excavation, stratification and the like. They will always be relational to being human. The denial of God, if we make it, will be a willed interpretation of ourselves. If we affirm Him as living it will be by our understanding of why and how we are ourselves alive, in that we could not even deny Him if He did not exist. Or, contrariwise, our 'exclusion of God' – to use the Qur'an's repeated phrase – will be a decision excluding ourselves from evidences that, however we read them, are always about our own being.

Either way, and in the simplest terms, it is clear that divine transcendence and human experience inter-relate, which brings us back to theology as 'the conceptual account of the existence of man as being determined by God.' Much, for us as Christians or Muslims, will turn on the word 'determined.' Is it large enough, generous enough, adequate enough? Could we say 'undertaken,' 'enterprised,' 'desired,' or even 'risked,' by God? And what if we reversed the formula and spoke of a 'conceptual account of the being of God as . . . by man' – what would be the word to place there? Clearly, not 'determined.' For transcendence, in both our theologies, must transcend. 'Experienced by man,' 'cherished . . .' 'adored . . .', 'received . . .' – all these might fit, but clearly the 'feel' of any theology would be greatly affected by whether we could go beyond the rigorous 'determined . . .' while firmly acknowledging total divine Lordship, 'the God, King and Master' of mankind (Surah 114.2–3).

I think that I came more and more to see that all that was crucial for us both turned on what words were most proper to describe this divine-human situation we both confessed but by differing perceptions of its character. It plainly involved all those themes of creation, law-giving, providence, prophethood and mercy which made the Bible and the Qur'an, on that account, such kindred Scriptures, however far they might diverge elsewhere. I was at pains to try to assert that kinship both to retrieve the Qur'an's people from their too ready dismissal of Christian faith as incompatible, and Christian perceivers of Islam from their too facile neglect, ignorance or disavowal of the Qur'an. This was especially the case with *The Mind of the Qur'an* which studied carefully the sacramental giving of the natural order into the 'dominion' of man, through the reality of 'the signs of God,' which enshrined the intelligibility of nature to mind and the sanction of divine 'given-ness' on all material things, as these yielded into the economies and politics of human society under God.

It was these fundamentals of all human experience when read as 'determined' by God, bestowed mercifully, graciously, lavishly by 'the Lord of the heavens and of the earth,'[6] of which Christians, by and large, seemed not to be aware as also Islamic. This left their perceptions too often, and too far, negative or dismissive. If we could clarify how close, in this particular, were the doxologies of the Qur'an to Biblical psalmody, how akin to the New Testament dictum that 'every creation of God is good if it be received with thanksgiving' (1 Timothy 4.4),[7] would we not have enlarged our sympathies, not by compromise, still less by easy patronage, but by genuine acknowledgement of truth?

There is no need to repeat or elaborate the case here, since it has been fully argued and documented – as far as in me lay. If it became for me somewhat of a repetition, this was only because the realization of it seemed often so tardy and reluctant. Perhaps the only duty here is to face the suspicion that Christians had no business anyway appreciating the Qur'an, still less citing it for Christian persuasion. People who did so, it was said, were either 'Christianizing' the Muslim Scripture, or discriminating at will the parts from the obligatory whole, or playing into the hands of Muslim understanding of its status. None of these charges were true. It was not 'Christianizing' to note what was already there, in its own right, and plainly integral whether we saw it or not. The question was not of 'choosing' this from that within the Qur'an but heeding it intelligently. Its final status (faced elsewhere in proper context) was not at issue, seeing that truth is not finally determined by where one reads it but by what it says. Talk of 'playing into hands' was the language of prejudice and polemic.

To be joyfully aware of how far Bible and Qur'an shared the 'being of man as determined by God,' in respect of creaturehood, guidance, vocation to rule things and defer to God, destiny to appreciate mercy in every form of cognizance and experience, as liable, beneficent, and mortal, from 'the Lord of all being' – this was the common perspective in its kindredly Semitic form. Acknowledged as such, it led directly into the distinctive indictment of Christian theology by the tribunal of Islam. It was precisely an honest mutuality which incurred the utmost stake at issue. What was the charge?

Christian faith had carried too far the implications of 'the being of man as determined by God,' had carried them into measures of divine self-giving, of divine risk and compassion, that unwarrantably compromised, indeed denied, divine transcendence. So doing, it had also too far miscued as tragic, distorted as radical, its reading of human being. The two travesties – for such they are accounted – go together. How, we have to ask, had Christian faith offended in its perception of how 'God's being God' related to 'man's being man'? We can defer till later the Christian tribunal as to how Islam had offended in confining to law and judgement its measures of how great God might be and in limiting what human experience of that greatness might comprise.

iii.

It is very clear that, from every angle, Islam in its origins was pre-occupied with the insistent assertion of divine unity as necessitated by the prevailing idolatry in Arab-Meccan belief in many deities. This plurality of worships was not incompatible with belief in One supreme Lordship, *Allah*, at the apex of divine, or semi-divine, beings. It was, however, intolerable to belief in the sole, undivided, undiverted, sovereignty of *Allah*. All deviation from that single worship was *Shirk*, the cardinal evil in Arab society, the evil which spawned its political and social ills. The total veto on *Shirk* became the central theme of Muhammad's mission.

Perhaps it was inevitable, in context, that the Qur'an should see the classic Christian understanding of God as falling under the same anathema. It could not see Christian Christology as truly within its own Islamic 'jealousy' for divine unity, nor allow it to belong with what might be 'proper' to God in relation to 'the being of man.' Christian faith and theology, we must say, incurred misunderstanding and rejection in consequence of the urgent Quranic encounter with Arabian paganism, and the direction this gave to all its perceptions. It is fascinating to ponder what Islam might have been, in temper and tradition, if its wholly authentic mission against idols had been situated, not in the crude tribal superstition of the original Hijaz, but in the agnostic sophistication of a modern culture given to the subtle idolatries of the market, of power and of ill-applied science.[8]

Muslims, however, believe that the incidence of the Qur'an in time and place, forming the whole stance of Islam this way, was integral to what divine revelation purposed and contained. Thus, it has to be accepted that Quranic verdicts against the Christian Gospel were paradoxically tied in to a wholly Christian concern, namely emphasis on the divine unity. Muslims proved unable, or unwilling, to distinguish between the way in which Arabian paganism denied the divine unity and the perceptions by which Christian faith affirmed it. Those perceptions – as we must see – had to do with the Incarnation of the Word and the redemption by the Cross, these being the corollaries of how truly One God was. That Christian Oneness was to be understood, not as arithmetical statement (as if the speaker was stopping short in a series which could have gone on to two, or three, or more, as one might count bricks in a wall) but as a spiritual mastery, the responsible 'power and wisdom' none could rival and no other authority usurp.

Islam and Muslims, it seems fair to say, were required by the Qur'an and its Arabian context, to focus faith as to the divine unity on a singularity over against countable idols and pseudo-worships, but *not* also on a sovereignty reckoning duly with all that defied it, with the sort of reckoning for which human history called, if God as One was to be divinely vindicated. In its anathema for how Christian theology saw such reckoning, did Islam fail to register how deep and rich a metaphor was unity itself?

The question is one we have to explore with the Quranic text, realizing as we do so that, though the issue of the divine unity divides us sharply, the theme of it unites us. It is vital also to see and acknowledge that so much is already in agreed place – creation, creaturehood, divine guidance in law, prophethood for our education, and perennial 'signs' for our heeding of divine mercy in a *privilegium humanum* whereby all our arts, technologies and cultures subsist and accumulate to make history urgently significant. Nowhere is this divine-human situation more finely expressed than by the Persian poet, Hafiz, with whom we can all concur:

> 'In wide eternity's vast space
> Where no beginning was, wert Thou.
> The rays of all pervading grace
> Beneath Thy veil, flamed on Thy brow.
> Then love and nature sprang to birth
> And life and beauty filled the earth.'[9]

The many doxologies of the Qur'an confirm the sentiments of one of Islam's most celebrated poets whose very name denotes a 'memorizer' of that Scripture.[10]

If what is shared in each Semitic theism is so far-reaching, why should antipathies arise? Ought the reality of divine unity to provoke division in confessing it? Given the Qur'an's preöccupation with *Shirk*, the answer takes us to failures both of mind and patience, with much in the Christian scene that abetted them. It is right, after careful study of the actual texts and terms of the Qur'an, to conclude that it does not explicitly deny the classic meaning of Christian Christology. It may be assumed to intend to deny it: in point of fact its language denies something else. The several most important passages are those which repudiate any notion of 'the Eternal taking to Himself a son.' The verb here, *ittakhadha* means 'to adopt,' 'adoptionism' being a heresy – as Christian 'orthodoxy' believed – which in fact reversed what the faith meant by 'God in Christ.' *Ittikhadh*, or 'adoption,' meant a sort of 'deification' by which the human Jesus was, at some point in life, 'taken' for 'divine son' which he had not been before. This runs counter to 'and the Word was made flesh,' '. . . and was made man,' where incarnation, not deification, is affirmed. If what is truly divine has condescended to 'our low estate,' to confess it so cannot be included within *Shirk* or denied as such. For the confession does not have to do with a human 'divinizing' alleged by idol-making men: it has to do with a initiative from God entirely consistent with His unity, indeed – in Christian terms – necessitated by it.[11]

It is, of course, that 'consistent' and 'necessary' which Islam excludes though, mostly, without pausing to consider how divine unity requires them. That is the issue of theodicy to which we must come. Here we must stay with the charge the Qur'an presses around Christology.

Just as there is perplexity around 'adoptionism,' so there is around the term 'begotten.' It is a term the Christian Creed deliberately contrasts with 'made,' in order to insist that 'God in Christ' is not to be understood as in the chain of contingency as creaturehood is. It tells of self-giving in love which, being such, has in no way forfeited divine identity. The Qur'an means to rule out such condescension into human need by insisting, in Surah 112, the Surah of Unity, that God 'does not beget and is not begotten.'[12] That, too, is essentially Christian theology. The divine reality is not 'derived' and 'deriving' as are the succession of fathers and sons, mothers and daughters, of human transience. The divine in Jesus is not displacing, succeeding, or supplanting, a divine original now relegated to a past. Nor is divine initiative of grace within the divine being any sort of supersession: rather it tells the dynamic unity of love. So understood, 'begotten' in credal Christology is in no way at odds with the theme of Surah 112, telling of a unity we all alike confess.[13]

Rightly perceived, this is the sense of the word 'only' about the Incarnation in Biblical and credal language. 'Only,' after all, shortens 'onely,' 'unitarily,' 'entirely,' 'inclusively.' If, indeed, the divine is Self-revealed in our history, in time and place, that revelation must be as 'one' as God Himself. It cannot be disparate, diverse, plural, inconsistent. Seeing that time and place are the 'where' and 'when' of incidence (many issues here) it will, of necessity, be particular, but if it is of and from the Eternal, it will be as 'One' as God Himself. If God is Self-revealing, then God is Self-revealed.

iv.

It is, however, just that crucial 'if' about which the tribunal of Islam demurs. Even when we have removed misconceptions that stem from terms and perplexities, there is still a built-in instinct to reserve God from this measure of condescension. Given its proper vigilance against idols in its own context, the Qur'an sees something like calumny against God and against the pure Prophet, Jesus, in the Christian Christology. In my task as Bishop in the seventies I became increasingly occupied, through *Jesus and the Muslim*, and other writing, with this aspect of two sincerities at odds about what was precious to each. The Islamic tribunal said that Christian faith had done violence to Jesus and violated the majesty of God. The two charges, of course, were fused into one. Fair enough – Christian faith could only do right by theology if Christology was inside it, could only express Christology on warrant of theology.

Some of the issues here we can defer until we reverse the tribunals, as earlier promised, and try to see Islamic judgements through Christian eyes. Trying now to look through Muslim eyes, of what was Christian faith guilty? Unwarranted deification we have already assessed and seen to be 'no case.' Christianity is not *Shirk*. Our inter-theology becomes a question about the length of divine reach, the criteria of divine mercy, the capacity of divine love. In a word, we are asking what it takes for God to be God? The answer of Islam is power, wisdom, mercy in creation and the natural world, mercy in given law and guidance, watchfulness and mastery, beneficence and final judgement. These, broadly, are – if we may so speak – the human relationships of God.

Beyond them and within them Islam sets inhibiting

reaches of divine immunity, of divine Self-reservation, because of which we must beware what analogies we use, what metaphors we employ, like 'father,' 'shepherd,' 'redeemer,' which might seem to soil the divine hands or compromise the divine serenity. It is important to distinguish here between due acknowledgement of transcendence, of God, in John Donne's phrase, 'only and divinely like himself,' and a concern to withhold from God, in the interests of His exaltedness, different credentials of 'power and wisdom' which He might well possess. Denial to God of attributes that in fact belong would be as heinous as the *Shirk* which falsely associates what does not belong. *Shirk*, in fact, works both ways. It occurs, either way, when God is not adequately acknowledged for the God He is.[14] Everything turns on the criteria and these on the discernible credentials. It will take God to assure, and ensure, us about Him. The question is where and how, wherein and whether.

Is there, in the end, we have to ask with Robert Browning, 'too much love' in the Christian faith about God, 'a bridge too far' into our human crisis?[15] Islam, by and large, holds that law, guidance and a providence that keeps its own counsel, suffice for us and fulfill what the divine can properly mean. For the rest, Muslim theology feels it must not be too troubled, over interrogative, unduly intellectual or ever spiritually distraught. The Qur'an's Ayyub, Job, is a brief paragon of patience, not an anguished interrogator of omnipotence. Its Ya'cub, Jacob, wrestles with no angel. Theology does not have to reckon with the crown of thorns.

On the contrary, the emphases of Quranic narrative and direction are assured, as a Book 'in which there is nothing dubious.'[16] The right posture for the reader is to submit, to defer to the indubitably 'given' of revelation, and not to distract fidelity with queries which the silence of the revelation has ignored. Let its authority suffice by its own explicit sufficiency. The sense in which God is God and our humanity 'determined by Him' is known, as far as it need be, and finally so. Obedience is then the proper business of theology. It is this simplicity of writ and duty, of authority and destiny, which the Christian 'liabilities' of God in the Incarnation and the Cross as perceived in the New Testament, distort and encumber. By its own criteria of what it takes God to be God, Islam finds those Christian dimensions of the answer improper, illusory and deplorable.

'A bridge too far' seems to leave between us no bridge at all. Before we so conclude, however, it is necessary to take the issue for theology into the kindred theme of Christology and then examine both in the light of what it takes for man to be man, where the third part of the tribunal of Islam has Christianity accused.

v.

That there are strenuous tasks of scholarship and of believing integrity around the New Testament faith in Jesus as the Christ is emphatically the case. It is also true that Islam is very deeply involved in the study of whether there was some great aberration whereby the 'Jesus of actual history' (as the phrase goes) was transformed into 'the Christ of faith,' or whether what happened was the authentic perception of truth. One has to note that, crucial as the issues are for Muslim and Quranic depiction of Jesus, they have rarely been taken up by a Muslim scholarship equipped with the skills necessary for the pursuit of them seriously.[17] The themes of Christology deserve much livelier perception and much more patient discerning then they have received – qualities which the complexities demand and which an authoritarian Qur'an tends to discourage.

Jesus and the Muslim (1985) and *What Decided Christianity*, (1989) represented my own effort to accept the obvious – and the less obvious – liabilities of a Christian scholarship about Christian faith. It had longed seemed to me that the root question was: What sort of an event must the entire impact of Jesus have been to have had the consequence which the New Testament embodied as, at once, document, community and conviction? All those three were actual, remarkable and inter-dependent and they had come about in the throes of deep factors that might have been expected to preclude, annul and refuse them. These factors were the rigorous Judaic monotheism in which faith in the divine Incarnation in Jesus had come to birth, the apparent incredibility of Messianic fulfilment via a crucified teacher who could not even save himself, and the bold, decisive association of that Messiahship with the very nature of God so that one could truly speak of 'God in Christ' or avow that 'Christ is God's.' (2 Corinthians 5.19 and 1 Corinthians 3.23). Despite all that might have been expected to make such a faith inconceivable, indeed preposterous, it had, nevertheless come to pass. It had made itself plain in a document – Gospels and Epistles – at once its witness and its lasting credential, a document which told a history, educated a community, and lived in prospect out of retrospect.

There was something else, near incredible yet supremely eloquent, about that faith-community, namely its instinctive accessibility to all and sundry of humanity. Jewish Christian initiative had itself transcended Jewish privacy, seen itself intended for universal grace and acknowledged itself joyfully one with a 'kingdom open to all believers,' in which the Jew/Gentile distinction was obsolete. The fact that majority Jewry never shared – or later drew back from – this inclusive 'people of God' could not detract from its actuality, while immensely complicating the burdens it carried. Those burdens were honestly, even grimly, reflected in the New Testament document itself. Controversy, running so deep about Messianic fulfilment, or its denial, open peoplehood, or its abortion, at least were witness to the convictions that fathered it.

Given such surprising-ness about the nascent faith, community and text, stemming – whether validly or perversely – from 'the Jesus of history,' it would be right for scholarship to examine whether there were alien, misleading factors responsible for what transpired so that 'the Christ of faith' would have to be declared a travesty and the New Testament a fraud? A mischievous gnosticism might be a candidate for this perverse role, or the temptations of Hellenism in a variety of forms,[18] or perhaps a strange psychology compensating for the sheer tragedy of crucifixion by some myth of dying and rising visitants from heaven. None of these conjectures, however, seemed credibly to agree with the Jewish matrix of the New Testament, nor with the solid sanity, *joie de vivre*, and spiritual quality of the early Church.

Faith in the authenticity of the Christ-event and in the Church-event which followed it, could not, of course, clothe itself in any sort of 'guarantee' which would make careful scholarship redundant and exclude that final quality of 'trust,' not 'proof,' appropriate to love and to religion. The New Testament writings did not pretend to be 'impartial' any more than a husband and wife could be impartial about their wedding. However, the 'partiality' that made the writings 'witness' – for all its very significance as such – could, and should, readily submit to honest study about how the intricate processes of recollection, oral memory, text-formation, redaction, editorial cares and much else, had attended on the final shape of Gospels and Epistles.

I had long seen that a readiness here for arguably loose ends, factors in church-dispersion bearing on Jesus-situations, was properly due from Christian believing. I made what effort I could to bring that readiness into its distinctively Islamic tasks, given that the Qur'an had very much its own account of 'a Jesus of history' who was in no sense 'the Christ of God.'[19] But it often seemed a forlorn task. The prejudices were so massive, the necessary resilience of mind so far to seek. Yet the effort was imperative and it had a major place in all my travelling studies both in the fifties and seventies of my task as a Canon and a Bishop in and out of Jerusalem. The difficulties were compounded by the fact that the Qur'an so strongly cared, in double narrative, for the Virgin Birth of Jesus but cared in so little detail for the ministry to which it led and for the climax of suffering to which that ministry came.[20] So much at issue here still awaits an adequately mutual attention out of a common caring for the two Scriptures defining the two faiths. We turn to that other angle of their duty, namely the human as reciprocal, in some sense, to the divine.

vi.

'Reciprocal' may be too strong a word for many in Islam relating 'man being man' to 'God's being God.' Unless we are happy with metaphors like the artist needing his art, we may be disposed to insist that 'God has no need of man.' Islam is committed to concepts of sovereign omnipotence which incur no necessary moral liability in respect of our creaturehood. *Allahu akbar*, 'God is greater,' covers all. It may even be hinted that human *zulm*, or defiance of God, human *Shirk*, or falsification of a true, obligatory worship, are perverse elements in humanity God has Himself willed to be, by His prerogative as Creator 'to make man in whatever form He pleased.' (Surah 82.8) Divine transcendence in Islam must disallow our human categories of what it might take for God to be God in respect of justice, right, compassion and love. In the end inscrutability must come to the rescue of all ardent enquiry by simply excluding it.

Nevertheless, it is clear on every ground in Islam of creation, law, prophethood and revelation, that there *is* a human autonomy, however limited, about which the divine will is concerned to those lengths, but for which the divine will waits as something, namely human *islam*, human conformity, which only human will can bring. Were this automatic, it would not need to be enjoined. Were it instinctive, axiomatic, there could be no *Shirk*. Plainly, there is that, turning on human will, which God seeks and will not receive unless we bring it in freedom. There *is* our *khilafah*, our 'dominion,' our earthly 'imperialism,' (Surah 11.61). Divine law has claims on this – hence prophethood to enjoin them. Those claims wait on our consent.

Despite the Qur'an's evidence of the obdurate disobedience which attends on all prophethood, including Muhammad's, Muslims, by and large, see this human situation, as either culpable and duly retributed, or manageable and amenable, given the pre-requisites of knowledge, discipline, polity and habituation, which Islam provides. They therefore accuse Christian faith of excessively tragic views of the human predicament. My experience seemed to tell me that there was here an almost unbridgeable gulf of perceptions. I found Muslim writers resolutely excluding pathos and tragedy from their analysis of man. To see tragedy was a Christian temptation. It contradicted the organizational, political, legal formulae of Islam by which Muslims could be regulated away from 'occasional' lapses and pass muster successfully. Or to see any depth in human perversity was to approve the Satanic scepticism about the dignity God had conferred on the human vicegerent.[21]

By contrast with Christian redemption which it had to accuse on every ground, Islam was an eminently practical faith. It had no place for a Christian radicalism. Sin was not rightly understood as calling for interventionist grace, or advent from heaven (which would compromise God anyway). Islam could police us into due conformity by the private suasion of law and the public success of political constraint. So much the Prophet himself had demonstrated and achieved. For he

> '. . . saw no good reason why a resourceful sovereignty should be denied ultimate success in the world merely on account of certain utterly baseless qualms about the recruitment of force. As long as coercive measures were legitimately and properly applied, the use of political power was not only not wrong, it was positively right.'[22]

There was no sin that a political order, reinforcing a moral code, could not remove. Man might, indeed, be created 'restless,'[23] but this argued, not Christian redemption and grace, but what Islam historically exemplified. If Christianity would only shed its extravagancies of the Incarnation and the Cross, its Jesus could be properly perceived as a precursor of what Islam made finally evident and actual.

Otherwise, it must remain with the futility of its tragic vision, falsely comforted by its picture of 'a God come to earth,' and forfeiting a robust faith in the feasibility of human good by its indulgence in the pseudo comfort of a pathetic theism. It had no warrant to claim that 'God is love.' What could be known of Him was limited to the implications of His will for humanity, as revealed law enjoined it. The rest had to remain inscrutable. Muhammad's finality confirmed all that could, or need, be credibly known about Jesus' meaning and mission.

So the indictment ran and there the case stayed. Much of this was a deeply personal predicament for me. These paragraphs are only a trenchant (as I hope) summary of what has been more fully treated elsewhere.[24] The immediate point is what they meant inwardly as emotion, as well as mind, had to bear with them. Under the impact of them I was negotiating with the theological credentials to which such contrasted appeal could be made. There was necessary pain in their incidence. In perhaps minimal ways the issues were joined in reference to my own writings and there were accusations of theological naivete, incoherence, confusion and excessive theological romanticism. My 'An Exploration,' being the sub-title of *Jesus and the Muslim*, was judged 'a work of the fully Christian *imagination*' for all its effort carefully to document its contents. *Muhammad and the Christian* was 'marred by Christian theological preconceptions that militated against impartial enquiry.'[25] In any event, Christian faith was essentially incoherent, a religion in which 'trading on pathos' only registered a loss of the good faith Islam had right. Indeed, it would need to be seen, in some Sartrean sense, as 'bad faith,' inasmuch as it clung to deceptive delusion and had no heart for *Allahu akbar*. In some quarters the personal attacks called in question not only the content of my Christian faith but the integrity with which I held it and, for its sake, ventured into Islam.

Repeatedly, during my peripatetic years the thought came to me: What was the point of it all? Why persist with concerns that seemed locked in impasse and the impasse beset with personal distresses? I knew Biblically that there were, and are, numerous vocations pursued always close to futility, which could be neither abandoned nor attained. What practical significance could the theological points have, urgent as they were in their own right? Christians indeed had duties in respect of the Qur'an they had sadly failed to appreciate or fulfill. Muslims were still far from any inclusive register of the New Testament, its meanings and its invitation, its relevance to all that made them Muslim. Why not leave it all fallow? Why not defer to how inhospitable the times, how vexing the onus, how taxing the themes? It was tempting to concede that all could well be set aside as irrelevant. The two faiths persisted, the two Scriptures were there: let there be no more tribunals either way, only inarticulate co-existence entirely sceptical of any sharing in the common world.

To concede futility, however, would be to ignore another's faith and to disown one's own. Neither could be marginal in that way to the other and remain serious to themselves. Any surrender to despair ought to be deferred until there had been a provenly futile relating of the faith about 'God in Christ' to who and where the Muslim was. Perhaps 'the provenly futile' would never transpire: it had certainly not yet been reached. For what reasons should the Christian continue to care?

vii.

They are deep in its perception of the reality of God, which means finding them, in turn, in understanding Jesus and his being 'the Christ' through birth, ministry, word, suffering, death and resurrection. If, as promised, we reverse the assessments, what stock is classic Christianity required to take of Islam in the same three realms of God, man and what is properly between them? It will be well to resume where we just ended, namely with the sanguine or the radical in the human situation, whether divine law and human amenability readily prevail, or whether there is about us a perversity capable of negating law, revelation and, exhortation, a *dalal* saying, with a strange inscription in Westminster Abbey: 'Hang the law and the prophets.'[26]

With the crucifixion of Jesus so central to its genesis, Christian faith has always been alert to the depth of human evil. So also have some Muslims.[27] What it there and then identified as 'the sin of the world' (not the sin of such and such) was its constant index to how wrong mankind could be. Nor was that focus of the evil capacity of human politics, religion, society and selfhood, however climactic, some isolated or untypical event. On the contrary, it had to be intensely recognized as definitive of human ways because of its evident continuity with prophetic experience through the centuries. Was it not clear from Biblical story, which Muhammad's career in the Qur'an confirmed, that to be on behalf of God was to incur hostility, rejection, and suffering? Precisely where the voice of divine summons was heard there was the counter cry of human self-will, of an autonomy resenting and resisting what law from God prescribed.

Had Muslims taken proper stock of the *Shirk*, and *zulm*, and *nifaq*, their own Qur'an accused, the false worship, the gross injustice, the deep hypocrisy that necessitated and spurned the mission of God's messengers? Those were not evils which could be waved or willed away, for they persisted in the very society of revelation. They did not indicate some condition beyond repair. For they only mattered because the human calling was positive and critical and 'highly favoured.' Yet were they susceptible of correction by command, or exhortation, or protest, or threat? Perhaps, as the Christian might suggest, those evils identified by the Qur'an in the very midst of final revelation had some kinship with the sense of things in the New Testament, namely that law itself could, and did, somehow bring out the will to flout it. In enjoining and forbidding, law kindled into defiance the very autonomy to which law paid tribute precisely in addressing it. Autonomy was, therefore, always in the crisis implicit in its very nature – namely that of freely doing what was necessarily required. Was Islam right in reading history, including its own, as warranting any confidence that this conformity always happened? Was not prophethood itself, and the need for it, witness to how doubtful, how devious, how despairing the human case could be?

When Christians tried to keep that urgent question in place, it was not out of any basic misogyny, some morbid distrust in the whole enterprise of creation, or some suicidal surrender to existential doubt. On the contrary, they were keeping faith with the logical sequence of an intelligent theism – God, creation, creaturehood, 'dominion,' 'messengers with law' and then . . .? Unless these were all illusory, did not coherence, credibility, require that history should 'achieve' them all in the divine rule, through the human obedience, which was their evident intent? But could history be said ever to have attained, or currently to manifest, that achievement? If not, how not? And, if not, was there not a question which needed to be carried back – along that sequence of theism – from history, to law, to messengers, to 'dominion,' to creaturehood and creation, and so to 'the sovereignty of the heavens and the earth'? Would it not be part of honest faith to see that there were questions fit for God in the very confidence with which theists worshipped?

There comes at this point the whole issue of what used to be called 'theodicy,' the need for the reverent interrogation of God. Did Islam have no need of theodicy? But, before that aspect is taken, it is important to explore how Muslims react to the need arguably urgent from the thoughts just summarized. It would seem that they offer three considerations which might obviate the need to take the questions into God, or – if not – to draw much of their sting. They can insert the Islamic State, claim that broadly, satisfactorily, history does – or can – yield human rightness, and thirdly 'justify' God by His writ of final judgement in requital and retribution.

As a confidently political faith, Islam from its beginnings in the Prophet-Ruler has stressed the implementation of its theism and faith in, and through, the mechanisms of rule and statehood, of the *Ummah* and the Caliphate.[28] Though there have been many Christian versions of the same confidence in the power-aegis for divine ends, Islam has long reproached Christianity for the cult of 'meekness,' 'long-suffering,' 'tragedy,' as leading to other-worldliness, supine tolerance of the changeable as if it were not so, acquiescence in an unwarranted acceptance of ills that power could subdue. Much of the contrast between the politically 'finalized finality' – if we may so speak – of Muhammad and the Gethsemane of Jesus, the vindication of 'rapture to heaven' for him, rather than 'manifest victory' on earth, aligns with these Islamic instincts. There may be a nobility about Gethsemane but there is also a certain futility. It is well not to stay there, still more well not to trace divine and sovereign ways back there. A 'crown of thorns' may arouse emotion and kindle poesy but, in the harsh world it tells, it tells no answer.

So Islam. That power and politics have a due place in ethics, in society, in the human economy, it would be foolish to deny. There are aspects of 'good' which are properly enforceable, of 'evil' which are legitimately restrained. There are, in Quranic terminology, limits and bounds not to be violated, with power seeing that the writ runs. Law, divine or human, which carries no penalties, judges no situations, or lacks sinews to enforce, is thereby effectively abrogated. It is right for all theists to salute the realism of Islam in this context. 'Thou shalt,' 'thou shalt not' have to be in some measure institutionalized if they are to obtain at all.

What a tribunal on Islam has to ask, however, has to do with those reaches of good and evil which what is institutional can never identify, still less retrieve and may well accentuate. There is no true conscience that can be codified into legal pros and cons or honoured in solely judicial terms. 'Sins,' we may agree, are what we commit: 'sin,' more radically is who I am. There has to be a clear distinction between 'crime' and 'wrong.' Just as reason is often perverted by motive, so conformity to law may be sullied by pride, hypocrisy, and deceit. What is between us and the divine will can never be fully probed, still less ensured, by legal conformity and state control. The problems that history presents to the credibility of theism are not sufficiently resolved by leaving them to a political régime divinely ordained and constituted as being all they need.

Furthermore, apart from the limits of any régime in care of 'sacred law,' there are the temptations of power itself. These are implicit anyway: they are heightened when power is construed and wielded 'on behalf of God.' Just as a false worship 'deprives' God of what is 'justly due,' so does a subtle invocation of His Name, when it effectively turns the servant-role into the master-state. Nowhere is the force of *Allahu akbar* more urgently relevant than to those who say it. There is surely a very subtle associational issue when the Qur'an refers to 'the party of God,' *Hizb-Allah*, in contradistinction to 'the party of Satan.'[29] How is the 'construct' (in English grammar the 'gentitive') to be understood? How is divine sovereignty possessively related to 'partisans' on earth, especially if these are politically defined? The whole concept poses sharp issues about 'the ways of God with men,' and whether the divine and the human can be so complacently, so monopolistically, aligned, seeing that 'in the vastness of the heavens and the earth His throne is established.' (Surah 2.255).

The Qur'an, for its part, is, nevertheless, truly aware of how perverse human evil can be, how far it can, and will, defy the constraints of revelation and deny the restraints of power. We have already noted the concepts of *Shirk*, *zulm* and *nifaq*, so frequent deplored and denounced in its pages. The Muslim Scripture, carefully read, allows no facile optimism about the human crisis. It does not, of course, comment – except by implication – on the content of subsequent, post-Quranic history but its whole panorama of the pre-Islamic generations is a *mise-en-scène* of warnings disregarded, prophets spurned and of peoples and cultures that went down into retribution leaving behind them the wrecks and ruins of their folly. Such judgement, whether historically meted out or prospectively in waiting beyond death and time, is the final dimension of divine reckoning and, thus, of 'the being of man as determined by God,' with mercy always also in that future.

viii.

It would seem clear that human history, including Muslim history, returns us squarely to the question of theodicy and that, reluctant to face it as Islam has been, there are, nevertheless, aspects of the Qur'an which imply that it is real and not to be evaded. Via the sequence we studied through creation, 'dominion,' revelation and law, God *and* human history, how the 'and' is understood becomes the vital theme of a responsible faith. It seems clear to me that the central concern of Christian faith for Islam and Muslims – insofar as thought alone can care for it – will belong precisely here in a perception, and commendation, of what it takes God to be God in relation to what humans are.

If faith and life are really to 'negotiate' in the sense that each takes honest responsibility for the other, and if 'God' is the proper theme of such 'negotiation' – as we both assume – then there would seem to be two options for believers, for theists. The one will be to insist, whatever the contrary evidence, that somehow life and history are, or will be, or can be, what the divine will intends irrespective of how they *seem* to violate what ought to tally with divine wisdom, power, justice and mercy. The other will be to concede that they do not tally, and therefore to ask how authentic faith, nevertheless, sustains conviction about all those divine qualities evidently flouted as they are by what history discloses of evil and human nature demonstrates.

The first will be less than honest about the real world, in the interests of an emphatic faith: the other will accept what has to be radical in the interests of a questioning one, or – perhaps more truly expressed – it will let the questioning enter into the emphasis of doctrine. It will have the need for theodicy central to its conviction and theism itself will turn on being satisfied. Otherwise, agnosticism, even atheism, would have to be preferred.

So much of my personal inner wrestling with Christian/Muslim issues focussed here. Muslims, it seemed to me, could not be Islamic in rejecting theodicy altogether, nor did they. Creation and the 'deputy-creature' told of a divine purpose history had to vindicate. There was the cosmic, primeval human assent to the divine question: 'Am I not your Lord?' (Surah 7.172) That could not ride with any divine neutrality about humanity, embracing – as the question did – the whole saga of history. Nor could it hold with the repeated confidence of the Qur'an that God was both 'the mighty and the wise,' If one truly held the two descriptives together (as the Scripture did more than forty times) then one could not read history as a tale of 'power' not accountable to 'wisdom,' nor as an intention of 'wisdom' lacking the power to achieve. Could any realism about ourselves and our story, our religions most of all, think the two attributes fulfilled? Maybe the credentials would need to go farther and delve deeper if each were to be compatible with the other and both with honesty.

Of course, one could fall back on mere assertion or insist that our criteria did not, and could not, be applied to God's vindication. Yet would not to do so be to go out of *our* world, the world to which all revelation related and all doctrine concerned? Moreover, the Qur'an did speak about divine liability of which we could properly be cognizant. Particularly in Surah 4.165 it spoke of 'a case *against* God' as truly to be made had it not been answered by the messengerships that had been sent.[30] In the absence of 'guidance' to us humans God would properly have been seen as in default. It was just at this point that life as we knew it required us to go further. Further Christian faith had gone, in anticipating what there ought to be if we were to be authentic about either life, or faith, or God. That going further had to do with the adverse reception guidance plainly received, with how human will defied it, human motive disdained it, human mind disowned it. If God's being God involved Him in guidance of us by law and messengers, in what did our non-amenability to guidance involve Him? Non-*islam* could not not matter if He was in truth *Allahu akbar*. Where His 'power and wisdom' were at issue, what further form could they take or had they taken?

ix.

It was evident that 'sending' – to us on the part of God – was a common factor in both our convictions. The question was in what would 'sending' adequately consist? 'Messengers' were sent: and so, as the Gospel had it, was 'the Saviour.' Perhaps the significance of 'sent' words could be personified in a 'sent' life-event, in a personhood comprehensively set where that for which it was sent and meant could truly be recognized and grasped because the setting, in its very realism, called out from 'the sent one' all that we would need to know. This was what Christians believed had happened in 'Christ and Him crucified.' Therefore, could not the Quranic belief in divine 'sending' somehow carry the Christian faith in incarnation?[31]

I realized anew that the obstacle lay in the confusion between us over the proper – and mutual – anathema on *Shirk*. It was one thing to translate *Shirk* as 'association,' i.e. the sin and error of 'associating' idols with God as if divine sovereignty could ever be 'shared,' diverted, or usurped. This, for us all, the faith in the divine Unity forbade. It was quite another thing to imply that there was 'dissociation' of God from the world, or to exclude God from human relevance because it was imperative to exclude idolatrous 'sharedness' from our confession of divine Lordship. To 'dissociate' God from the world would end all belief in creation, messengers, law, guidance and compassion. It would also render illusory our human register of all these. So the question was not some 'whether' about 'God with us, for us and on-behalf-of-us,' it was how far it might be so, how generous, how embracing.[32]

It came to me that in a will like this to a genuinely conversing theology between mosque and church, we were truly back at some *multazam*. What was it we were 'embracing' when in *shahadah* we acknowledged God? What was it that was embracing us? Was the very word too intimate for divine transcendence? Yet what could be more intimate than those aching arms out-stretched to feel and know the Kaʿbah? From the divine side, could the sense of being embraced by the arms that endured the Cross be rightly acknowledged as God's *ekpetasis* of us?[33] We all had the conviction, as theists, that theology was about 'the being of man as determined by God.' There *was* this *iltizam*, this 'necessariness' between us and God, in any definition of either Him or us. Without Him we could not be who we are: without us, in our given dignity, our quality as a responsibility for Him, He would not be the God His creating and His sending tell us He is.

It must belong with Chapter 9 to ponder the Christian dimensions of this 'conclusion,' and to do so as an interior confession, not as an exercise in inter-faith. For being 'theological' is not finally the will to dialogue, nor the art of words, nor the logic of concepts: it is the worship of the Lord who seeks by the heart He finds and knows itself in being found. Nevertheless, there was a desire and hope to think and pray for what might mediate between the *iltizam* of the Kaʿbah (though disallowed me in my Christian *kufr*) and the embrace of the Cross. It remained a positive, if often distressing, factor in my Christian believing. If faith lives, and means, and feels, and moves as poetry does, it may perhaps prove similarly untranslateable. Yet, if it is true poetry, the effort is imperative, and sometimes it may succeed.

The sceptic may find this a revealing way to end. For is not poetry a luxury, abstracted from the prose of life and so like all theology today, an indulgence in the private, the intimate, the elusive, the unreal? What does it matter if those who embrace at the Kaʿbah see only futility in the broken-off arms of Jesus' Cross 'branching off indefinitely'? Muslims will always prefer a transcendence excluded from such imagined associations, such bizarre alignments of majesty and pathos, such tracing of any divine 'power and wisdom' in a sad miscarriage of human justice. What difference will it make anyway to the vagaries of the day-to-day world, to the cynics in corridors of politics, to the millions in the misery of keeping alive for lack of perceiving the absurdity of the attempt? Will it not be open to Muslims to point out that the 'imitation' of the Cross succeeds no better than the 'imprimatur' of the Qur'an: indeed that it avails less well and incurs the greater hypocrisy when it is violated.[34] All in all, the sanest thing has to be some practical live-and-let-live between faiths, a rivalry in good works that leaves aside all 'whys' and 'hows.'

That, to be sure, is wiser than polemic but it does not make faith-issues pointless. On the contrary, it engages them the more radically. Surah 3.65 invites all theists to 'a word . . .' that is 'the same' between them and identifies it in divine unity and non-association. At once we are back into the confusion we have just examined, namely whether a proper anathema on idols makes impossible divine condescension into our deepest need. Divine unity, too conceals the urgent question whether, and how, the contradiction of evil to it is overcome – assuming that we have not confined it to a sheer numerical singular.

There should not be conspiracies of silence in the transactions of love between us. There is a price to be paid in suffering and weariness.[35] There may be a sense in which the terms of reference that judge our failure in them are the more true for their very ability to indict us. That will always be the case if life is for the learning of love.[36] We may more readily succeed if we are held to lesser demands. That, however, will be no exoneration. It will not justify preferring a theology that eases our self-reproach by relieving conscience and vocation. These will surely be at their most critical, their most authentic, if 'love is their argument,' and if they can ground that 'argument' in faith that 'God is love.' Has faith any ground for that conclusion? 'The tribunal of Islam' conveys us to an exploring Chapter 9.

Chapter 9

Life's Faith - Conclusion

i.

In early Tranmere days I remember pausing abruptly at two words in Matthew's narrative of the passion of Jesus. 'Him there' (27.36) stood out starkly from the story demanding total incredulity. The verse was about the Roman soldiery 'sitting down to watch him there,' no doubt the normal routine of crucifixion anticipating a long vigil. 'Kings of the Jews' would not be dying quickly. As they watched, they may well have been gambling, dicing, lounging, swearing, yet also awed and cowed at the sight, especially if they had ever served in Galilee. History ever since has found the Cross of Christ a spectacle for vigil and perplexity. 'Him'? 'there'? – this person in this place? Was this where the Beatitudes had landed Him? What Pilate 'had written' in the *titulus* explaining condemnation hung over what Jesus had said about 'Come to me . . . and I will give you rest.' Everything about who He was where He was seemed utterly incongruous, obscene, incredible.

There was no denying it was He – Jesus of Nazareth, so the placard said.[1] So there was no escaping the enigma, the scandal, of His being there, hung to die between two terrorists. Whatever 'why?' could fit this who and where? It was in the very forming of the answer that the Christian faith was born. The purpose here is to seek it out afresh and know it for what it truly was.

First a point about the word 'conclusion.' It may have to do with what is closed and ended – which faith can never be. That is not the meaning here in mind. For love is ever open to faith's future. From the Latin *claudo* and *concludo* it means also 'to encompass,' 'to close upon,' and so 'to comprehend and comprise.' 'Let us hear the conclusion of the whole matter,' said the Preacher, Qoheleth (Ecclesiastes

12.13), the summary he had 'closed upon.' The only thing that faith's 'conclusion' ends is inconclusiveness. There was always 'not yet' in the great 'but now' of the New Testament. So the hope here is to say where I now am in the faith that has accompanied me through all the undertakings it involved and the experiences it underwent. How looks a boy's faith in the man's retrospect? Any answer has to carry forward the relationships examined in Chapters 6, 7 and 8. For those anticipated this one in points it will not be necessary to repeat if they are kept in mind.

My point of departure from 'Him there' is deliberate. Arresting as they are, the words also focus dramatically the intense particularity that characterizes Christian faith. 'Christ, and Him crucified' was, and is, a well-nigh incredible concentration of significance. This has been a perpetual source of demur and disbelief for sceptics and critics on every hand. Do not Christians read far too much into far too little? Is not that 'little' quite incongruous as a world's salvation or even as a tolerable symbol? Had Pilate's brief tenure as Procurator of Judea from 26–37 C.E. not been memorialized in the Christians' Creed by the cruel fate of Jesus of Nazareth, he would have passed rapidly into oblivion, with uncounted other travesties of Roman, and every sort of, justice, through all the centuries. As the central point of a world's redemption, all seems remote, minute, negligible, in Roman times entirely customary, routine and incidental in a brutal age.

That Pilate *is* there, fixed for ever in credal recital, thanks only to his victim, is the very paradox we must explain. To be sure, the Creed forestalled oblivion for all concerned but why should it have emerged to do so? The event can be so differently perceived. Has it not given occasion to every kind of parody? 'Custer died for your sins,' wrote Vine De Loria, quoted at the end of Chapter 7. The allusion meant to celebrate Indian Chief Sitting Bull's slaughter of white American forces led by George Custer, at Little Big Horn, in the very year of the Centennial Exhibition of national pride in Philadelphia. The ambush was only a brief halt to the massive, blood-stained superiority of whites over Sioux and Cheyenne Indians. What could it have to do with Gethsemane, by the satirical link of that preposition 'for' (to which I will return) about a dying and 'sins.'?

Was it well for Christian faith to be so vitally linked to an event so far open to readings that mistook it, or – like much Palestinian poetry in recent years – used it as a paradigm of victimization, fitting their own tragedy into it?[2] It could so easily be bent to contravene its meaning. Ought the sovereignty of God – as Christians said – to be subject to such associations and confusion? What of those, from Pliny to D.H. Lawrence, repelled by blood and wounds and nails and all things morbid? Do we need a crucifix to interpret the world, a victim by whom to come to God.?

That these are very Jewish and Muslim questions we already know, with many sympathizers elsewhere. They find themselves quite incredulous about the Christian version of the Cross. Jews, for their part, writing about Jesus, hover between dismissiveness and fascination – the latter for the puzzles of His person, the former for what has been done with His death. Arthur A. Cohen is not untypical.

> 'Jesus . . . obscure origins . . . moral insouciance . . . ecstatic gift, hieratic arrogance . . . charisma . . . comes to the attention of power and is rubbed out as cruelly as a gnat . . . comes to be crucified, condemned by some Jews and slain by some Romans . . . the single madman redeeming his acre of life (becomes) the Son of God redeeming the universe.'[3]

The madness was even greater on the part of those who preached that through this event and its antecedents in those 'obscure origins' God had exemplified all history's meaning.

Others, more sensitive to how universal bearings may be had from minute particulars in their own faith, whether at a burning bush, or under the Bo Tree, or in an Arabian cave, may allow that Christian perspective too can have specific siting yet still find the Christian 'site' overplayed. Even if we revere the manner of Jesus' dying can we accept the matter of it as redeeming the world? Has not

Christian theology greatly overloaded one event? Can we locate 'the sin of the world' at any one point or see its forgiveness consummated in a single lonely sufferer? 'Watching Him there' can we ever credibly see other than what the soldiers saw – a day's work, a sorry scene, a bitter end, a page to turn, not, emphatically not, 'God . . . reconciling the world.'?

The proximity of 'holy places,' not to say also an ear for such voices, made me acutely aware of the case my Christianity had to answer and to heed first, before answering. Mere rebuttal is not attention: only attention can refine it into witness. I tried to think as one who meant to listen.

ii.

What, however, was immediately clear, was that the incredulous themselves had 'somewhat to answer.' The faith dubbed impossible had at least occurred. The sequel to 'Him there' had belied the verdicts of negligibility, futility, transience, or the shrug of the shoulders about unfortunate tragedy. Messianic conviction had greeted it as the Christ-event and in under three decades there was a church-event – a community rejoicing in both across the eastern Mediterranean world and communicating in a literature and a liturgy. Paul penned his hymn of Christology – or perhaps quoted it as embryonic elsewhere – in Philippians 2.5–11 as if Gethsemane were only yesterday, as indeed it was, the yesterday of one man's maturing mind.

We have, then, again to ask, as in Chapter 7, what event must the living and dying of Jesus have been to have had this consequence in His Name? The legitimacy of what ensued will always be the concern of honest faith, but we may not ignore the fact of it. Both the Christ-event and the church-event were against all the odds, i.e. a 'Messiah' who could not save Himself – or did not, and a Jew/'Gentile' unison around Him. These are history. We have to reckon with the speed and the assurance with which the one event followed the other, the faith-community from the lonely Cross. A Jewish happening, with Jewish 'disciples' transformed into 'apostles,' inaugurated a Christology in simple redemptive terms which would later readily take on the language of the Greek mind.

Evidently the words and acts of Jesus had the significance capable of generating what became the faith of the first Christians and of sustaining that faith through all the following generations. Those words and deeds were imbued throughout His career with the issues of Messiahship – issues which dogged the attendant controversies about the Sabbath, the Temple, healing and forgiveness.[4] As Gerhard Kittel observed:

> 'The New Testament takes account of no Christology which is not related primarily to the historical Jesus. The historical interest belongs to the essence of Christian religion. The Christ of faith has no existence apart from the reality of the Jesus of history ... Anyone who attempts first to separate the two and then to describe only one of them has nothing in common with the New Testament.'[5]

Attempts to separate them have been many and continue today. Historicalness, it is said, need not matter because Christ calls us to existential decision. This cannot turn on what requires criticism, as history always will. Or lack of will to live with the nature of the event and its evidences intimidates some minds into retreat from reliance on them. Thus Denis Nineham asks:

> 'Is it any longer worth-while to attempt to trace the Christian's everchanging understanding of his relationship with God directly back to some identifiable element in the life, character and activity of Jesus of Nazareth.?'[6]

The question implies that it *was* once appropriate, 'Understanding,' as we will see, is not 'everchanging,' nor are 'elements' – one or many – 'unidentifiable.' Let us not disown the historical because it runs us into risks but rather hold to it because it invites us into trust. Ours is not the kind of world where we can demand guarantee, nor is faith congruent with infallibility. Christianity is bound into what is open to doubt and the New Testament, in its very quality as 'Gospel,' is the product of 'criticism,' of a desire to investigate and rely only on what is reliable. Relativity, to be sure, attaches to *all* historical knowledge, but take faith out of history, and history out of faith, and you go out of this world. Also you hold to God – if you do – as being in entire outsider-status in respect of time, of who we are, here in flesh, on conjecture, in sin, in tragedy, in the very things with which Incarnation has to do. Incarnation means history. Or so my own slow, timid relating of faith to doubt gave me to see and understand. Alternate Greek tenses in John 20.31 suggest that the Gospel was written out of faith and so as a call to faith. It looks back to event and forward from it. In confirming faith, the record aims to awaken it. The sequence is always properly alert, critical, reverent and in liberty. There is a sense, as we have seen in Chapters 7 and 8, that we have to cry with S.T. Coleridge 'No Christ, no God,' and realize that there is no Messiah except in history, in life, in act, in ministry, in death. The Church eventuated, as it did, because Jesus had been the Christ He was. He was known as such by virtue of what it became because of Him.

iii.

To see things so readily undertakes responsibility to history. The faith that accepts the invitation into trust does not thereby opt out of necessary scholarship. However, before broaching the obligation to history in believing the sequence – Jesus, the Cross, the Christ, the Church – and trusting its appeal to faith, it is well to clarify a basic factor in so doing. It is one that I was slow to understand. It explains why I began with 'Him there.'

Christian faith about the person and work of Christ is all retrospect to happening. We can only arrive in creeds at Chalcedon – if we do – by starting at Galilee and Gethsemane. Christology, in this sense, is afterthought. We have it presented in the Gospels as divine forethought – as, indeed, properly understood, it truly was. We may miss the gradual unfolding because we have the clue already. It was not that way in fact. All began with a man preaching, not with a then, known virgin birth. We are conditioned to see it otherwise. We understand a 'a visitor from heaven,' descending among us. We are in the mystery from the beginning and so we scarcely take the actuality for what it first was, and could only be, if we were ever to have the light by which we could identify its nature. It is as if we had all Shakespearean criticism before we had the plays.

It took me a long time to appreciate how urgent it was to have the perspective right. The 'visitor from heaven' perception stemmed from *a* sermon on *a* mount, from 'loaves and fishes,' and from 'bread and wine.' Christology, as Latin has it, was *ex eventu*, *post facto*. It demands to be understood that way. I recall an early Christmas sermon soon after my Ordination. It was from the text 1 John 4.10: 'He loved us and sent His Son . . .' I spoke via the analogy of a 'journey,' and on 'the length of it,' (i.e. from heaven to earth), 'the love of it,' and 'the lessons of it.' All was well meant but I do not now know how I conceived it to be. Nor did I then see that 'journey' was a risky word. For journeys are between two places over measurable distances. Was 'heaven', therefore, a locality? What could 'sending' be? And how did 'His Son' relate to one, Jesus, being here?

It helped me later to realize that this language, *ex eventu* as it was, affirmed that in the historical around Jesus the eternal could be read. What had transpired, the events in place and time, in word and act, had their source, their origin, their meaning, in the same sovereignty to which we attributed the world. We should know metaphor about 'journey' and 'Sonship' for what it was. There was the factuality before there was the knowing of Christology explaining it, though Scriptures told it the other way round. 'The beginning of the Gospel of Jesus, the Son of God,' was how Mark could announce his narrative. It was only by hindsight that he knew how to tell the thing that had begun.

For it did not begin historically in One promptly hailed as 'virgin-born,' or 'trailing clouds of glory,' but in One to whom those mysteries would be seen to belong only in the aftermath of lowliness and pain, of patience and compassion. The scepticism that feels more at ease with a purely human Jesus is only rightly answered, by us who hold the faith of 'God in Christ,' if we let the truly, fully, human Jesus necessitate that faith, by who and how He was, rather than invoke such faith on any grounds of pure miracle, or arbitrary authority, or some mere 'say-so' about God.

The unhappy ambivalence in some Christian credence in this regard may be sensed in a remark of the philosopher, Ludwig Wittgenstein. He wrote:

> 'Christianity is not based on a historical truth: rather it offers us an historical narrative and says: "Now believe," but not "believe this narrative with the belief appropriate to a historical narrative," rather "believe through thick and thin."'[7]

My whole point is that true faith *does* believe appropriately to historical narrative, and needs to do so, if the appropriateness is alive to how history can duly yield theology only in first being history. Only then can such history be told, *ex eventu*, in terms that incorporate the Christology it always was. This is what happened in the Gospels and was elaborated – on the basis of them – by the Fathers. Then we are not believing 'through thick and thin' by sheer assertion of miracle but 'through love and hope.' That history yields theology, and that theology waits on it, is the very principle of the Incarnation. Samuel Beckett once wrote of 'the transcendent . . . whose Providence is not divine enough to do without the co-operation of humanity.'[8] 'The God and Father of our Lord Jesus Christ' is transcendently divine enough to recruit and to indwell 'the co-operation of humanity,' and the human Jesus is where it happens. Being human among humans in the way He was took Him to a cross.

This leaves the disciple with two alternatives about how to take the form in which the actual historical was and is Christologically perceived. As long as we have 'Jesus came, preaching, healing, suffering . . .' we can understand the story of His birth as fittingly inaugural to what we alone identify by His so coming, comprehending the birth narratives as a profound symbol.[9] Or we may understand the whence and whither of Jesus' significance as suited to such an actual inauguration. Credal confession will be consistent either way. If we opt for the second we shall not be adding anything fortuitous or extraneous to whom and how Jesus was. We shall have the birth-story only in the life-significance. We comprehend motherhood because of Him.

Similarly, the emptiness of the tomb wonderfully comprehends the ultimacy of the love that suffers. It does not further that conviction but rather obscures it, if we lose ourselves in detective-style enquiries as if their positive issue added anything to 'the glory' that followed 'the suffering.' That 'death has no more dominion over him' has to control how we understand Who moved the stone. Clearly the Christian Creed sets itself firmly in the factual: 'born . . . suffered, crucified, dead, buried . . .' For better confirmation of these it acknowledges motherhood in Mary and a régime in Pontius Pilate. It is birth that preludes being: only a procurator signs a Roman death warrant. When we pass to 'coming down from heaven' and 'ascending into heaven' we are framing the historical between them in the prologue and climax of divine grace. We are understanding a history as telling a theology. Virgin Birth and Empty Tomb are the portals of their whence and whither.

> 'The belief that God's self-expressive activity was supremely present in the person and the decision of the historical Jesus implies the belief that Jesus was supremely sympathetic to God and that God is supremely compatible to Jesus.'[10]

iv.

Yet should we think the 'sympathy' credible, the 'compatibility' trustworthy? And what of that 'decision' in 'the historical Jesus.'?[11] Had the faith fairly recorded it when it saluted it as Messianic? This *ex eventu* faith – why should we hold it as the index to God, why should the credentials of God require what it contains? Can what it contains really underwrite them?

Theodicy again – as in Chapters 7 and 8? Indeed: if we

are to have theology theodicy is vital. Why is it proper to associate 'the power and wisdom of God' with Jesus crucified? Reflection makes us realize how deep the reasons and how significantly they converge. Though in isolation they might not suffice, in convergence they persuade. What might they be?

There is first the uncompulsiveness of the Cross. 'A truth that must use violence to secure its existence cannot be truth.'[12] For, in having its forcible way, it leaves remainders of unsubdued evil. It does not incorporate its enemies, as the Cross does, in its 'salvation.' Nor has it taken the full measure of what human wrong signifies. As the Hebrew prophets and psalmists well knew, there is that about human perversity that wishes God were 'not there,' that divine rule did not exist.[13] To be sanguine and hortatory is not to plumb these realms. As Camus has it, 'faith presumes the acceptance of the mystery of evil.' If Christian it harbours no illusion about our being readily perfectible.[14] There is much Pauline realism in the words of Edgar Allen Poe:

> 'Have we not, in the teeth of our best judgement, a perpetual inclination to violate that which is "Law" merely because we understand it to be law? . . . This unfathomable longing of the soul to vex itself, to offer violence to its own nature, to do wrong for wrong's sake only, urged me to continue.'[15]

Gethsemane and the Cross happen in this truth of human things. They for ever deny to Christianity the luxury of mere ideology, of superficial or facile reckonings with society and the heart within. They measure how far sin can make us blind to awareness of its meaning. ('They know not what they do.') To have a victim of the human situation at the very heart of a perception of it is to end, and to begin, where, if at all, faith has to be found. If we can say that the very idea of God contains that relation to humanity that is expressed in Jesus as the Christ, it is because we also say that a true reading of humanity contains the relation to God explicit in that same Christ's suffering. Truly, as Disraeli has it in his novel *Tancred*, 'omnipotence has shed human tears.' They flowed from human ways. If we are saying with Paul: 'Christ died *for* our sins,' (1 Corinthians 15.3), the first meaning of 'for' must be 'because of them.' Without that, no other meanings could follow.

Furthermore, the Cross dramatizes the principle that love cannot be love and immunize itself from risks love necessarily runs. For it is always vulnerable. In and by the church-event with which I started, the suffering of Jesus was interpreted as being central to the logic of the prophetic suffering that preceded it and of the suffering of the community to which it gave birth. A remarkable passage in Isaiah 43.24, where God disclaims requiring 'sacrifices' from His people, tells them: 'You have made Me a burden-bearer by your sins.' The meaning may seem cryptic but is plain enough. The prophets, as messengers from God, incurred 'the contradiction of sinners,' against them. The human perversity we have noted above cost them dearly in pain and travail. These, though visited on them, were plainly meant for God. They were part of 'wishing He did not exist,' of denying that He had any claim upon them. The messengers bore them vicariously on behalf of God. Clearly when they did so, and when rejection supervened upon their ministry, it cannot be that God deserted them. On the contrary, in some sense, He participated – by virtue of their sending – in their suffering. To think otherwise would mean a callous God whose commission of the prophets was fraudulent and fickle.

Could it be that 'the Messiah,' whom prophethood awaited, and whose significance, however read, would achieve all that prophethood affirmed, be exempt from the same experience? However we understand 'the suffering servant' passages in Isaiah 42, 50 and 53, echoes in the Gospels clearly suggest that they had a deep place in the consciousness of Jesus. Christian conviction, at least, quickly recruited them to interpret what the death of Jesus meant and how it should be understood in the economy of God. The Cross had to be comprehended within those same parameters of 'suffering for sin,' of divine agency meeting the brunt of human denial. From all those precedents it was a sublime, but not a distant, step to 'God was in Christ reconciling . . .' The God who was 'in' the teaching as the voice of His claim, and 'for' the teacher in what he underwent because of the claim, was 'with' him in the anguish, and therefore 'through' him on behalf of righteousness.

It has sometimes been whimsically said that God and humanity resemble a pair of lovers who cannot find each other, with no place for their rendezvous. Biblical religion sees a situation of lovers estranged by our unreadiness for the relationship in the terms creation willed it. The place of rendezvous, therefore, will be the point where our unlove relents and divine love has borne what we have been. The Cross is that place. For

> 'Whereto serves mercy
> But to confront the visage of offence?'[16]

and where it is admitted ours in penitence, there the divine face of grace.

We need to remember that when, early in the church-event, this reading of 'the mind of Christ' was reached and preached, those involved were themselves in adversity because of what they represented. The New Testament records this dimension very clearly. They set what was happening to them into the frame of what had happened to their Master and sought to 'take it' in the same mind. Saul's vision en route to Damascus identified his victims and Jesus as one. 'Why are you persecuting me?' the voice asked. Saul had, in truth, been doing that, for his hostility to them was enmity to their account of Him. When Saul became Paul he was himself to become 'a partaker in the afflictions of Christ.'[17] In reading the Cross, Messianically, the Church was simply experiencing that 'Messianic community' – as it believed – which was always part of the Messianic vision, so that – as we saw in Chapter 7 – Messiah could be 'all of us.' The Cross was thus the clue to who they were, but only because, in priority, it had proved the clue to who He was. The key that opened their faith informed their life. It is hardly necessary to add that these growing perceptions in my mind about my once innocently simple faith owed much to the utter doubt of them in what I perceived of Judaism and Islam – a fact which only made me the more anxious for conversation.

It is further significant for this understanding of how the Cross saves that, in some quarters the title of 'Messiah' was attached to Jesus as 'false accusation' for purposes of abuse. Its use in this sense reproached Him for pretension, blasphemy, deception, even megalomania. That paradox entitled the first Christians to glory in it when, having recognized its reality in the truth of Him, they were themselves caught in the same obloquy. The martyrdom of James, the Lord's brother, and Stephen, and others, were to be understood as confirming the reality of the faith in Jesus and of the insight on which it rested.

When, in its Gospels, the Church presented the teaching and ministry of Jesus, it always linked 'following' closely with the Cross. The significance of this should not escape us. Rabbis, if Jesus could ever be considered one, were followed in the relation of pupil to teacher in Torah. 'There was no bridge form the rabbinate to following Jesus,'[18] at least not after the Cross. 'Following' then meant resembling the Lord in 'having His mind.' Law itself, as we find in Romans 13.8–10, became *imitatio Christi*, in what some have called the 'Christ mysticism' of being 'crucified with Christ.' It is there our selfhood finds its clue.

v.

I cannot hope that the foregoing has fully explained the maturing my faith needed, and perhaps acquired, by reflecting long on how it came about that the church-event followed hard on the Christ-event in the way it did, and how it so confidently found the Messianic clue where all these things converged. There were three questions, at least, I still needed to ask, namely, now in fact does suffering 'work' redemptively; whether it was 'in all the Scriptures' in the way that Jesus had fulfilled them or how well the Gospel was served by its own antecedents; and thirdly, how it might all be credibly stated theologically as entirely consistent with the glory, sovereignty, majesty and unity of God and, if consistent, then also necessary.

What has already been said is on the way to the first answer. If it is sin that makes the need for pardon, then the two must be commensurate. There is a story, perhaps apocryphal, that on her death-bed, Gertrude Stein cried time and again: 'What is the answer?' but, shortly before she expired, sat up and asked: What is the question? What question is forgiveness asking before it can be the answer if not something adequate to how wrong we are and something worthy of God all holy, all righteous, all loving? Wrongdoers themselves know that their sin is not measured if it is merely condoned. It has to have the tribute of being truly condemned. Atonement is somehow necessitated by the very nature of evil. For sin is not merely about withholding the fruits of the vineyard one year: it is scheming to own it for ever. (Luke 20, 9–16). It is not merely about a broken law: it is about a lost relationship. It is not, finally, what I did as deed; it is how and who I am as 'me.'

'Forgiven-ness,' therefore, cannot be some casual hand-out, like prizes at a fete. The 'forgiving-ness' reciprocal to it has an overcoming to undertake within itself – an overcoming of injury, of pain, of anger, of hatred and revenge, of hesitation over rebuff or doubt about the sequel. 'Forgiving-ness' is risk and hope in one, and these are costly things. Redeeming evil means bearing what it has meant in the vicarious principle that wrong necessitates of all who undergo it, who pay its costs and know its shame and take its enmity. On all counts it shapes into a cross.

This bearing does not mean that wrong is somehow arbitrarily transferred to make a scapegoat or fictitiously to 'free' the sinner. It remains where it always was as guilt and condemnation. But if it is not 'justified' by retaliation,[19] or left festering in alienation, or fallow in evasion, then it is indeed 'borne,' taken, carried by the wronged and, only so, 'borne away.'

The distinction just made between 'forgiven-ness' and 'forgiving-ness' is important. For the two are often lost in the single word 'forgiveness,' which comprises them both. When we say we 'believe in the forgiveness of sins,' we speak about an active practice as well as of a mercy done to us. There could not be the one without the other. Such redemptiveness is happening all the time where-ever love responds to wrong in forgiving terms, when it 'bears' to 'bear away.' We are not going to suppose God incapable of what dimly we attain ourselves and have from others – thanks only to God's own paradigm of how it happens.

In trying long to understand the Cross of Jesus – and aware how far other faiths in the Middle East excluded it because Law sufficed, or because God, being Almighty, made forgiveness effort-less – I often fell back on resources from both parts of the Bible. My hope was to understand, and perhaps explain, what lay in that one word 'for' in the claim that 'Christ died for our sins.' 'On account of them' was an obvious sense, but what more? My mentors were how 'the suffering servant' was 'justified,' and how 'the prodigal son' was 'brought home.'

About the former, there is much potential confusion as to 'justification.' Habakkuk's confidence that 'the just (man) shall live by his faith' becomes, in Paul: 'the unjust is justified by faith' in the Saviour.[20] There is here an evident shift of meaning. When, in the great prophets and the Wisdom writings, the righteous man holds out against evil, at the cost often of his own life, he ensures that evil does not prevail or, crudely put, is not allowed 'to get away with it.' By his tenacity through pain the good endures, it is 'not overcome of evil.' It lives in his very wounds to bless another day. His suffering, albeit fatal, leaves behind it a perennial rebuke to evil. Wrong is allowed no hiding-place as if it were not what it is, no palliative that lets it masquerade as legitimate. It is arraigned for what it truly is. The fidelity to truth of 'the righteous man' means the vindication of good. He saves society for a future by the quality of his agonized antithesis to what would pervert and corrupt it. 'He lives by his fidelity.'

Some in his community live to see it so, to acknowledge that he has retrieved for them that which evil would have extinguished had it not been countered in the way he countered it. 'He was wounded or our transgressions,' they learn to say. 'He has carried our sins.' He has made us know how mistaken, how guilty, we were. 'All we like sheep had gone astray but . . .'[21] In such recognition there is a loosing from sins, a blessed impulse to renounce them, to realize their shame and to find their pardon. The fact of 'not being overcome of evil' leads to 'evil being overcome by good,' insofar as suffering righteousness is understood as both indicting and redeeming those who did the wrong. We are near to the Gospel if we can think this happening on a cosmic scale.

For when Paul applies this to the Cross and 'justification,' he turns the logic round. It is we wrongdoers who are 'justified' by 'faith' (now 'trust' not 'fidelity') precisely in recognizing what has transpired in redemption. It was keen perception on Paul's part to read his source this way. 'With his scars we are healed,' has now a double meaning – the one the Isaian passage meant and the one enlarged from it by Paul's realization in Christ crucified of the same principle inclusively enacted. Jesus, 'up to the Cross,' as Peter had it (1 Peter 2.24), had taken 'the contradiction of sinners against Himself,' comparably to Isaiah 53 and other passages in psalm and Wisdom. It may well be that these had guided and sustained Him. In the church-event, Christians – thanks to all they understood of Jesus – made those precedents the light by which to see a world's redemption. Love proving stronger than evil was the meaning in the apparent tragedy of His death. They were taking the secret of the suffering prophets into a theology of the divine nature. They were 'risen with Christ' on 'the day of resurrection.' 'This is the victory, even our faith.' We should not be surprised at the lively speed with which this Gospel kindled an assurance minded to give it to the world as grace unlimited by place or race.

vi.

One of Jesus' best remembered stories, from another angle, can help us further. Appeal to it has the further point that it is often assumed to give the lie to everything 'Pauline' and 'redemptive.' For, in the story of the father and the wayward son in Luke 15.11–32 the father – as it seems – just forgives. How often have Muslims said to me: 'Where is the Cross in your own parable: it is so Islamic. God simply pardons and receives. He is "the merciful Lord of mercy," having a prerogative of effortless forgiveness and needs no scheme about a "saviour" who will make it possible. To think He might is to impugn His majesty and power – He who "only says: Be! and it is." Creation itself shows us how direct, immediate, authoritative, is divine will. Do not clutter divine mercy with precautions about atonement. Jesus never did so.'

Taking the point of such case-making against my sense of being forgiven only through Christ, and wanting to be open to the theology, not to say the friends, that made it, I came nevertheless to realize that the Cross *is* there in the story – there deeply and clearly if – as we must – we read between the lines.

The two previous stories (v1–10) about sheep and a coin, lost because they are merely grazing sheep and chance-prone coins, give us to realize that the son is 'lost' by asserting his own will. That autonomy, as any parent knows, confers a certain helplessness which a parent must bear. He cannot obviate the break in love – given a son so minded – unless he imprisons him. If we are persons, even under God our volition has its way and uses its right. So the son claims his inheritance and promptly turns his back on home. The helplessness of the father continues and deepens as the grape-vine – presumably – brings word of what ensues – the descent into penury, misery, futility and the plight of a young Jew at the swine-trough! Of what irony was Jesus capable.[22] In this situation, we may say, the father has two options – to be careless or caring, to accept the 'gone-ness' of the son (whether angrily or casually) or to yearn continually. If, doing the latter, he continues to love then, by the same token, he continues to suffer. For only the former would let go the pain though only in leaving the resentment.

It is evident from the sequel that he continues to care, to

wait, to believe, to hope and pray – in a word, to be the father. This, of course, is the only basis of the son's return. He, for his part, perceives the old abode as unchanged. He has no reason to suspect that his father has written him off or ever said, or thought: 'Good riddance.' Humbled by his own sin and folly he says: 'I will arise and go to my father.' Happily the father he can go to still exists but only as a suffering one. The returnee banks altogether on being received, albeit as the lowest of the servants, those paid by the hour with no tenure. That measure of contrition, however, is reciprocal to the other sort of 'extremes' in the fatted calf, the shoes, the ring, the robe and the feast. Forgiven-ness receives forgiving-ness but only at the price of a pain-bearing, shame-bearing love. The Cross is at the heart of the story and Jesus Himself put it there.

This is clear via the elder brother, though so simple is the telling that we can easily miss the point. 'This your brother is come.' The father presses on the older son the same will to renewed, indeed unforfeited, relationship. The other son will have none of it and will not use the 'brother' word. Twice he tells his father 'This your son . . .' 'Call him that if you are still crass enough to do so. I can be no part of all this celebrating of what can only be repudiated.' The Cross in the father's heart only sharpens, but the point is clear, and the rejoicing is not stayed. So it is with God in 'Jesus Christ our Lord.' We begin to understand how redemption works, how forgiveness avails, how Christ suffers and how love wins.

vii.

Our second question waiting answer had to do with whether, and how, the old Scriptures served this new faith. It is clear already how magnificently they did so in respect of 'the suffering servant,' the fidelity of the righteous and the travail of good against evil. It is less clear in respect of animal sacrifices as precedent for Jesus crucified or metaphors that stem from the warriors of Israel. In my early auspices I had been nurtured on 'Christ in all the Scriptures' and took typology, as it was called, quite trustingly. 'Paying the price of sin' or 'blood cleansing' meant no problem. However, the time came when I had to realize that metaphors could well disserve, rather than serve, the meaning, that they were very 'coded' language and liable to engender deep misconceptions or make crude and superficial what they intended to convey. I found myself wanting to tell people that there was nothing less like a lamb than Jesus in Gethsemane. He was, indeed, such in meekness, or as victim, but in no way such in the volition that said: 'The cup my Father has give me shall I not drink it.'

The maturing was painful. Some for whom I cared saw it as disloyal. Nevertheless, it seemed to me imperative that faith should keep firm control over its metaphors and that what had transpired in Jesus as the Christ should master its antecedents and not the other way round. In part, it was coping with the perplexities – or worse – of other faiths which made it so. I became particularly chary of interpreting the Cross with language from levitical altars and animal holocaust in the Temple. It might be true, as imagination had it, that the sheep the shepherds were guarding in their fields at Bethlehem were intended for the sacrificial ritual. That did not make any analogy compatible. For me it became paramount that the will to suffer, as an obedience of love to the factors we have studied, must be central to our preaching of Christ crucified. Animals forcibly immolated could be in no way adequate to comprehend the real Cross. Also they might lead to something purely arbitrary, and therefore, non-redeeming, in the way we read: 'The Lord has laid on Him the iniquity of us all.'

There was the same problem with the scapegoat which had, of course, no inkling, and no option, about what it was carrying off the guilty and away into the wilderness. To see that comprehending Calvary was to carry truth itself into a wilderness of vacuity. Outsiders, too, needed to be rightly alerted, not bewilderedly confused, by what we meant when we told them that 'His blood cleanses us from all sin.' (1 John 1.7), the more so if we compound the metaphor further and sing: 'Wash Thou our wounds in that dear blood.' Blood in fact only stains and, doing so, also tells the guilt of those who shed it. To say that 'it cleanses' is, in context, blessedly true. But in what context? only in the experience by which we are 'loosed' from our wrongness through knowing how it is taken into that forgiving-ness in which Jesus, at the Cross, suffered for it – present as it truly was in the evil factors that conspired to have Him suffer, these being forever representative of how wrong we all are.

Such 'unpacking' of meaning is urgent if the vivid, and sacred, brevity of Scriptural form is to reach the soul. Otherwise strangeness goes on making strangers. Our theology is never truer than when it is wrestling to be understood, never more sterile than when it merely rehearses: 'It is written.' Being 'bought with a price' is similarly opaque for many, if not misconstrued. To whom was the price paid? the curious ask, supposing, in 'a nation of shopkeepers' that there is always a till and a check-out where 'prices' are 'paid.' It is not so with redemption, nor with the price of liberty as eternal vigilance, nor of the price of coal in miners' lives.[23] Such prices are paid *for* without being paid *to*. They are simply 'paid.' So it was with the Cross as 'the price of sin.'

Some have thought that the *Aqedah*, the 'sacrifice' of Isaac in Genesis 22 could be a 'type' of Jesus but we would need to know much more, in that mysterious story, of the mind and attitude of Isaac on the way to Mount Moriah and during the building of the altar and the binding. Perhaps there was a sort of Gethsemane here – a Gethsemane of apprehension, even terror, but not a Gethsemane that had ensued from a plot against a preacher. It had come about from some strange, apparent, aberration of his father Abraham. It could 'carry' Calvary only remotely. Probably Calvary would be better alone in its own stark light.

All in all, it came to seem to me that a typology of 'Christ in all the Scriptures' should subject them to Him, rather than He to them. This was especially so where-ever the old ethnicity was at odds with the open grace of 'no more Gentiles.' (Ephesians 2.19). Jesus and Joshua could not be reconciled, for all the oneness of the name. If we use (as in note 4) the imagery of 'ore' smelted from the

Biblical earlier Scriptures we must do so with the alloy of all that Gospel grace commended, knowing that only alloy gives precious metal currency. The imagery here is not derogatory. The New Testament gloried in being in common Greek and in transacting its meaning in the ordinariness of Philippi and the seediness of Corinth. We have to invoke the 'Christ in all the Scriptures' as the 'Christ in all the world' and let our borrowings of conveyance be drawn as widely, in full loyalty to the Hebraic quarry from which the church-event first drew them. As Auerbach wrote in his *Mimesis*:

> 'In principle this great drama contains everything that occurs in world history . . . There is no basis for a separation of the sublime form the low and the everyday. For they are indissolubly connected in Christ's very life and suffering . . . there is but one place – the world and but one action – man's redemption.'[24]

All Christians surely often repair to Luke's narrative of the road to Emmaus and the sequel in the house. All Luke's artistry is in it. Do we have to understand 'the same day at evening . . .' as on the clock of one twenty-four hours? Or is it the 'day' of resurrection, the spiritual morrow of the risen Lord? The 'church-event' is older than it used to be. It is 'toward evening' – the parousia may be near. But there has been space to ponder and to say 'We trusted He would redeem . . .': we were in deep trauma about that aweful climax of His dying. Its after-math has haunted us. Instinctively we searched the Scriptures but could not find the clue. Yet, in all our wistfulness to understand, there has been a Presence walking with us – the One who is at once our only theme and our present quest. 'The bread and wine' is where we recognize Him because it is there we find His wounds by which the Scriptures can be confidently known as well.

Is Luke, in his conscious authorship, compressing into a single 'day,' precisely that movement into faith we have been at pains here to understand, the movement by which the Cross-event, in all its devastating incidence, brought forth the church-event? Perhaps so, perhaps not. Scriptures and sacrament together, Luke assures us, contained and told 'the mystery of Christ.' For it was He who handled them.

viii.

However, – our third question – is that Christ-event as housed in the church-event properly the inclusive credential of God? We have seen it strongly disavowed by two staunch theisms with whose people we Christians are kin. We might simply turn the question back and ask whether, without such credential, or denying it, we do not find any intelligent theism impossible. For an implication of divine indifference to who we are and where we have got ourselves must make theology a romance without a lover, wilting in illusion. It would be the end of our own credibility as creatures in creation, still more as lovers in community. It would mean that what is most authentic about us – our capacity to love and to be loved – was falsified into futility. Theism as a living faith must surely either stand or fall by the truth, or otherwise, of the manner of credential present for us in the Incarnation and the Cross. For these are where the answer is if we are asking: 'In what does being God involve the God who is?'

It has often been urged that divine suffering is incompatible with divine sovereignty and that, in technical language, God must be thought impassible. True enough, if we think of suffering as derived from some external power proved, by ability to inflict it, greater than God. Not the case, once we realize that inward impulses of love may prompt and take initiatives that cost and tell in inward travail. If God be impassible in those terms faith is impossible. Its eyes cannot negotiate with a merely onlooking God.

Nor should we be deterred by the 'negative theology' that bids us abstain from all question of credentials about God and from daring to contrive or require them ourselves. For it will be part of how far divine reality transcends them to know how properly they are given into our enquiry and our capacity to love. Are we not invited to seek Him 'where He may be found.'? The invitation does not mock. He will be found nowhere if not in our tragedy.

But, if we can hope to know divine relationships and the nature they express, can they go as far as Christians think they know in 'the Word made flesh,' in 'God in Christ reconciling.'? We have seen in Chapter 7 how there were deeply Judaic, as well as Greek, clues to those meanings in the concepts of divine 'wisdom;' of 'agencies' whereby the divine in action issued from, and for, the divine will; of 'presences' in which the divine mercy was known to be 'derived from God's deriving' and 'desired by God's desiring.' These significant realities in no way compromise the truth of unity. They mean that unity was at work. Yet there was need for the working distinction in human thought about them – God revealing and God revealed, God acting and God's action, God's will in end and God's will in means. Islam, in its own idiom, was in no way exempt from these features. They are inseparable from any theism. 'God's speech, God's Word, God's will, God's Book,' were all in some sense 'His,' and, therefore, mysteriously 'part' of Him. To know it so was in no sense idolatry. Even the Names of God in Islam meant that – in some sense – adjectives with human connotation were properly applicable to God. The Qur'an had enjoined their use upon the faithful. Worship would be impossible without them. Adoration was their vocal use, theology their conceptual employ.

These realities of theological discourse do not demand that belief in the incarnational form of them must follow. They do rule out any denial of the possibility – as distinct from the fact – of it. Christian faith, as the Christ-event and the church-event comprised it went further to God revealing and God revealed, God finding and God found, in 'Him there,' learning in the school of that story how 'the Christ of God' was 'God in Christ.'

To be sure, it went that farther. There are many who would hold back, insisting that though God may be apprehended in the powers and means that are consequent upon His being, these do not present His nature or His essence but only presage His existence. 'Essence' and 'existence' may be subtle niceties of distinction for those with idle leisure from the conscience and the conflict of religions in our time. For the love of God's sake, 'existence' will suffice: the 'essential' will then simply be trust in the truth and tryst with ministry and, for me, all these – open, warm and joyful – 'in Christ.' The twin 'event' we have been studying is home and heart.

ix.

For all my misgivings over certain psalms, I was never out of love with the 23rd, though it is well always to keep its neighbour the 22nd in view, 'the green pastures,' with how 'they pierced my hands and my feet.' For 'the good shepherd' is both. I often pondered the words: 'You spread a table before me,' especially when in 1972 I was briefly in Capetown as a guest at Claremont, the Archbishop's residence on the slopes of Table Mountain. 'The table spread' can be Christian Eucharist with its fourfold meanings. It is 'spread' in the guest-house of the good earth and thanks to birth. The natural order, by human hand, technique and will, yields the economic order and so, in turn, the social scene. These are the first meaning of the bread and wine – reverence, humility, gratitude, exploitation – to be sure, for only so do we survive, but also consecration, celebration and the unfailing wonder that gives music its voice and colour its brush.

In and for that order of creation and repairing its misguided waywardness, its selfish autonomy, is the order of redemptive love, the central meaning of the bread and wine. 'Do this in remembrance of me.' The Cross as the place of our re-making, of 'loosing from our sins,' of knowing where forgivingness is God's and forgiveness is ours.

There at once follows the food analogy of faith. 'Take and eat,' 'make this your own,' 'taste and see that the Lord is good.' Nothing makes me so inalienably me as the place of food and drink in my existence, where in digestion only me has what is mine and only mine can be the metabolic me. So it is with faith, personal and proxy-less. It is I who have to say: 'The Son of God loved me and gave Himself for me.' He is 'my Lord and my God.' Thus, to each in their personhood – 'into their hands' – will go the bread and wine.

The fourth dimension holds the other three. We all eat of one bread and drink of one cup. Here is 'holy communion,' each with the other and all with the Lord. Where we hallow birth and being, we remember Christ crucified, we make His truth our own, and we find ourselves 'one body in Christ.' What Blackpool held for me in boyhood is still where my conclusion has arrived, knowing it the larger and the deeper for what it has traversed.

When Leonardo Da Vinci painted 'the table of the Lord,' he took the faces of the Apostles from the features of some worthies of Milan, merchants, citizens, whom he thereby patronized perhaps in hope they would reciprocate. Were they there on false pretences? actors in spite of themselves? playing a part? decorating what they did not share? The suspicion that it might be so with us should give any Christian pause. Where we conclude in faith we must proceed in ministry. If 'we preach Christ Jesus as Lord' it must be that we ourselves are 'servants for Jesus' sake.' (2 Corinthians 4.5.) The Gospel where God is on-behalf-of-us needs us on God's behalf. False pretences have no place in either.

Chapter 10

Faith's Life - Ministry

i.

'Ministerially yours' – one must assume – is not a frequent usage with the signatures of politicians in government or of clergy in parishes. Both, however, are designated as 'ministers,' whether of 'the State' or of 'the Word and Sacraments.' That both spheres are 'ministry' is vital to any due discharge of office. 'Magisterial' is a different word which has acquired sinister overtones of dominance and the heavy hand. The original Latin distinguishes between 'lesser' and 'greater,' between heavy portentousness and modest self-awareness. 'Ministers,' according to Paul in Romans 11.13, 'magnify their office,' yet are, by definition, 'little ones.' Humility is appropriate to a right esteem of power or status.

In the faith-conclusion of the previous chapter we saw that a being-on-behalf-of was at the heart of the Christian comprehension of the divine. We acknowledged a manwardness in the very being of God and read it as the central clue to an alert theology. To be sure, we reserved to transcendence dimensions of majesty and mystery entirely beyond either the reckoning or the relevance of humanity. In that sense we conceded whatever can be meant by the so-called 'negative theology' – all those aspects of the divine which have to be exempted from the claims, or the pretensions, of affirmation. But we made that reverent and wise concession only on the understanding that we did not thereby doubt, compromise or impugn the knowledge we confessed and possessed in the divine human inter-society of love. For were we so to cancel our integrity in the timidity of such reservations, we would be playing with meaning and letting enigma negate not only divine magnanimity, but our own human experience. Faith was never called to be its own laughing-stock. We are bold to 'believe in belief' – given the due pre-requisites of the lowly in heart.

We identified the divine manwardness in our reading of creation and the acceptance of creaturehood, in the divine solicitude for human society in the given 'law of life,' and ultimately in the divine self-giving into human tragedy evident in 'the Christ of God' and, therefore, in 'God in Christ.' Via the Christian Gospel we understood God to be signing 'ministerially yours' in inclusive address to human awareness and in our terrestrial experience of nature and grace. We coined 'on-behalf-ness' as a way of apprehending this sense of things and related it to the whole shape of Biblical theology in both Testaments. We read in creation an 'annunciation,' a 'call into being,' which made the world of birth, nurture, discovery, delight and destiny an invitation to become true selves in response to a magnanimity that had so intended it. Being in the world we would be at the world not – as Karl Marx had advised – in exploitative terms alone, but reverentially in viable hope and grateful wonder. With all our physical, sexual, social and intelligent endowment, we had been 'let be,' to undertake the venture and appreciate the crisis of our selfhood. There was, on behalf of us, a creative, redemptive compassion, a caring grace, which had spared no risk and evaded no travail in bearing with us and bearing for us. We were creatures of an incredible generosity and objects of an irrepressible love.

This was a verdict of faith which some sceptics might attribute to amenities of culture and cushioning, to immunities of affluence and fortune cruelly withheld from multitudes of Asian poor and African distress, from all the oppressed of the earth in privation and despair. Not so. The verdict had come to its first full confession centuries ago around the Mediterranean. It had affirmed itself in catacombs beneath the earth of Rome. Its confidence was not a rationale of circumstance. It took its ground from the Christ-event where it had discerned the ultimacy of love at the very epitome of human wrong. It enabled a courage, a humour, a resilience – as its record proved – which held good in any and very context of place and time.

If we were right in this perception of things vicarious in the very nature of God, then things vicarious must be the stuff of our human response. If God undertakes us in creative purpose and redemptive love, we must undertake each other in comparable terms. If we affirm that 'God is love' then 'love one another' must closely follow. The outgoing into need which, through Christ, we perceive in the very heart of God must be the clue to inter-human society. Life's faith-conclusion requires faith's life-ministry. The Church which was launched in the one can only be fulfilled in the other. In the Epistles of the New Testament we find emphatically this inter-association of what is believed about God and what is required between humans. The Christian ministry is the corollary of the Christian theology. It has to be seen as a new dimension of the old associationism between 'God and his people,' now no longer understood in ethnic or exclusive, but in open and inclusive, terms. 'Let this mind be in you which was also in Christ Jesus,' (Philippians 2.5) was the logic it obeyed but only because 'thinking like God thinks' – according to Jesus' exchange with Peter at Caesarea-Philippi – had been the heart of a Messianic readiness for the Cross (Matthew 16.23).[1]

Many issues implicit in the experience of Ordination were left in Chapter 3 for maturer perspective, for the hindsight that was then lacking. These call for exploration now. In the naivete of a twenty-third birthday how could I appreciate the measure of what I had undertaken? I had assumed an untried competence to pledge a future. I had not asked how I could hold in constancy the morrows of my own faith, ignorant as I was of what such constancy should entail. The one thing that saved me was the fact that faith responds as it proceeds. For it belongs with an enterprise of trust in which it is junior partner to 'the patience of God.' Only dependence on open-ended assurance about God sustains such once-for-all commitment, promising tomorrows while it steadily recedes into yesterdays. What might 1937 be in 1973? 'Take thou authority . . .' was – as the grammarians say – a present-simple bound to pass into a present-continuous. Time that made it prospect would also make it retrospect. What, through the flux, would be the unity? Are vows improperly presumptuous? Do I ever know myself dependably or my faith decisively? Might a pledged vocation spell a closed mind? Was it appropriate for faith ever to become 'professional' or for ministry ever to be 'official'?

In the immediacies of Manchester's Bishopscourt and Chester Cathedral these queries were muted in the anticipations of youth and in an evangelical sense of sure warrant. I need not revert to 'the time of embrace.' What matters here is the intervening 'education' variously assessed in all the foregoing. If Ordination meant being patterned on the vicariousness identified as the nature of the God of the Gospel, one's assurance could only lie in the Holy Spirit translating that truth into ministerial incentive. There would have to be something reciprocal between what was believed and what was ventured. Any 'work of love in the world' would live only by that transcendent referent.

The clue was there in the case that Jesus made in the Sermon on the Mount from 'sun and rain,' from the very elements themselves.

> 'I say to you: "Love your enemies, bless them that curse you, do good to them that hate you and pray for them that despitefully use you and persecute you, that you may be the children of your Father in heaven. For He makes his sun to rise on the evil and on the good and sends rain on the just and on the unjust . . . Be you therefore perfect (inclusive) as your Father in heaven is perfect."'[2]

The undifferentiating generosity of God does not turn on our merits or demerits. Were it to do so our autonomy – and so the possibility of integrity – would be at an end. We are free to blaspheme even in Grasmere and to ply ourselves with drugs under awesome Alpine peaks. Our flagrant violations of the benedictions we inhabit do not weary the divine fidelity towards our creaturehood. Nor is the suffering love of the Cross such as to exclude its very perpetrators. It is there we learn how 'inclusive' 'our heavenly Father' is – and at what cost. It is precisely in *not* being condoned or exonerated that evil remains the arena of unfailing pity and vicarious pain. In that sense of things Christian ministry finds its commissioning logic and its ability to last.

In his 130 C.E. Apology to the Emperor Hadrian, Aristides explained this habit of mind:

> 'The Christians, O Emperor, . . . do not do to others what they would not wish to be done to themselves. They comfort those who wrong them and make friends of them. They labour to do good to their enemies . . . He that has gives freely to him that lacks. If they see a stranger they bring him under their roof and rejoice over him as if he were their own brother. They call themselves brethren, not after the flesh but after the Spirit and in God.'[3]

'After the Spirit, and in God,' and only so. Aristides, however, was not writing about clergy, priests or deacons, aside from their inclusion among common folk. Even if we suspect him of idealism he knows where the core of Christian identity belongs and links it organically with the being of God. It is only in that inclusive, community-wide, vocation and in the theology which gives it being, that any 'ordered' ministry, any 'Holy Orders,' can obtain. 'Ordered' offices and those ordained to them only have place and meaning serving the entire 'body of Christ,' the company of the faithful in any and every place, and never as 'lords over God's heritage.' It is such solidarity alone that gives the clergy being and validity. Whatever is received in office by tradition and succession belongs only with, in and from, the whole people of God. There is about it neither comfort nor legitimation on any other count. The moment it seems or becomes a perquisite it stands betrayed.

The sense I have always had about the paradox of being ordained which, at times, I assume all clergy must share, was painfully renewed one day as, in company with his wife, I drove to visit in hospital a cherished colleague who was dying of a brain tumour. As we negotiated the traffic, she explained how she had first noted a confusion in his speech. 'You know,' she said, 'we always pray together at breakfast. I read the Bible passage and he prays. I leave that to him: he's the professional.' I was deeply moved and after a painful pause I said: 'When it comes to prayer there are no professionals.'

Yet, it may not be denied, there *are*. There *are* those ordained to be ministers of the sanctuary, trustees of the faith, holding the solemn commission of 'the Word and the Sacraments,' and all in the tumult and anxiety of the world. These 'Orders' mean recruitment into what God in creation and grace has been doing all the time but doing in a patience that makes room for our partnering relevance so that ministry may reproduce the 'on-behalf-ness' of Christ himself.

Though the *Bodhisattvas* in the Buddhist realm are 'on-behalf-of' frail humans within the prescripts of that faith, the Christian institution is distinctive in its deriving of the human 'ministerial' from what is ministerially divine. This makes Christian priesthood different from the ritual priesthood which the Hebraic ethos abandoned for the dual Torah via the rabbis, after the loss of the Temple in Jerusalem in 70 C.E. Experience in Ordination gave me steadily to realize that – while scholarship is relevant – ministry in Christ can never have a merely academic or tersely declaratory form. To be sure, the metaphor of 'shepherd' may be anachronistic among very sophisticated 'sheep,' but the pastoral and the kerugmatic[4] are no less liturgical than the Eucharist. Ministry is everywhere 'truth through personality,'[5] so that what is 'nounal' in the faith is 'pronounal' in the serving. *Accipe curam meam et tuam:* 'Receive this care, both yours and mine' can only be the ordainer's words in first being Christ's.

ii.

It was not unwise to write in the paragraph above: '. . . all in the tumult and anxiety of the world.' Only in retrospect did I fully realize how potentially insulated the ordained ministry could be from the throes of the lay spheres. I imagine there are many other clergy too who sometimes wish they moved in more evident 'corridors of power' where they might take the travail of justice, compassion and conflict more immediately. There is something remote in singing psalms or making intercessions or 'summoning by bells.' Furthermore, the inner warmth of a parish community, with the rhythm of its seasons and its array of occasions of togetherness, readily conduces to a satisfactory sense of meaning which does not always wrestle with how obdurate the world may be or how elusive from our reach are the wider population.

It had been so in Tranmere. Sustained visiting kept us close to the unchurched and the 'Rites of Passage' brought them critically into our cares. But the distances remained and could only be tolerated by the sense that the ministry which was ordained, pursued in and around the sanctuary, was also authentic in its incisive bearing on the ministry we call 'lay' – the ministry to which the other must be handmaid and servant. Only in the inter-action of both ministries, rightly grounded in theology and truly joined in life, can clergy be saved from the complacence which feels no distress or from the oppression of a perceived irrelevance.

For what is implicit in unchurched society must always bring disquiet to what is explicit in holding 'Holy Orders.' To be pre-occupied, as I have been, with how the Christian faith and fellowship should relate to the acknowledged pluralism of religions and their co-existence has not saved me from the pain of secularity. Indeed the secular 'negligence' of God – if we may so speak – is far gone in every culture. For some people it follows from what they perceive as God's 'negligence' of them.[6] They have settled into what is seen as a bilateral indifference. Others live with an anodyne and do not even bother to suspect either the transcendent or themselves. Others again adopt a philosophy of necessary futility from which there is no rescue but their own courage, witness that incorrigible rationalist, Bertrand Russell. Writing in 1911 to Lady Ottoline Morrell, he protested:

> 'I love the sorrowing race of mankind but I have little to say to help – only courage and gentleness, and I fail sadly in both . . . I grow cold and intellectual . . . I am filled with love and longing for service but . . . I hate the furious

> persecutor in me, but he is terribly vital . . . I worship your devotion, your love, your tenderness, but it is not for me . . . Turbulent, restless, inwardly raging I shall always be – hungry for your God and blaspheming him. I could pour forth a flood of worship – the longing for religion is at times almost unbearable.'[7]

Would that all secularity was so self-aware, for 'he that seeketh findeth.' Dylan Thomas might wrily remark: 'No man believes who does not wonder why.'[8] We can readily take his point but, sadly, he is wrong. There are strong believers who have never wondered why they are and, likewise, the nonchalantly unbelieving who have never interrogated their unconcern. All are measure of the task of Christian ministry. Why-ever and how-ever distant from lively membership 'in Christ' – or how-ever near – in despair, apathy or perplexity, all secularity is ministerial liability.

It follows that, without forfeiture of hope, something like 'pain' belongs too with that situation. If the agnostic can know 'pain' about what eludes him, the faith-servers must know 'pain' in what is elided for the closed mind or the restless heart of popular secularity. It springs from a sense of the depreciation of human worth, the deliberate or the unwitting disvaluing of dimensions of wonder, joy and mystery that attend our mortal way, the blight of perversions which blast the treasures of delight and gratitude that ought to wait upon our sexuality, upon our selfhood and our capacity to love. Ministry that feels the onus of countering what demeans us all and of restoring its ravages could well speak itself in terms like those of John Ruskin in the different world of art.

> 'I have not written about clouds and flowers because I love them myself, but because the energies of mankind are devoted all around me to the pollution of the skies and desolation of fields: and I have not written of pictures because I loved pictures, but because the streets of London were posted over with handbills and caricatures and had become consistent and perpetual lessons in abomination and abortion to every soul that traversed them, so far as it used its sight.'[9]

Of course Ruskin 'loved clouds and flowers and pictures.' He denies it only rhetorically to make his 'mission' sharper. Perhaps, for our purposes, he makes a doubtful ally in analogy.[10] But, as the prophet Joel had it (2.17) it was 'between the porch and the altar' that 'the priests of the Lord' were to weep. Their tears would concern the aching distance between the consecration of the sanctuary and the desecration beyond the portal and in the street. To be in the world 'on behalf of the love of God' is to register the discrepancy between the terms in which 'God so loved the world' and those by which the world so dis-loves God.

We are not thinking of some 'counter-culture' that fails to love in mounting only reproach, nor of some do-gooding to which the cynic might scathingly respond: 'They are in the world to do good to others: but what do they think the others are in the world for?' Nor is it some urgent idealism that romanticizes itself. Did the great Edwardian Fabians, Sidney and Beatrice Webb, really inscribe *Pro bono publico* on her wedding ring?[11] The ministry of the Gospel is none of these. It incurs and undertakes a brooding sense of things unheeded and ever ready to be found. It wants to arrest an imperception far sadder than that of which Ruskin accused the Venetians among whom he so assiduously cherished 'the stones of Venice.'

> 'Through century after century of gathering vanity and festering guilt that white dome of St Mark's had uttered in the dead ear of Venice: "Know thou that for all these things God will bring thee into judgement." . . . The Temple from afar off like the star of the Magi . . . The sins of Venice, whether in her palaces or in her piazzas, were done with the Bible at her right hand . . . done in the face of the house of God burning with the letters of His law.'[12]

Marcel Proust thought Ruskin 'arrogant' for writing so. But some Hardyean 'Spirit of the Years,' conceding the co-existence of divine creating, redeeming grace and human history – unless sunk in Hardyean aloofness – would find the Venetians by St Mark's only a minor example of the guilt of 'impercipience.'[13]

Features of our secular forfeiture of authentic, credible, joyous being and becoming are all around us. Christian ministry has to be vicarious about the vacuity, the ennui, the unease and the disease that ensue. Interviewed in *New Writing*, over his sleazy novel *London Fields*, Martin Amis explained that he had no interest in disapproval. He was merely 'hooked on decadence,' not out of choice but out of realism. In the novel everything is in decline. It is 1999, the expiry of a century, of a millenium. All else too is a-dying. Sheer decay is fascinating. Novelists anyway – unless they are Tolstoy – cannot make goodness or happiness 'read well.' 'With a weary shrug that (decay) is my subject.' There is no occasion for regret, still less for remorse, still less for retrieval. Did not Somerset Maugham in his *Summing Up* describe his writing as 'one great shrug of the shoulders' about 'human bondage'? Literature should capture a scene and then 'have done with it.'[14] All is a far cry from vicarious ministry – except in being the urgent case for it.

iii.

It must follow that Christian ministry is no negative propagandism. Faith must negotiate with life's follies as well as with its enigmas, just as life negotiates with faith about faith's capacity to 'come clean' in honesty and truth. Ministry does not concede any legitimacy to evil but its calling is from 'the God of patience.' There is no bearing with – as we learn at the Cross – that is not a bearing for. Who in the theatre has not witnessed the web of malice Iago weaves around the Moor and not ached to cry out to Othello how grossly he has misread his Desdemona, how blindly succumbed to machinations he ought to have discerned as treacherous, how tragically he carried his martial dignities into the maelstrom of racial prejudice that seethed around him? But it will not avail. In that context there is something inexorable about Othello's decline into suspicion, his inability to doubt damning negation and to hold the dependability of love as he had once known it.

Dramatic necessity contracts into an evening what is writ large in the human story.

> 'Nothing, or so little, comes of life's promise.
> Out of broken men, despised minds,
> What does one make – a roadside show,
> A graveyard of the heart?'[15]

G.M. Hopkins wrote: 'This seeing the sick endears them to us, us too it endears.'[16] This is ministry. What the tragedian only portrays the Gospel retrieves. There is 'the Word' to unmask the deceits and delusions that plague the selves we bring to one another. There is the Holy Spirit to identify the 'loss-making' in society, not measured brutally in dividends and markets but crucially in homes and marriages, in minds made angry and wills malign. There is a grace to reverse the travesties that break pledged trust, prejudice childhood, defile sexuality and store up future ills by present sin. There is community in vicarious engagement around the human predicament – 'the body' patterned to perpetuate the Christ. It needs all the allies it can get from those credally outside itself who, though perhaps sceptical of its doctrinal credentials, can generously concede those doctrinal intentions.[17] Such partnerships may help reduce the institutional pretensions of the Church – a point to which we will return. They will never obviate the centrality of its vision of God and the ministry it brings to pass.

Surrounded – at least in the West – by caring professions, by skills of surgery and medicine, by agencies of social analysis and provision, and related anywhere to active services of compassion in famine relief, technical aid and human succour, the Christian ministry via formal Ordination seems often amateur, proximate, even groping in its ways and ends. Clearly its situations are not susceptible of the precision we expect in surgeries nor of the finesse that goes with every sort of engineering. Clergy often wish they were. The cure of souls and the commending of faith and the art of human redemption must always be taxing, puzzling and resourceful.

Private reflections on a long retrospect of these exactions

personally known may yield us little. Unreviewed, they will yield nothing. Let me try to resume them under three heads – intellectual, institutional and 'considerate,' using that word in a special care for its origin.

iv.

'Perhaps one of the greatest handicaps Christianity has to contend with is Christmas.' What could the comment imply? Does the speaker mean to do away with the poetry and the choirs, to abolish the *Oxford Book of Carols* and extinguish yule-logs, to ban Dickensian mirth and dismantle all the trees, to take that ridiculous red-robed Santa out of all the supermarkets and forbid all our mid-winter celebration? No more 'Good Kings,' calling for 'flesh and wine' to rescue snow-bound peasants and put heat into the snowy sod? Are there to be no more conversions – if only seasonal – of those scrounging Scrooges? Let us have none of such misogyny.

Yet the point behind the comment is clear enough. Is it all a fairy tale? Have we forfeited the meaning of the Incarnation in the business of its alleged celebration? What is this ritual of Christmas cards – a 19th century innovation anyway?

> 'In ambush by the merry board
> The mystery dwells anonymous . . .'[18]

'Do they the burning glory learn that easy fancies fondly turn?'

The Christian embarrassments of Christmas only focus the perennial problem for Christian intelligence. The Christian ministry has to contend with forms that impede, with usages that obscure, with vocabulary that has become archaic. Time has overtaken aspects of the image it presents and how it seems tells against what it holds. The faith is indeed 'committed to the saints,' as Jude insisted in his Letter (v.3), but his word *paradidomai* means 'put into your hands.' It does not conjure up a picture of gold bullion lying secure in a bank vault. It has the imagery of the relay race where the baton is 'in tradition' from hand to hand. Even that analogy does not fit. For the baton is unchanged throughout. It is more apt to think of 'passing on the torch' for then one is liable for it staying alight in the 'tradition.'

That there are occasions for such vitality – or evidences of the lack of it – is clear on every hand. The Aristotelian word 'substance' which the Creed uses for the inter-society of 'the Father and the Son' has long ago ceased to belong intelligently with our understanding of matter. 'One in being and one in doing' more aptly captures the unity of God. We need not rehearse here the faith as to 'God in Christ' which we have rigorously explored in Chapter 9, but it is not always clear how 'God of God, light of light' fully or readily conveys it. Creeds may well suffice and 'carry' for 'insiders,' but is there no onus on them to interpret or is it somehow on the 'outsiders' to fend as they can with our obscurities? If we understand ministry we can be in no doubt where the obligation lies.

We have always to ask what the world is 'hearing' via what the Church is 'saying.' Points in question are innumerable. A friend of mine was receiving priest's Ordination late in a long and distinguished career as an academic. Commendably he invited his many secular associates to attend and, readily, they did so. They were deeply moved by 'the laying on of hands' and warmed by what was undertaken by their colleague, except that they heard from the consecrating Bishop: 'Whose sins thou dost remit they are remitted: whose sins thou dost retain they are retained.' What, they mused, was this discretionary power of life and death, of forgiveness granted or withheld, thus committed to their friend? What the Ordinal means is not what it is heard to say, for it belongs with an ancestry of 'binding and loosing' in the Hebraic world. That personal crisis in bound up in the things that ministry transacts is not in doubt, but it is expressed in terms that might suggest to the uninitiated that ministry has arbitrary control of divine forgiveness or that grace admits of custodian-monopoly.

Earlier we noted how, in New Testament scholarship and comprehension, there runs the inter-play of history and story. It is plain that they inter-relate. History is given in narrative and is certainly storied in the heart. Story, too, belongs equally in the context of what happened. How far, however, does being 'storical' have to do with being 'true.'? It is evident that there is a difficult tension between the historian and the theologian. The tension turns on the nature of 'fact,' – whether 'fact' is 'bare' and 'concrete' or whether 'fact' is pregnant and poetical. Do we not rightly speak of 'the truth of fiction?' One does not ask about Dostoevsky's *Crime and Punishment* whether Rashkolnikov and Sonia 'ever lived' or whether his redemption 'ever happened.' Pure fiction speaks entire truth. We properly insist on the historical all around our Lord but we say it in 'storical' terms when we tell of Him 'coming down from heaven.'

When Jesus speaks of the imagery of Jonah is it 'historical' about a real whale-belly sojourn and a fortuitous swallowing and vomiting, or is it 'storical' about an unwilling people-emissary (Israel under divine mission) held in 'monstrous' exile and finally emancipated for a repentant (but still churlish) fulfilment of the original errand? We are free to decide but the world needs to know what we think the options are.

Why does John's Gospel apparently move the cleansing of the Temple to the beginning of the story, while the other three evangelists place it as the climax precipitating Jesus' condemnation – a role John assigns to the raising of Lazarus which the others ignore? Was the Fourth Gospel moving in an editorial freedom with history in a 'storying' of the confrontation it perceived to be the essence of the history? Do we think we find New Testament confusion, or do we recognize New Testament genius? How did the evangelist mean us to understand that Lazarus 'story'?

Two Gospels are content to ignore the Christmas narratives of Matthew and Luke. When these treasured them did they 'historify' or did they 'storify'? Prophecies they cherished were important to them. What ultimately mattered about their narratives was not that these might be merely 'story,' but that they deeply told what was known only in sequel to Gethsemane and beyond, concerning a divine enterprise in human terms where the human was indeed recruited but the initiative was wholly 'from above.' The meaning of the Virgin Birth can only be significant within the reality of 'God in Christ.' It is no extraneous history divorced from the story of eternal grace, where 'He who made the fire now feels the cold.'[19] What we acknowledge is a history-story. Faith is responsible for its own perceptions but it is also responsible to a querulous and quizzical world.

There was about the dying of Jesus an unmistakable quality of event, 'under Pontius Pilate', ending in a sepulchre. The faith and the Creed were always insistent on the clause '. . . and buried.' On the far side it passes into '. . . and ascended into heaven.' 'Rose again' mysteriously conjoins history and story, which is its perennial fascination. The risen Christ does not become an astronaut nor does being 'seated at the right hand of majesty' admit of a rendezvous in space. 'Entering into his glory' throws us back upon the dimensions we studied in the previous Chapter concerning the ultimacy, the sovereignty, of the love that suffers to redeem, and its achievement in time from within the eternal being of God. The sequence of the Creed passes exactly through that connectedness between what transpires in the crucifixion and what happens in the eternal mind. The empty tomb, then, is actual enough in the reality of that inseparable fusion of what had happened at the Cross and what happened 'in God.' It was not possible that the death He had accepted should imprison Him. The emptiness of the tomb is eloquent token of that meaning, but let not imperceptive faith read it as the riddle of an unresolved detective story. It serves to depict a faith having independent evidences, a faith which responds directly to the risen-ness of Christ and corresponds to his unfailing presence as one who 'overcame death.'

Christian faith-presentation means a living trust with meaning which has to mediate intelligently between study and pew, between what scholarship debates and preaching commends. The task calls for lively intelligence and imagination, rooted at once in the living Word and sensitive to the way the time thinks. Knowing that its Gospel is both history and story it does not lose sight of the Jewish/ Palestinian Jesus whose person, mind and mission are at the heart of all else. Though alert to how recoverable those dimensions of Him are, it knows that they are vital and does not despair of them. Yet it recognizes that they have become a *kerugma* that has storied them into the Church's faith. That faith, however, is not as some have alleged, sufficient to itself, as if a mere 'being believed' made a 'being true.' It sees itself as a faith issuing from event and the event as issuing into faith and finds neither independent of the other.

The trust of the resulting task as Ordination enjoins it is, therefore, no easy dogmatism, no lazy recital by rote, but a joyful, strenuous exercise in being articulate with Christ. It has to engage with obsolete vocabulary and deepen the ideas of the naive. It has to draw its meanings through, and beyond, the bias of the unheeding, or the dubious, mentality it meets. It has to do, here and now, what the New Testament apostles and writers did in their own there and then, knowing the range of the difference. Though its faith-commendation will always be in the context of that other 'proclamation' which is liturgical and sacramental, it will not see these as displacing all that must be verbal and eloquent in 'ministry of the Word.'

That something like a displacement has occurred seems clear from current practice on the part of some. The pattern of the Eucharist as the central, even the only, liturgy in parishes – soundly motivated as it is – diminishes the Church's reach outside itself. Not that 'liturgical preaching' (though abridged) is to be discounted, but it occurs in a context of provision for those already there. The partial, or total, abandonment of Evensong has further reduced the chances of drawing in the outsider, or those who are as yet unready for a sacramental presence. Are we too self-centred in the very arts of worship? Have we lost the crucial role of thought audible within the holy places of the soul and of 'the bread and wine.'? Casual acquaintance with numerous vestry books where no themes or texts are ever recorded makes me wonder whether the clergy keep no check on the balance of their verbal ministry or maybe consider the detail irrelevant. In that event perhaps it is negligible in both pulpit and pew.

Paul at least was convinced that preaching was a priesthood. Indeed, the only place where he uses priestly vocabulary, in Romans 15.16, has to do with preaching as his *leiturgia* in which, *hierourgounta*, he is 'priesting the Gospel,' so that 'the offering,' or presentation before God, of the fruits his hearers are may be 'acceptable' as 'made holy by the Spirit.' All the verbs and nouns are sacramental but the theme is verbal ministry. Does he not rebuke the separation which – architecturally and conceptually – we make between altar and pulpit, between what is seen and handled and what is handled and heard? So ought it not to be. I am not here pleading to turn the house of God into an auditorium nor to 'stage' an orator. God forbid. But nor is sacred ministry a stageing of 'mysteries' that have no truck with mind and thought, with the need to understand, while swaying censers and ringing bells. 'Thou shalt love (and serve) the Lord with all thy mind.'

V.

There are two exacting areas of an intellectual ministry fit to give us pause. The one is the way of metaphor in the language of faith: the other, not unrelated, is our perception of Biblical loyalty. In both it is well to be alert to what the outsider 'gets.' The wayside pulpit announces comfortingly that 'The Lord is good to all that call upon Him.' What, the passer-by properly thinks, about those who don't? Does the Lord only love those who love Him? Is there some sort of bargain relation with the Lord? The verse is true in its lovely positive: it is not true in its implied negative – not if we hold with what we have in Christ. No doubt we could wish that people did not read perversely, but they read only what we give them in these realms.

Or what of that Tenth Commandment which in the admirable business of forbidding covetousness sets 'his wife' after 'the neighbour's house' and lists her among 'everything that is his.' This cannot ride with Galatians 3.28 nor 1 Corinthians 11.11. What strange capacities we have to be oblivious of what, did we come to it newly, would distress or amaze us. 'Enemies' and 'foes' come so monotonously in a Concordance of the Psalms. Should we not suspect that the psalmists are over-occupied with enmity to themselves and wonder what in them made it so, whether it was legitimate and whether, in the end, our vindication is always the obligation of God seeing that our enemies must be also His? Doubtless, we can allegorize the 'enemies' into temptations and spiritual besettings of sin. But then, the psalmist meant the Philistines or the renegades. How ought we to live with the mandate to Joshua to exterminate the inhabitants of the land or say after that lection: 'This is the Word of the Lord'? Even if it was not altogether *in situ* as the chronicler thought at least he thought so. Either way the problem persists. If we ignore the questions, our constituencies do not – if they are Biblically concerned at all.

We have to acknowledge that our Scriptures are geographically located and historically confined. That need not preclude them from their role and the Canon requires us to believe they can discharge it. If so, however, it can only be by vital partnership now between the Holy Spirit and ourselves. We noted in Chapter 4 the onus of a 'Hebrew, Greek and Latin' ground-work of faith, when meeting that 'sifting East.' For Christ did not stay, Virgil like, in the Mediterranean, nor in the first century of recognition of the faith. What was once transparent readily becomes opaque. 'Sacrifice,' for example, once central to the Biblical mind via Leviticus and priesthoods Aaronic, may well now be no more than an exaggerated term about a clearance sale. What, or who, we must ask, is this 'lamb of God,' unless we know already and understand the sharp vicariousness of prophetic suffering and how tortuously meaning passed from brazen altars to the Messiah of God. Otherwise, 'the little sheep of the Lord of heaven' will avail us little.

Misconstruing how 'blood cleanses' or 'price of sin' is paid was noted in the previous Chapter. We can still sing with Charles Wesley. 'Can it be that I should gain an interest in the Saviour's blood?' but can all viewers of *Songs of Praise* explain it to a world of dividends and profits? 'Ransom,' also, is a puzzling word, much as we may enjoy the herald coming for it in Shakespeare's *Henry V*. Or there are all those sheer archaisms of the Prayer Book about being 'miserable sinners,' or God having the 'property' of mercy. In the devaluation of their currency time has inflicted, 'misery' is no longer a realized need for pardon, nor is 'property' anything but 'real estate.'

'Only' in credal language about the Sonship of Jesus is another verbal stumbling block, noted in Chapter 8. We think numerically of 'only alternatives' and 'only children,' though both these can readily be plural too. That misleads us. What the Gospel and the Creed are saying is that God revealed in Christhood, there in time and place, and God eternally, are truly One. 'Son to Father,' 'Father in Son,' are how faith tells it, as 'the fulness,' or *pleroma*, of God. (John 1.16, Ephesians 1.25, Colossians 1.15 and 2.9).

The question of the Ethiopian in Acts 8.30: 'How can I (understand) unless some-one guide me?' will always be near when Scriptured faith negotiates with the perplexed. Ministry of the Word is a sustained, imaginative mediation of a 'many splendoured thing.' Alive to the incomprehension that attends it, it becomes 'a dayspring in the dimness of us.' It is where we understand Christ's Gethsemane, taking the brunt of all that grieves the Spirit, no less than in the ministry of bread and wine.[20]

We pass from the intellectual in ministry, from the trust of faith, Scriptures and Creed put into our hands and minds at Ordination, to the institutional Church where those tasks are set. It has already been emphasized that all is 'priestly' where every thing is 'ministry.' Where truth and personality – as the psalmist might have said – 'kiss each other' in preaching, priesthood is there in the sacrament of language. Priesthood is no less present in the art of pastoral care – tending the sick, supporting the lonely, serving the bereaved, seeking out the alienated. The visit, the handshake, 'the word in season,' the letter written, the token left – all these, in their prosaic given-ness, are sacramental, no less than 'bread and wine.' To import the last, as it were extraneously – and by another hand (if the main ministrants were only deacons) – has always been a sort of astigmatism, looking different ways. What culminates in the sanctuary, in the sacred chalice, is everywhere extensive in the transactions of grace. Whatever Luke may have intended about the Eucharist in his Emmaus story what he narrated was a simple travellers' supper. Sunday is not holy for the desecration of Monday, nor 'Holy Orders' meant to consign the laity outside 'the people of God.' The Sacraments we rightly capitalize tell of the sacramental everywhere.

This leads us into things institutional, but with the warning that they must not aggrandize themselves beyond their calling and their proper meaning. Arnold Toynbee, as we must see below, in his monumental *The Study of History*, and elsewhere, wrote often of the bane of 'institutions.' Humans could not dispense with them, but nor could they stop them from gathering vested interests of prestige or indispensability such as to disqualify their ends. His understanding of *kenosis*, as evident in Jesus as the Christ, led him to require of the institutional Church the same kind of self-giving. There were aspects, for him, of its being 'institutional' which made such genuine humility impossible. The Church would always be over-pretentious.[21]

We have reason not to share Toynbee's Christianity here for it was one that stayed in Gethsemane and disallowed the Resurrection. Yet it is wise to keep always in mind how far from self-aggrandizement was – and is – the way of the Cross and firmly to apply the lesson to our understanding of the Church and, in turn, of the ministerial priesthood she possesses and perpetuates. In his earliest theological writing, Michael Ramsey, in *The Gospel and the Catholic Church*, wrote of 'the Cross as the place where the theology of the Church has its meaning.' 'The Church of God and the Passion of Jesus' were 'themes central and inseparable in the New Testament.' Indeed: but in that deep evangelical emphasis, he sought also to argue that 'the Episcopate' declared – by its very nature – 'something integral to the Gospel' so that 'truth about the Gospel' would be 'obscured if the Episcopate was lacking.'[22] In that verdict, did not the pride of the 'institutional' invade the 'organic' he was anxious to substitute for it? Could one well plead 'dying and rising with Christ' as a warrant for indispensable Episcopacy? It is melancholy to reflect that the exposition of 'the Gospel' and authentic 'Catholic Order' in *The Gospel and the Catholic Church* as bonded into one in 1936 was not unrelated to the failure of the Anglican/Methodist re-union hopes in 1969.[23]

I had just been made deacon when the book appeared and it was to the future Archbishop, as an Examining Chaplain of Chester ordinands, that I had to submit essays. As noted in Chapter 3, I was much pre-occupied with the issue of 'authority.' I now recall his apt comment on an occasion in 1964, in the Common Room evening at the Central College, Canterbury, to a question about *Soundings* – a book of theological Essays then in vogue. He said: 'There is all the comment I need in a verse in Acts: "They went further and sounded again" (27.28)'[24] It would have been apposite enough for my youthful prose-on-faith. It might be proper, too, for any venture making the institutional or organic 'form' of the Church crucial in the way of 'grace,' or having no patience with the distinction between the *esse* and the *bene esse* of the Church in respect of ministry.[25]

What is meant in present context is not to wrestle with the complex issues of ecclesiology with their minutiae of scholarship and the loaded-ness of debate. Having lived four years in old Longworth Rectory it is a work of piety simply to cite one of the 'lights' of *Lux Mundi*, R.C. Moberly and his *Ministerial Priesthood*. His insists that priestliness is much more than being (his word) 'a sacrificer,' i.e. an officiant over 'bread and wine.'

> 'A Christlike cure of souls . . . can never be exhausted by anything in the sphere of ceremonial method . . . It is the unreserved offering, the total self-dedication of what is . . . wise oversight, anxious forethought and rule, an unwearied guidance, preaching, teaching, discipline . . . of an utterly loving pastor, a shepherd who . . . is ready to die for the souls of his flock. All this belongs exactly to that inner reality of the spirit and the life which . . . should be the

> true inwardness of the outward representation of the sacrifice of Christ.'[26]

It follows, therefore, that ministry must be ever watchful of the bearing of its 'official' dignities, the rights of rites, on the inner secrecies of personal self-esteem, lest there be subtle usurpation at the very core of our servanthood. It is true enough to know, and swear, that the ministry belongs to Christ alone, 'our great High Priest,' and because of Him to 'all the people of God.' True enough; it does not suffice, however, if we promptly contradict it by the conventions, the deferences, the contrary assumptions, with which ministry too easily conspires. Even sartorial usages can betray us – those apparellings which John Milton, in his controversial writings, used to suspect had emerged from 'Aaron's wardrobe.' Ministry does well not to be too often mitred, since the flames of Pentecost are not amenable to millinery. I remember Bishop Graham-Brown of Jerusalem (1932–42) telling me that Jesus' only headgear in Jerusalem was 'the crown of thorns.' In the sanctuary he preferred to be bare-headed.

Lay-people, of course, have much responsibility in this regard. It is sometimes those who feel most loyal and most committed who are most indulgent of clerical pride. There are notions of authority that connive with complacence. The health, for example, of Christian nurture within the churches, needs a lively challenge, a temper that is demanding and not docile in its willingness for instruction and leadership. The old Catechism may have served its ends in an illiterate society with its set questions and answers. Does not the very word derive from the Greek 'echoing'? So the Catechism determined what was proper to be asked and how it was properly to be answered. A teaching Church now needs something more strenuous than this and perhaps today's juveniles and adolescents are better set to evoke it – unless indifference and the T.V. mind have already overtaken their capacity to think or ask uncomfortable things.

The liveliness of ministerial priesthood, on every count, has to be responsive to the actualities of the day-to-day world as only unremitting immersion in them can ensure.

If we are musing on 'life-ministry' only life will sift its motives and test its sincerity. It is the immersion of 'me' into the 'me-aning' of Christ. The will to believe is implemented in the will to relate believingly to all that belief confronts, suffers, pities, loves and undertakes, whether in mind as to truth, or in heart as to hope, or in will as to deed. William James, who gave modern currency to the theme of 'a will to believe,' confined the idea to philosophic ambience. He wrote:

> 'The Divine, for my active life, is limited to abstract concepts which, as ideals, interest and determine me, but do so faintly in comparison with what a feeling of God might effect – if I had one.'[27]

It is not so with the Christian. 'What a feeling of God' might effect is documented in the faith and community of the New Testament – 'a feeling of God' informed and enthused by the measure it has because of Jesus as the Christ. That measure is indeed a theme of faith but it is in no way a mere concept to 'interest' us. It moves only by ministry – ministry in which credentials we can hold become credentials we must live. In terms of 'Holy Orders,' such ministry belongs in the larger world of politics and power, of economy and markets, of sciences and arts, mainly by the proxy of the lay folk it may cherish by the Word and nourish with the sacraments. Such lay folk, in turn, must hold it to an honest realism and a steady scrutiny of its self-assurance.

Having heeded Arnold Toynbee's reminder about 'the corn of wheat that dies' into the ground (John 12.24), we are ready to disallow his exclusion of Easter from the significance of Jesus' Passion. For it is not the sheer triumphalism he thought it to be. On the contrary, it is 'the glory inherent in the suffering,' and that suffering-glory alive in an ongoing 'Body of Christ,' bearing it into the human future in 'the priesthood of all who believe.' Only so does the meaning abide in openness – both for recognition and resemblance.

To be sure, there *is* a hidden-ness, a 'privation' (we might call it) in this secular world, of that divine Self-disclosure we studied in the previous chapter. It is a hidden-ness poetically captured in Alice Meynell's lines:

> 'And will they cast the altars down,
> Scatter the chalice, crush the bread?
> In field, in village and in town
> He hides an unregarded head.
>
> Waits in the cornlands far and near,
> Bright in his sun, dark in his frost,
> Sweet in the vine, ripe in the ear –
> Lonely, unconsecrated Host.'[28]

Ministry will always be in league with that perception, when it is most 'in distresses . . . as unknown' (2 Corinthians 6. 4 and 9), but it will not stay there, still less find improper solace in the paradox of its 'beloved/unwanted.' For it serves in the joy to which 'evil report and good report,' the 'season-out and the season-in,' are equally occasions of a risen Presence and renewal of life. It has apostolic precedent to hearten it – surely the first and most urgent dimension of any apostolic 'succession.' The first Easter was about walking the roads, kindling fires, sharing meals and 'being of one accord.' Only before Easter was love about spices for burial and winding sheets for remorse and repining.

> 'A legend told above his head, a king in language three,
> A crown in thorns about his brow, the kind of king was He.
>
> There came this King to Olivet with comrades of his mind,
> The virtue of his sovereignty, new birthing of mankind.'

The rest was, is and ever will be, ministry in that new birth.

vi.

It was suggested earlier that 'considerate' might be a third descriptive after 'intellectual' and 'institutional' in the exploration of priesthood in this Christ. If we mean to use the word we had better first rescue it. For it has fallen on hard times and may therefore seem oddly meant in present context. 'Taking into consideration' has a hackneyed, possibly dismissive, ring. 'Consider,' however, comes to us from the stars (sidera). To gaze, to inspect, to view attentively – all these are its range. It is a better word than 'contemplate' which may imply withdrawal. It might bring to mind the psalmist 'considering the heavens' and – by the same token – marvelling at the significance of mortal self-awareness in doing so.[29] Or John Milton, writing years after his meeting with astronomer Galileo, of how

> 'Through optic glass the Tuscan artist views
> At evening from the top of Fesole,
> Or in Valdarno, to descry new lands,
> Rivers or mountains . . .'[30]

on the surface of the moon.

There has to be in ministry a comparable intentness as it registers the social and intellectual scene around it, takes stock of how contemporary literature mirrors human vagaries, and strives to appreciate what lay folk face, in their ministries, in the complexities of politics, of commerce and employment – or the lack of it. All of this is what Karl Marx called 'the appropriation of human reality.' As King Lear said to the blinded Gloucester: 'If you would weep my fortunes take my eyes.'[31] There has to be in ministry a capacity, like Ezekiel, to 'sit where they sit.' (Ezekiel 3.15) '. . . astonished among them.' 'Whether the Church knows it or not,' wrote Kingsley Amis somewhere, 'she has obligations to my sort of person as well as to her own communicants.' Among all and sundry, the Word that was once made flesh has to be made word again in those articulate with its present tense.

We have broached earlier what this means intellectually. Its demands in the daily intercourse of parish and street, of hope and tribulation, are no less ministerial. According to Paul in Romans 12.15, we are to 'rejoice with them that do rejoice and weep with them that weep.' In this sometimes trivializing and cynical world, we may also have to rejoice and weep *for* those who do neither. Celebration is far from the sciences that are only exploitative and the arts that are only vulgar. One of the reasons for faith in God is to leave ourselves with the possibility of praising and giving thanks and – equally – the ground for being vicarious in sorrows and in the love they should command. For only in being vicarious is love itself. That truth is seen to be also transcendental in its range or, in Hebraic terms, 'underneath are the everlasting arms.' (Deuteronomy 33.27). If such is our theology then our living must be its counterpart. The task of Holy Orders, therefore, is to concert this everywhere in the wider 'orders' of a common humanity.

This means a passion against attitudes and beliefs that only operate at the expense of honesty. It means remembering with William Blake that 'every harlot was a virgin once,' in order to keep faith with hope. It cares about 'arms that ache for their own void' as it registers the situations that ache and voids oppress. Where economic realism reckons only with what accrues in the market-place of dividends, truth must care for what these entail in society, in marital infidelity, in sundered families, in child-abuse and blighted relationships. It knows the detritus of moral compromise for what it is and reads in the wasteland of industrial decay a wasteland also of the heart. It is aware that behind crime and enmity there often lurks a fester of injustice or deprivation and that things present can be neither understood nor redeemed without reference to things past. Overtaking and reversing these dark sequences is where the will to believe has to take shape in the will to relieve. Redemption is no abstract doctrine: it is the kingdom of God actively liable for its own meaning – the meaning where the Church lives and has her being.

'Some idea had seized the sovereignty of his mind,' wrote Dostoevsky of his character-hero in *The Brothers Karamazov*.[32] The phrase aptly describes what this and the preceding chapter have intended to 'consider.' We have tried to identify where, in Christ, faith concludes and where, in sequel, life ministers. We found it in the event of 'God in Christ' illuminating and enlisting the meaning of ourselves. We could even accept the caveat of the unsure, namely that 'a proof tells us where to concentrate our doubts.' From the latter we sought no immunity. Finding them either contained or resolved, we took 'the proof of love' to be telling us where to concentrate – and consecrate – our purposes. 'Here,' we could hold with Ezra Pound

> '. . . error is all in the not-done,
> All in the diffidence that faltered.'[33]

Ordination would always be diffident, approximate, faltering, both in the receiving and in the continuing. 'Error' would be in the not-done, not in the withholding of doing at all. Ministry of the Word and sacraments was riskily entrusted and received. It was clear from the Christian past that there was continuing business and that it invited to be undertaken.

> 'I saw the Son of God go by,
> Crowned with the crown of thorns.
> "Was it not finished, Lord?" said I,
> "And all the anguish borne?"'

He had left his disciples in no doubt about the answer.

Chapter 11

'Some Strange Divine Complicity.'

i.

Excluded by my maleness, I have often wondered what it must be like to know within oneself the stirrings of birth, to register in signs and emotions the waking inwardly of being yet to be. Perhaps in some remote way the coming into mind of a book or a poem or a purpose may be a hint of what transpires in physical conception. Truly the female body undergoes what ecclesiastical language calls an 'annunciation,' an apprehending of meaning, a message to the self that is at once an invitation and an imparting, set to take a course and reach a climax – a climax of fulfilment. In one sense all sentient life is this way – which is why the Christian faith has *the* 'annunciation' as its clue to sexuality and to the divine love for us – all and sundry, male and female, Jew and Greek alike.

I came one day across a passage from a sermon of Saint Bernard on the Feast of the Annunciation. It was in an anthology given me by our son, John. It thought of Mary as hearing these words:

> 'Answer the angel speedily . . . Speak the word and receive the Word. Offer what is yours and conceive what is of God. Give what is temporal and embrace what is eternal . . . Let your humility put on boldness and your modesty be clothed with trust . . . In this one thing, O Mary, fear not presumption: open your heart to faith.'[1]

In the several paradoxes of that 'one thing' I realized that all of us, in Christ, are in 'annunciation,' each their own 'Mary.' Some lines oddly came to me in which I mused on her reaction.

'How can a maid of Nazareth beatitude conceive?
The urge that would my womb awake
Moves only to deceive.

There is no quality in me such merit to attain.
In love by troth to Joseph bound,
Plain Mary I'll remain.'

She became confident, even suspicious, in her resistance.

'Who is this lord to hail me so?
What might his greeting spell?
What burden in these arms that take
The pitcher to the well?'

Incredulity and apprehension occupied her thoughts.

'Conception of the Holy Ghost,
Say creeds that yet will be.
But, here and now to bear and care,
Are creeds intending me?

My mother love could well suffice
The time of infant need,
But what of manhood's hidden risk? –
This call I cannot heed.

The girl who would be dedicate
To Messianic birth
Might forfeit in Gethsemane
The son she gives the earth.

His task will leave her home bereft,
His mission haunt her mind,
At length, beside a felon's grave,
Her broken self to find.'

'Annunciation' remonstrated, urging how any and every divine purpose will need a human means.

'Emmanuel, the vision said,
Here seeks nativity,
The travail of your low estate
His own necessity.

It is his love's prerogative
To come by need of you.

In every enterprise of God
Some human part is due.'

Mary is finally persuaded by an awesome sense of the divine humility in finding her indispensable as she responds

'Partnering purpose, have your way,
My soul and body yield.
This strange divine complicity
My readiness has sealed.'

The final lines were meant to be ambivalent. Was it the 'divine complicity' which had contrived the 'readiness,' or was it the 'readiness' which had allowed it? That both were responsible was the truth of either.

If, in faith and life, we are all parties to 'annunciation,' 'divine complicity' will always be crucial to our story. Yet it is always well to be diffident about discerning, still more about claiming, divine providence, special guidance, or explicit heavenly interventions, in our circumstances and careers. There are always temptations in thinking ourselves favoured of the Lord, or recipients of arbitrary privilege. For such thoughts will always have to incur their negative implications of why what we identify as interventions were denied to others, why the 'accident' which so arguably aided us worked so darkly and sadly in experience as others knew it. Is it not a dubious thing to be always, as the American novelist has it, 'examining everything for the fingerprints of God.'?[2] Do our prayers, as a poet asked, imply 'an eavesdropping God' in the sense that we possess some special claim upon divine attention?

Nevertheless, if that warning is always in mind, who can fail to be aware of an ordering and ordaining, if only in retrospect, thanks to which disaster was retrieved or fulfilment found? That life is vicissitude faith cannot deny: that faith is relevant life cannot doubt. How we perceive their inter-play will be the crux of both.

The purpose, then, of this final Chapter is to ruminate on orderings of things which it would be graceless and churlish not to recognize and faithless not to ascribe to divine mercy. These will also afford opportunity to incorporate some aspects of story-study that have escaped inclusion elsewhere. It will be important, over-all, to have Paul's meaning right in the oft-quoted passage in Romans 8.28, in which he is supposed to have written that 'all things work together for good to them that love God.' That reading might suggest a complete passivity in which we await the good providence, somehow divinely contrived, by which adversity proves to have been 'a blessing in disguise,' or a seeming chance altered a sorry picture.

Such arbitrary or fortuitous meaning was not in Paul's mind. His Greek was about a divine-human 'complicity,' an inter-working. It ran: 'God works together in all things unto good with them that love Him.' All situations were capable of yielding 'the fruit of righteousness,' given divine grace finding human partnership, human obedience affording divine ends. It will not then be a matter of 'the fingerprints of God' detected in answers to our prayers, but rather 'the hand of God' in ours shaping what transpires. As Robert Browning has his Johannes Agricola warn us, there are no private bargains with the love of God, no cheap, proud assurance that

> 'Ere stars were thundergirt . . .
> . . . God thought on me, his child,
> Ordained a life for me, arrayed
> Its circumstances every one
> To the minutest.'[3]

We have always to reckon with inter-acting will, human and divine, whereby the doing in the becoming has us 'fellow-workers with God.' (1 Corinthians 3.9 and 2 Corinthians 6.1.)

This is not to say that there are never things that are, or seem, entirely fortuitous. It is to say that, where they are significant, faith has to undertake them, reckon with their meaning and act in its light. The guidance for which we yearn is often elusive but if 'we intend to get to God' who is 'the God of patience,' negotiation and situation together bring us on our way. Sometimes a way has to be taken before its rightness is confirmed and sometimes the sequel will spell disproof and require redemption.

As told in Chapter 3, we were sure that any unity in love meant a unity in vocation. Very soon, it became medically clear that one of us could not have vocation where, geographically, we had first thought it should take us. Sharp crisis presented itself hard on the heels of the intentions we felt sacred between us. Had their very intensity misled us? If so, why did we have them so intensely? It was both distressing and honest to put them on hold. The crisis yielded an answer only in being undergone. Vocation, we finally concluded, could – and by these tokens should – be found elsewhere. Otherwise we would never have come to belong with Arabic and the Middle East.

Another negotiation soon presented itself, less emotionally charged but no less critical. Bishop Graham-Brown was unsure of the form of the proposal under which we would be going there. I remember vividly the oppressed state in which his letter put me, with its seeming veto on that future. I recall the warmth – and the length – of the letter I promptly wrote and the presumption, if such it was, with which I tried to overcome his scruples. Being the Bishop he was, and with the pledge I had made about the feasibility of 'due obedience,' and with the help of others, the course, as narrated in Chapter 3 was finally cleared. Hurdles hardly taken can become the stuff of better confirmation.

Both these crucial negotiations were overtaken nine months later by an episode which might have wrecked them altogether. Though no more than an episode now, the story meant the tensest negotiation I ever had with the misery of indecision. It began with my departure from Jerusalem in late August, 1939, leaving behind my first impressions of sandbags and check-points and the air of uneasy vigilance around holy – and unholy – places and the tragic distance between *Shalom* and *Salam*[4] in the paradoxes of 'the city of peace.' At a farewell tea for the Summer School, at the home of Canon Marmura of St Paul's Church, we learned of the 'Pact' between Germany and Soviet Russia which made world war imminent. 'Battle and murder and sudden death,' in my newly Arabicized familiarity with Cranmer's Litany, loomed into a present tense.

It had been arranged that I would take pastoral care during the month of September of St George's Church, Baghdad, close to the River Tigris. Armed with the tediously acquired visas and permits, I made my way to Beirut, cresting again that northern hill in the reverse direction, grateful to have known the sacrament of geography as it then was before suburbia took its toll of the imagination. For landscape desecration finds no atonement in the devotion of museums. A very different scene awaited me in Iraq where history, too, was at odds with itself. A pair of enterprising New Zealand brothers had organized 'Nairne Transport' across the desert from Damascus, via Rutbah Wells to Baghdad, in an over-night journey of about twenty hours, using a trailer-coach pulled by a cabined-car after the fashion of an articulated lorry. A food basket was supplied en route. In the absence of paved roads, oiled tracks were used across the sand. As we pulled out of Damascus, a hysterical passenger bewailed Hitler's invasion of Poland of which we then had news. The night air of the desert, brooding and still at our stops, made a grim ambience for apprehension, despite the glowing sunrise over Ramadi at the Euphrates.

Sunday, September 3rd found me at St George's preaching on Psalm 77.10 about 'remembering the years of the right hand of the Most High,' though with what point I cannot now recall. The Counsellor at the British Embassy kindly took the lonely chaplain home to lunch. He was summoned from the table after we had enjoyed the soup. I awaited his return. After some forty minutes he appeared with the word that we were 'at war with Germany.' Chamberlain's warning to Hitler had been ignored. The famous broadcast about 'the evil things,' the perfidy which had compelled us to it, duly came to the bulletins. It was everywhere assumed, by high and low, Cabinet and War Office, that shooting war would promptly ensue, that bombs would rain down and make massive evacuation immediate. Only the last transpired, the rest awaiting eruption after eight months of 'phoney war.' How were we to know? Had I not helped to hand out gas-masks in School in Tranmere the previous September?

I was housed in the dingy quarters of the Baghdad Y.M.C.A. How I rooted through its equally dingy library for things to read including books of war-time resonance like *A Student at Arms* and *Vain Glory*. Temperatures by day exceeded 105. Mercifully we could sleep at night on the flat roof under the stars and perhaps say with the poet:

> 'There's heaven above and night by night
> I look right through its gorgeous roof . . .
> I keep the brood of stars aloof . . .'[5]

Sleepless thoughts I could not keep aloof. The month in Baghdad was desperately vacant yet pre-occupied to the point of agitation. What was the point of teaching in Shimlan with dire emergency in England? Had I been misled in January, 1939, when more perceptive minds might have foreseen that if I cared about war tribulations it was folly to have left at all. But then was not 'peace in our time' the famous promise? In any event 'hope springs eternal . . .' Now, as I walked the dusty suqs of Baghdad, mused around the crowded coffee-shops, the book shops of Rashid Street and the domes of Kazimain, 'hope sank infernal . . .' My Arabic, I reasoned, was still partial. Ministry should go where need was greatest. I argued my own near-redundancy in the Bible School, far from the war-zone. In my first week I wrote – where it was necessary – for visas and permissions in a resolve (?) to return to England.

We held thrice weekly intercessions in St George's and I tried, as best I could, to discover my temporary congregation. I lived through four patient and impatient Sundays regaling them with texts like 'knowing how to be abased and how to abound,' being 'an ambassador in bonds,' or 'the simplicity that is in Christ.' The last for me was then very far to seek, as I moved from hesitancy to decision, and from decision into doubt.

There was, of course, the complication of my love-story. I believed sincerely that my motive was ministry and *not* short-circuiting the risk of prolonged impossibility of marriage through war-induced separation. Melita was not due to leave for Lebanon, at best, until late April, 1940, when her College studies would end. However, I could not prevent what I deeply held as integrity being otherwise interpreted and that added to my burdens.

I left St George's, Baghdad, on Monday, September 25th and made my way via Beirut, to Shimlan and then Jerusalem, receiving only reluctant permissions for my purpose as I went, but no determined or firmly reasoned opposition. In Jerusalem I had word of a Japanese vessel due to sail from Port Said. Ignoring any sea-analogies from Jonah, I decided I was meant to go. The Bishop gave me his own visiting card, inscribed on the back 'To commend the bearer,' naming me. This would be my credential at the War Office, and its Bureau for Chaplains. I would pay my own expenses and believe the sequel would justify my resolve. Train took me via Kantara to Port Said and the good ship Hakozaki Maru put out to sea early on October 4th, bound via Naples for Marseilles. As, like Aeneas, we breasted the Tyrrhenian Sea I thought of my journey down the Adriatic nine months before. The ship was not crowded. I could pace the deck at night with little to divert my thoughts from the quandary in hand. Misgivings beset me which it was too late to heed: assurance sought to convert fact into truth. I found the Bay of Naples a legend overdone, the more so as we loaded crates of tomatoes through the small hours and set foot in dockside confusion.

From Marseilles I went overland to London and within a week arrived at the War Office, only to be told what I could have guessed, namely that there was no immediate need and a waiting list would inconsequentially record my name. Total anti-climax followed, made worse by the reception I received from the Mission Committee when they duly summoned me to appear. Apparently not gauging the agitation I had lived through, they enjoined my prompt return to 'the field,' as one who, otherwise, was a renegade, a stranger to all discipline, indeed a deserter from 'the mind of Christ.'

My whole sense of mission and vocation was shaken by this response. If they had only remonstrance for my action and its logic, what was I to think of my obligation? Had I wasted all the painful process through which they had recruited me? Had I acted in precipitate haste and impatiently betrayed their trust? Meanwhile, 'phoney war' gave the deserter no vindication. My business ought still to be with the minutiae of Arabic.

I was stunned and perplexed, even felt betrayed myself. Could evangelical purity of faith assume such a monopoly of the Holy Spirit in the quest for integrity? The veto on my logic for a while clouded the essential issue. A mood of rebellion overtook me. I went down to rural Dorset where Melita's College had gone to find solace and take stock. The College was kind to us but the perplexity only deepened. Parishes, we thought – since I had come anyway – were just as danger-fraught as trenches, civilians as soldiers. I returned to my parents to search for a curacy. I owed it to Melita to be decisive: to us both I owed a will to prove my coming right. Or so it seemed, and, otherwise, there would be the awful prospect of another parting, far more precarious than the first, and yet a consideration to be loyally suppressed.

Through weary weeks I sounded out no less than thirteen curacies, until finally finding one on Advent Sunday, for implementation at Christmas. It was at the Parish Church of Rushden in Northants. I duly took up residence. In the afternoon of Christmas Day, a deep disquiet seized me. Perhaps while I was prospecting the reality lay dormant. Once I was appointed it overtook me in devastating perplexity. Had I/we really meant to abandon an overseas vocation for years, perhaps for ever? Had my coming really been misguided? Maybe the 'phoney war' would go on months on end? If not, had I not made my gesture which would help, if and when I/we were far away from falling bombs? Shimlan and its antecedents fought in my soul with Rushden and its implications. I wandered around Rushden debating whether to go to the Vicarage and say I could not stay. That, too, would be embarrassing. I stood several times on the doorstep, too paralysed to act. Nearby, a policeman accosted me to know why, with what intent, I was loitering. Finally, I did unburden myself to my new

Vicar, clutching as I did at a straw which might decide for me what I could not resolve. He had told me that there had been another candidate. If he were still available, my desertion would be soon repaired. The Vicar agreed to find out at once. The answer was affirmative. I asked him to release me. I telegraphed Melita, spending Christmas with my parents, for her concurrence in my returning to Lebanon. Courageously she gave it. Enormously relieved, I returned home to be briefly with her before a new term, the final one, and made plans to return to Beirut. Yet another parting and still the ugly risk of war perpetuating our absence from each other.

Sailing, in due course, during January, 1940 on the Egyptian ship, Al-Nil, I reached Lebanon to be received like a returning prodigal and to resume the toils of Arabic, no longer a deserter and perhaps, perhaps, more wholly a recruit. But the experience had deeply shaken us. I might well have returned more promptly had my mentors shared in Christ the honesty of my aberration. The risk about Melita's journey which we had feared and consented to run, did not in fact transpire. Mussolini came just too late into the conflict to close the shipping lanes across the Mediterranean, but as Wellington may have said about his Waterloo: 'It was a damned near thing!'

ii.

How we 'work together with God in all things unto good' tests all our faculties as music does the resources of the instruments by which it is fulfilled. I have been self-indulgent in detaining the reader with a story which soon receded and deserves to be forgotten, except that its lessons stayed with me as critical both for the present of my faith and the future of my life. One should not romanticize, but perhaps there had been 'some divine complicity' brooding over mine. Complicity, ours, can be a sluggish or a roguish thing. There is 'the hill of evil counsel' among the hills around Jerusalem.[6]

In Baghdad, heeding that Psalm 77.3, as the Prayer

Book had it, 'When I am in heaviness I will think upon God,' I realized the mis-translation. The Hebrew was 'When I think upon God I am in trouble.' For awe, wonder, even dread, possess us and 'fellow-working' seems incredible. When Paul wrote of divine-human partnership he used the plural '*those* who love . . .' There is always comfort in community and danger for the soloist. Family meant much to me in this connection while time and place united us. To my elder brother I owed much, especially in the early days. His certainties were always more sure than mine and there were times, I think, when he feared or suspected that 'the sifting East' might be leading me astray. Arguing from Ezekiel 3.5, he believed what we then called 'the home ministry' was his right and only sphere.[7] Perhaps it was this, in part, that made me opt for 'overseas.' I could not blame him for not having to align his theology to experiences he had not known but there came, at times, a certain tension. I have the impression that he kept *The Call of the Minaret* in 1956 in the margin of his mind. However, in his last address at the Keswick Convention just before his death in 1980, he took from it a quotation I had always loved about 'rescuing a word and recovering a universe' and 'burying ourselves in a lexicon to arise in the presence of God.'[8] It was clear he had picked it up again.

So the 'those who love . . .' of Romans 8.28, if English grammar allowed, could well be the dual pronoun. Weddedness, of course, is the ultimate mystery of any human communion with the purposes of God. Of this I have said enough in Chap. 3. The world, since that partnership mortally ceased, has been a different world. Yet the instinct to want it to continue as it was is unabated. 'They took sweet counsel together' is a precious text even if its own context leads into a treason we had never known.[9]

The three redundancies we experienced were obvious and vexing occasions of trying to fulfill Romans 8.28. One could perhaps sum up that episode in the closing months of 1939 in the words of La Fontaine: 'On rencontre sa destinée souvent par les chemins qu'on prend pour l'éviter.' In our other cases of things abortive, 'the ways of getting out' were taken by others, or by events, all against the grain of one's own thought. Unwanted relinquishments, by 'divine complicity,' could nevertheless yield new discoveries and fresh adventures. What followed our first two 'disemployments' has already been narrated. As for the third in the mid-seventies, the context itself hinted at a resolution.

How the Anglican Archbishopric in Jerusalem gave way at that time to the Province of Jerusalem and the Middle East was told in Chapter 6. It meant that, as Assistant Bishop, I then became extinct with the demise of the office after the changes. However, it was suggested that if I could find a salary outside the area, with time to visit it, I might become an honorary Assistant Bishop to the new Presiding Bishop. In that event a modest item in the Synod's budget could be found for travel costs.

There seemed to me an ideal complicity in this proposal. It would mean that there would not be complete abeyance in the Muslim study aspects of my pastoral ministry which I was eager to sustain. It would also mean that jurisdictional 'hand-over' need not imply that love was only available when it had control. The Church would still be 'one in Christ' whose-ever the aegis. I had to act quickly as the post of Reader in Religious Studies at the University of Sussex was coming vacant. I was duly appointed and became solely an 'academic,' apart from such ministries as Bishop Roger Wilson of Chichester readily made available in his Diocese as 'assistant' yet again. The University did not see it as anomalous. To keep abreast of one's field was academically right and proper. So, at intervals in vacations, I/we returned where we belonged to help in Summer Schools or other tasks as opportunity allowed, while the new and local régimes had no reason to feel invaded. This pattern persisted through my five years in Brighton.

Contrivances are never ideal. It would have been a joy to have stayed as one had been, but as negotiation with a situation it was benediction to the mind and tempered the sense of possible unwantedness as well as enabling new perspectives. I found the Sussex experience an education. The University had begun in the sixties with a sudden fame for 'contextuality.' There were no 'Departments' of this or that, in splendid seclusion from the rest of knowledge. In Arts there were 'Areas' – English and American, African and Asian, European, and Cultural and Community. My Readership fell within the fourth, among the 'caring professions.' 'Subject Groups' were required to share half their time and accountability in courses deliberately contrived to bridge the disciplines. Thus 'Artist and Public' could comprehend the historians, the sociologists, the literature people and the jurists, while 'Images of Childhood' brought all these together with educational psychologists as well. This inter-mixing could be very salutary but it meant that the particular disciplines were seriously attenuated. When 'Religious Studies' – as distinct from (Christian) theology – took in its tasks, what it could comprise particularly, without the Biblical or other languages, was crippled in the extreme. The argument between 'less about more' and 'more about less' continues to beset the academic world. There is a price to pay for specialization, perhaps a greater one for contextual hospitality.

One feature of Sussex intrigued me from the start. Its heraldic 'legend' was the truncated verse from Psalm 46.10: 'Be still and know . . .' suppressing the sequel. It seemed odd for a university inasmuch as the Hebrew seems to mean 'desist,' 'hold off', or, even – loosely – 'go on vacation,' hardly apt for a place of learning. On enquiry, David Daiches, the veteran esteemed Professor of English Literature and a co-founder, informed me that the four words had 'sounded good' to the first Vice-Chancellor. Instead of 'vacation,' I went from time to time, to Cairo, Beirut or elsewhere in pursuit of the knowledge, found and shared, that 'God is God.'

Almost at the outset, I had a puzzling illness in the aftermath of change, but otherwise the five years went quickly and happily. They certainly required me to try to be more versatile and compelled me to take such notice as might be of Buddhism and its reading of the human self, which wound a basic interrogation mark around all the Semites, with their confidence in the reality of selves. To know religions for the vast continents they are is to realize how pretentious are superficial surveys. The contextuality which occasioned that menace could also supply the excuse.

It was, perhaps, expedient, but it was not satisfactory. Sadly, even before my retirement there were omens that, in the secular competition, Religious Studies would not survive at Sussex. Two years later they were withdrawn. I barely escaped a fourth redundancy.

What might 'complicity' then contrive? When the suggestion came, just prior to Lambeth, 1978, about Helme I could not even find it on the map. The Bishop of Wakefield's idea was that on the base of a small, solo, Pennine parish, suited to an iron in another fire, I might concert with his Community Relations Chaplain (then a Mirfield Father) in helping clergy and school-teachers in their contacts with the numerous Muslim populations in their parishes and schools across West Yorkshire. This was our semi-retirement for three and a half years until Melita's failing health dictated that we bring it to an end.

The terrain was rugged, the snows frequent and the folk superb. We were learning the first of the winter woes in the landscape of 'the last of the summer wine.' To the west of the village were the hills climbing up into the watershed that sundered the 'white rose' from the 'red.' To the east the fading elegance of Huddersfield. David Bernard Chamberlain and I teamed up to foster informed relations between the churches and the sundry house-mosques of the Muslim enclaves in every city within radius. In some areas, especially in Bradford, if one could forget the drab, grey weather and the rain, one could dream oneself into Lahore via the shop signs, the attire and the intimations of the streets. It was an elusive venture for, out of its instincts and traditions, Islam does not take readily to minority status. It finds much that is oppressive and bewildering, not to say also offensive, in the drift of western secularity and the T.V. invasion – long on exposure and short on exposition –[10] into its due God-mindedness. Hence the urgent claim on a Christian sympathy for its dismay and a perception of its spiritual claims on Christian neighbours.

It is hard to know what we achieved beyond a gesture towards a duty, but it was a benediction to be again *in parochia* after so long and, even till 1985, to be able to maintain in some form the honorary association with the

Province of the Middle East and Jerusalem. When Presiding Bishop H.B. Dehqani-Tafti completed his second five-year term it seemed a right moment to withdraw formally from that association making, however, no vow of absence. Through all the troughs of limitation which had punctuated our major chapters of obligation it had been possible to find the compensations of paradoxical fulfilment. It is imperative at every juncture to try to sense something like 'annunciation' – the theme and clue in all. For, as W.H. Auden has it,

'It lies within your power of choosing
To conceive the child who chooses you.'[11]

Paul, I know, has nothing to say about Mary or the narrative around her of his sometime travel-comrade, Luke. The terse 'born of woman' in Galatians 4.4. as life has us all, leaves him curiously indifferent to Mary's 'Annunciation' and the phrase has its own intention.[12] Yet what significantly has no place in his teaching is a clue to his heart when he writes of 'Christ being formed' in his Galatian Christians, Jews and Gentiles, later in the same passage. The imagery is exactly that of the embryo in the womb. In his ministry, both yearnings and hazards (from the legalists), translate into travail told in a rare metaphor. Writing elsewhere to Corinthians it is the 'father' language he employs (1 Cor. 4.14–15). Paul, we may conclude, was no stranger to divine-human complicity and the analogies by which it might be understood. There is no metaphor of travail in Romans 8.28. There could well have been if, like wombs, the places where things come to pass are the wills that let them take the shape they have divinely in them.

iii.

If we can be right in thinking with this imagery then may not conceiving, bearing, shaping, be the way to read life's story? These will mean the love that soul must have for body, the response that body has to soul and both in their bond with the Lord. Story-study then aims to bring together how the invitation came which is the faith and how the answer was which is the life. We know them, if at all, only as the transactions of our 'low estate,' for only there can we 'magnify the Lord.'

Such comprehension of things divine, realized and proven in leaving such room for our response, decides my faith in the majesty and mystery of God. It possesses me with the imaginative truth of Christianity. It is truth in its very priority as trust, an invitation to be traced in the Jesus story and told in historic faith. Only in drawing and commanding the affections can meaning take its place in doctrine for the mind and so tell itself in creed. This is the Christian way of the Incarnation and the Cross. If we heed Robert Browning's word about how 'hard it is to be a Christian,' it is only for the reason that there is no responding to this Christ on easy terms. One may not trivialize with the Crucified. There are no reduced prices in the Kingdom of heaven. If we have understood love by His measure, as faith discerns it, answer takes 'all that a man has.' It is only the will of a whole self that closes with grace.

> '. . . love of loving, rage
> Of knowing, seeing, feeling . . .
> For truth's sake, whole and sole.'

If God is read 'in Christ reconciling,' we are thereby acknowledged His and faith is glad it should be so. Negotiation has become capitulation. Life has found its meaning in the heart's devotion. The will to have it so is only ours because of His.

> 'You'll love me yet (He says) and I can tarry
> Your love's protracted growing.'[13]

Notes

Introduction

1 Robert Browning: *Poetical Works*, Oxford, 1905, 'Bishop Blougram's Apology,' p.444, col. 1. Cf. 'Does God love, and will you hold that truth against the world?' 'A Death in the Desert,' p.486.
2 The familiar dictum of A.N. Whitehead: *Religion in the Making*, Cambridge, 1930, p.6. 'Solitariness' was the word he used, On p.5 he wrote: 'Religion is the force of beliefs cleansing the inward parts.' If only it were!
3 The English title was *City of Wrong: A Friday in Jerusalem*, Amsterdam, 1958, paperback, New York, 1964. The author did not need to resolve the question at issue between Muslim and Christian accounts of the finale of Jesus' ministry, namely whether or not he was actually crucified. It sufficed for Kamil Husain to study the *will* to crucify which, in either event, must have been there. In that will to crucify he identified the inveterate enemy of human justice and integrity, namely 'expediency' over-riding conscience in the interest of 'collectives' (nation, state, office, community) which make men pervert themselves. It was in that sense, in the book's opening sentence, that he was able to write: 'Good Friday is the darkest day in human history.' See below, in Chap. 8.
4 Vol. xlvi, No. 2, April, 1956, pp.132–43 and Vol. xlvi, No.3, July, 1956
5 This, surely, is the right reading of the otherwise enigmatic: 'I am that I am,' in the Exodus passage. A metaphysical riddle such as that would never satisfy the anxiety of an oppressed people. God will *be*, and be present, only as the event will prove – 'there, as there.' The people can have no guarantee: in the going they will know. See Martin Buber's *Moses*, Oxford, 1946, New York, 1958.
6 William Shakespeare: *Hamlet*, Act 5, Sc.2, lines 298–301 and Act 1, Sc.1, lines 28–30.
7 A favourite saying of John Oman, whose chief work *Grace and Personality*, Cambridge, 1917, influenced me deeply when loaned to me with warm commendation of its worth by Bishop Graham-Brown in Jerusalem. He writes, for example, on p.41 of God as 'not circumscribed on every hand by considerations of His own dignity' but 'concerned with our need . . .' so that 'the first question' will not be: 'How would (God) seek to display His dignity?' It must be: 'How would He serve His children.' (See notes 8 and 16 in Chapter 2 on *kenosis*.) Elsewhere (p.67) he writes: 'If God's relation to us is irresistible power, acting so impersonally that a prophet may be a pen and a pope a mouthpiece, then uncertainties of revelation and the divisions of the Church are mere scandals of God's negligence.' It is that 'God is patient and not that He is weak. He will not have us accept His purpose save as our own . . . and learn His thought about His world save as our own blessed discovery.'

Chapter 1: Seaside and Season

1 Alice Meynell: *The Poems*, London, 1940, p.20.
2 Matthew Arnold: *The Poetical Works*, ed. C.B. Tinker and H.F. Lowry, Oxford, 1950, p.210.
3 See Lyndale Gordon: *Virginia Woolf, A Writer's Life*, Oxford, 1984, p.5.
4 Edward Gibbon: *Memoirs of My Life*, ed. G.A. Bonnard, London, 1966, p.3.
5 Thomas Traherne: *Centuries, Poems and Thanksgivings*, 2 vols., ed. H.M. Margoliouth, Oxford, 1958, vol. 2, p.22, stanza 4.

6 D.H. Lawrence: *The Man Who died*, London, 1935.
Lawrence pictured a dead and bandaged Christ coming, reluctantly, back from the dead only to repudiate the life of 'concern for others' which had brought him into tragedy: 'death had saved him from his own salvation.' He would cease 'giving without taking' and would yield to private bliss, serving love, not with a corpse but with a living, pulsing body.

7 Albert Camus: *The Fall*, eng. trans by J. O'Brien, London, 1963 ed. The canals are the concentric circles of Hell. The central figure, a judge, is inured to condemning others. His failure to respond to the 'fall' of a prostitute into the canal brings down his familiar self-esteem. Then he finds himself preening himself in his capacity to accuse himself, and a new form of self-satisfaction takes over. All is devious and even penitence has to be repented of.

8 Albert Camus: *Noces à Tipasa*, Alger, 1938. See also: *Lyrical and Critical Essays*, trans. Philip Thody, London, 1967, 'Nuptials at Tipasa,' pp.51–56, and 'Return to Tipasa,' pp.126–32. There is no real beneficence beyond the smile of the sun.

9 Albert Camus: *The Myth of Sisyphus*, trans. Justin O'Brien, New York, 1960, pp.16–20.
'There us no fate that cannot be surmounted by scorn.' p.98.
'There is but one serious philosophical problem – suicide.' p.11.

10 Germaine Bree: *Albert Camus*, New Brunswick, 1964, p.85.

11 *Entre Oui et Non.* See alternative translation in ed. Philip Thody, *Lyrical and Critical Essays* (of Camus), New York, 1968, p.36.

12 In *Noces* he writes of himself as often to ignore the whole claim to compassion which he registered in 'human being,' and surrender to merely sensuous private satisfactions. In *L'Envers et L'Endroit* he records the sinister temptation to abjure all effort after 'humanity,' Algiers, 1937.

13 Albert Camus: *L'Homme Revolté*, Paris, 1951, p.319. See Eng. trans. *The Rebel: An Essay on Man in Revolt*, Anthony Bower, New York, 1956, p.258. See also his *Retour a Tipasa*, see note 8.

14 See *L'Homme Revolté*, Part 5.

15 See the opening of *The Myth of Sisyphus*, p.11 and *L'Envers et L'Endroit*.

16 Albert Camus: *Lyrical and Critical Essays*, ed. Philip Thody, trans. E.C. Kennedy, New York, 1968, p.160.

17 Albert Camus: *Les Justes*, Paris, 1949, p.120 ed. of 1977. The play is a study in 'scrupulous murder' in which a group of assassins, ideologically motivated, find their own personal capacity to love disintegrating in a kind of nemesis.

18 As mirrored in Clamence, the 'judge-penitent' in *The Fall*, who is 'inclined to see religion rather as a huge laundering exercise,' (p.82) and who 'denies the good intention.' (p.96)

Chapter 2: A Window in the Turl

1 William Wordsworth: *The Prelude*, Book 3, Lines 80–81.

2 The Children's Special Service Mission which organized holiday Services at seaside resorts with house-parties and camps, to present the Gospel to the young. They tended to be closely identified with the Public Schools, as I discovered when, in my curacy in Tranmere, I sought their sponsorship for a Beach Mission we held in Penmaenmawr, North Wales, and they declined. However, we made our own banner, sought our own permission from the local authority and went ahead. The Scripture Union, however, closely linked with C.S.S.M., embraced all and sundry in its activities and was very welcome in our Parish.

3 The tireless Editor of these Surveys was Canon J. McLeod Campbell, General Secretary of the Church Assembly Missionary Council, who sustained its work almost single-handed at a time when the Missionary Societies maintained a robust independence of central offices. He lived in a fascinating house in Lord North Street, close to the Houses of Parliament.

4 I.e. Matthew 28.18–20 and Mark 16.15–16. It seems right to understand 'the great

commission' as finding itself in words only because it had already fulfilled itself in deeds. The developed baptismal formula in the Triune Name marks the decades that had intervened between the event of Jesus and its telling in the Scripture of the Church. The words formulate what had already been happening (otherwise they would not exist) – and happening out of that inclusive intention for the world apprehended by the apostles in the crucified form of Jesus' Messiahship. From him came the imperative, for them its enunciation as Matthew and Mark set it down for us. In John's terms: 'As my Father sent me, so send I you.' (20.21)

5 The 'simplicity,' of course, is *haplotes*, 'sincerity,' 'freedom from guile and duplicity,' 'singlemindedness.'

6 He became the Bishop of Salisbury in the sixties. See F.W. Dillistone: *Afire for God: Life of Joseph Fison*, Oxford, 1983. See also: Emily Dickinson: *Poems*,

7 William Shakespeare: *Twelfth Night*, Act 1, Sc. 5, lines 171–72.

8 The concept of *kenosis*, or 'emptying' (see also note 16 below), like all faith-terminology, needs to be rightly discerned. The image in mind is not that of 'emptying' (e.g.) a vessel of its contents, so that nothing remains. It is a divesting of what might normally be assumed to belong to a status so that standing, or dignity, or privilege, *might* seem to be no longer possessed but are in fact more superbly fulfilled. One might cite the lines in Shakespeare's *Henry V*, when the King leaves aside his crown, takes a borrowed robe and goes among his soldiers – 'a little touch of Harry in the night, thawing cold fear.' Is he still 'royal,' still 'kingly'? Less so? No, more so. Or the sweet story in Isaac Walton's Life of George Herbert in which the poet, usually a well-groomed, prim figure, arrived for a music session, all muddied and bedraggled. He explained, when reproved and misunderstood, that he had been helping a peasant whose animal had fallen down in the road. He could not, he said, 'tune his instruments for music,' had he not first laid propriety aside and 'soiled his hands.' There are some dignities that exist only to be laid aside e.g. that of shepherd or friend. They cannot be what they are and be self-preserving, self-immunizing. The Christian faith is that it is this way with God, with 'God-in-Christ' – and Jesus is the proof. The divine is not self-economizing, but self-expending. This is *kenosis*.

9 See Matthew 22.41–45 Mark 12.35–37, Luke 20.41–44 and Psalm 110.1 which reads: 'The Lord (in heaven) said to my Lord (His emissary or "agent") "Sit on my right hand until I make thine enemies thy footstool."' In the narrative Jesus has been hailed as 'The Son of David' and is being challenged to repudiate the acclaim. He responds to the authorities in the text-quoting they practice on Him. The psalm was recognized as 'Messianic.' The one to whom it referred as a divine emissary was called both 'Lord' and 'Son of David.' The latter, then, could not mean a natural 'son.' Jesus' question brought this out by making them see that the sense was not literal. So understood, Jesus could accept the acclaim. There was no need to assume that the actual 'David' wrote the psalm, or that Jesus so assumed.

10 *Essays: Catholic and Critical:* ed. E.G. Selwyn, London, 1926, with the hope to do for its generation what *Lux Mundi* earlier had achieved,

11 William Edwin Orchard, noted Congregationalist Minister of King's Weigh House, London, who turned to Rome's 'infallibility' as a secure haven from what he held to be 'the slippery slope' of a merely personal faith. I read him sympathetically at the time but failed to see either the panic of his misgivings or the veracity of his refuge as their 'solution'. See: *The Present Crisis in Religion*, London, 1928 and *From Faith to Faith*, London, 1933.

12 Matthew 3.17 and 17.5, Mark 9.7 and Luke 9.35. Like the voice in these passages, authority could, and should, attest and commend the whole significance of Jesus as the Christ but not trespass on more than the urge: 'Hear him,' lest it should usurp the final ground of faith. Cf. the lines: 'Faith holds to Christ the mind's own mirror out, to take his lovely image more and more.'

13 Roger Lloyd: *The Church of England in the 20th Century*, London, Vol. 1, 1946, p.111. He wrote: 'Longworth Rectory is one of the houses which will always be remembered in Anglican history.' I hope so: but I wonder? I am trying to have it so. Scott Holland, writing in *Commonwealth* after J.R. Illingworth's death, declared: 'Longworth became for us the symbol of all that was deepest in our lives. It acquired a

personality of its own. It stood for a certain habit of mind, for an intellectual type, for a spiritual fellowship.' Cited in: A. Mansbridge: *Edward S. Talbot and Charles Gore*, London, 1935, p.75.

14 Frederick Denison Maurice (1805–72), whose career enshrined many of the issues and problems of the Victorian Church, of Christian social conscience and the interpretation of the historic faith, published *The Religions of the World and Their Relation to Christianity*, London, 1842. He was ready to see extensive affinities between his faith and Buddhism (p.187) and saw 'denunciations of others as concealing a shallow faith.' (p.210)

15 W.H. Vanstone: *Love's Endeavour, Love's Expense. The Response of Being to the Love of God*, London, 1977, and the poem on pp.119–20. See also Chap. 9 below.

16 See Intro. note 7, note 8 above and: D.M. Baillie: *God Was in Christ*, London, 1948.

17 After his death and to commemorate his quality a triennial T.H. Green Moral Philosophy Prize was established in Oxford. From Beirut I submitted my essay on the assigned topic for 1947, namely: 'Morality and Religion.' The award of the Prize just as we were leaving Beirut made possible the 6 terminal fees required by the D. Phil regulations without which I could not have embarked on residence at Longworth.

18 R.G. Collingwood's remark – he being a notable Oxford philosopher of history and metaphysician – underlines how unusual amid Oxford's 'specialisms' was T.H. Green's versatility of mind.

19 Stephen Paget: *Henry Scott Holland: Memoirs and Letters*, London, 1921, 2nd, ed, pp.65–67.

20 Charles Gore, ed. *Lux Mundi*, London, 1890, pp.3, 5, 44 and 45.

21 *Ibid.* pp.202–05.

Chapter 3: A Time to Embrace

1 *Personal Recollections*, ed. R. Rhees, London, 1931, p.116.

2 A.R. Vidler: *Scenes from a Clerical Life*, London, 1977, p.40. 'There was probably a month or so when I was the youngest clergyman in the Anglican Communion'

3 William Shakespeare: *Love's Labours Lost*, Act 5, sc. 2, lines 576–79.

4 The other deacons were Cyril Ollier, who spent most of his ministry in the Dioceses of Chester and Lichfield, and Samuel Bird, whom I was to meet again in 1956 as the Chaplain at Izmir, Turkey. His sons were contemporary with ours at Rossall School, in Lancashire. In 1986 at his Vicarage in Horspath, Oxford, he arranged a renewal of vows Service in St Giles' Church where 'we three' came together again.

5 *The Poems of John Donne*, ed. H.J.C. Grierson, Oxford, 1933, pp.319–20.

6 Alice Meynell: (1847–1922), *The Poems*, London, 1940, p.179, 'To the Mother of Christ, the Son of Man.'

7 This seems to be the import of the story. *Barakah*, or 'a virtue with blessing and protection in it' was thought to be present for 'tapping' by the touch of the suppliant on any locus of sanctity, or a touch therefrom. It was, and is, familiar in the lands of the Bible and survived in England as a property of royalty until the reign of Queen Anne.

8 Among the Examining Chaplains was R.V.H. Burne, Michael Ramsey and M.A. Newbolt. The last made an interesting comment on my observation in a sermon that 'no one is interested in the vicissitudes of Hebrew national life in our modern world.' He suggested that 'we belong to the people of God. Abraham is our forefather. We ought to emphasize the *domesticity* of the Bible to *us*. It is God's dealing – not with a dead and gone race of Semites – but with our forefathers.' He had touched on a Biblical issue which was to loom large in my future cares. I wonder how far the Jewish tradition would accept Newbolt's account of us in Christ. Alas, I have no extant record of Michael Ramsey's examining perceptions.

9 Gustave Thibon wrote of her 'Though utterly and entirely detached from her tastes and needs, she was not detached from her detachment.' Indeed, when the 'ego' was 'effaced' it was also 'underlined.' See J.M. Perrin & G. Thibon: *Simone Weil as We*

Knew Her, London, 1953, p.119. 'The way she mounted guard round her emptiness still showed a terrible pre-occupation with herself.'

10 Emily Dickinson: *Collected Poems*, 3 Vols. Cambridge, Mass. 1958, Poem no. 1225.

11 See Chap. 2, note 19, p.63.

12 See Oliver C. Quick: *The Christian Sacraments*, London, 1932, 4th ed. pp.220–28. He argued: 'If the Reserved Sacrament is simply an external aid to devotion in more or less the same way as a crucifix or an icon, we are led to the conclusion that even in the Eucharist it is essentially no more than that.' He stressed as part of the confusion in the whole situation that 'the interest of many Anglo-Catholics is so exclusively fixed on the worship, not the doctrine, of Catholicism, that they seem willing to adopt the most apparently un-Catholic of doctrines, if only it can be represented as affording ground for the external practice of a Catholic devotion.'

13 It was all a conspicuous – and in the aftermath, sadly, an unhappy – instance of how faith and theology must discern wisely where, and on what case, they should 'contend for truth' and how a true 'contention' is alert on *all* fronts.

14 William Shakespeare: *The Complete Works*, Ed. W.J. Craig, Oxford, 1894, p.1135, 'The Phoenix and the Turtle.'

15 Dylan Thomas: *Collected Letters*, ed. Paul Ferris, London, 1985, p.39.

16 Many of Dickens' women are seen by critics as nothing more than ideal 'sisters,' too gentle, too pliant, too sweet, ever to be genuine 'wives.' He discerned better than his critics. How neatly, too, he outwitted those who demanded 'ever after' happy endings when, for example – reluctantly under pressure – he re-wrote the end of *Great Expectations* but only satisfied them with a deliberate ambiguity which retained the possibility he had always intended. 'I saw no shadow of another parting from her.' No one could accuse Dickens of the cynicism which sees all marriage as egoism.

17 Ignatius: 'The Epistle to the Ephesians,' in ed. J.B. Lightfoot, *The Apostolic Fathers*, Vol. ii, Part ii, London, 1889, pp.51–52.

18 Thomas à Kempis: *The Imitation of Christ*, ed. C. Bigg, London, 1898. The sentiment runs throughout: note esp. pp.228, 237, and 263: 'When Thou art present all things are delightful, when absent all things are wearisome.'

19 Note 6 above, p.123, 'To the Body.'

20 James Joyce: *Dubliners*, Penguin ed, London, 1956, pp.210–11. Or one might well say with Browning, 'I always see the Garden and God there, a'making man's wife, and – my lesson learned – the value and significance of flesh I can't unlearn ten minutes afterwards.' – or even lengthening years.

21 Ed. Ronald Gray: *Poems of Goethe*, Cambridge, 1966, trans. By G. Theissen, p.170.

Chapter 4: The Sifting East

1 *The Poems of Gerard Manley Hopkins*, ed. W.H. Gardner & N.H. MacKenzie, Oxford, 4th ed. 1970, p.52, Stanza 4 of 'The Wreck of the Deutschland.'

2 In that Europa was, in Greek myth, a Phoenician princess whom the god, Zeus, in disguise as a whule bull, took off to Crete, from which episode her name later was bestowed on a whole continent.

3 Robert Frost: *Complete Poems*, New York, 1949, p, 131, 'The Road not Taken.'

4 Alfred Lord Tennyson: *Complete Works*, London, 1920, p.103, 'Locksley Hall.' On prejudices about alleged prejudice see, e.g.: Edward Said: *Orientalism*, New York, 1978.

5 See, for example, the carefully researched survey of English missionary enterprise by A.L. Tibawi but entitled: *British Interests in Palestine, 1800–1901: A Study of Religious and Educational Enterprise*, London, 1961, to imply that all was politically motivated, 'interests' being a 'colonialist' term. Tibawi published in similar terms: *American Interests in Syria: A Study of Educational, Literary and Religious Work*, London, 1966.

6 Henry W. Longfellow in a poem entitled 'The Day is Done.' The notion that all 'Arabs' were 'nomads' who could always move, or be moved, on played some part in the Zionist idea of 'a land without a people.'

7 G. Basetti-Sani: *Louis Massignon: Christian Ecumenist*, ed. and trans. by A.H. Cutler, Chicago, 1974, p.116.

8 Henry James: cited from: Peter Cone, *An Outline of American Literature*, London, 1986, p.95.

9 Until the Second World War 'Near East' was the preferred term both in Britain and the U.S.A. (e.g. 'The Near East Foundation'). The usage 'Middle East' seems to have emerged in the forties.

10 H.H. Jessup: *Fifty-Three Years in Syria*, New York, 1910, 2 vols., Vol. 2, p.592. See also Elie Kedourie: *Arabic Political Memoirs and Other Studies*, London, 1972, pp.59–72. Kedourie takes a jaundiced view, holding that Universities exist only to 'increase knowledge' and have no business with either 'faith' or 'service.' He shows little awareness of the complexities faced in Beirut, nor of the credentials and criteria of 'increased knowledge.'

11 Cited from Stephen B. Penrose, Jr.: *That They May Have Life: The Story of the A.U.B. 1899–1941*, New York, 1941, p.181.

12 'Unravelling' in both senses, of deciphering mystery and the taking apart of an identity.

13 Note 11. pp.292–93, in his inaugural address, in June, 1923. He stressed that 'religion is not an ulterior aim of education . . . it is the consciousness of a spiritual power, controlling life and making good . . . The institution forms a link between East and West; a channel for the exchange of ideas between the two. Our University does not champion the cause of any one sect but she does bind on her armour to champion the cause of the spiritual.'

14 The Alliance Israelite Universelle was founded by French Jews in 1860 to foster education in Palestine and North Africa. Some six hundred thousand children passed through its schools in its first century. It was not Zionist prior to the rise of Nazism but Isidore Cahen (1826–1902), one of its founders, stressed that Jews, forming neither a nation, nor a race, nor a freemasonry, nor a commercial association, nevertheless had the right to consolidate themselves to resist injustice. Education, in the French mould, was crucial to this end.

15 See: Issa Boullata: *Women of the Fertile Crescent: Modern Poetry by Arab Women*, Washington, 1978.

16 *Adwa' Jadidah 'ala Jibran*, Beirut, 1966.

17 *The Criterion* being the literary Journal Eliot edited and inspired and, with essays like *The Idea of a Christian Society* (1939), fulfilled his spiritual migration in an Englishness through which American birth could believe itself retrieved beyond the malaise which *The Wasteland* (1922) had depicted as the post-war reality of the human condition in European terms.

18 See Issa Boullata in *The Journal of Arabic Literature*, Vol. iv, No. 1, 1973, 'The Beleaguered Unicorn: A Study of Tawfiq Sayigh,' Also my *The Arab Christian*, London, 1992, pp.261–65, with data on Arabic sources.

19 The reference is to 'the pool of five porches' in John 5.1–9.

20 Inasmuch as, in the late fifties and the sixties, U.S. Presidents were appointed at the A.U.B. who, far from being free of State Department nexus, had in fact found their careers in government service, i.e. Paul Leonard (1957–61) and Normal Burns (1961–65). This had never been true prior to those years and gave some ground for anti-U.S. suspicions. See My: *The Arab Christian*, London, 1992, pp. 222f.

21 Intellectual effort on the part of Muslim thinkers to be positive in response to issues that often had their sources in western culture was always attended by the political urge to be at the same time resistant. 'Modernists' were so easily dubbed as 'westernized' – a reproach well calculated, if not, at least, to deter them, certainly to compromise them. It always seemed to me that it was right for western Christian intellectuals both keenly to appreciate this nexus and do everything to 'dewesternize' their relations in a common humanity. Much western Islamic scholarship quite failed to do this.

22 John Donne: *The Poems*, Oxford, 1933, ed. H.J.C. Grierson, 'The Triple Fool,' p.15. Perhaps the title of the poem should have deterred my use of its analogy.

23 Marshall Hodgson: *The Venture of Islam*, Chicago, 1976, Vol. 1, p.29.

24 Surah 9.118. *Malja'* is well known in current Arabic for an air-raid 'shelter.' The context has to do with divine mercy bearing with deservers of divine judgement.

Only by 'repair' *unto* God could one find refuge *from* God. In Christian terms it was a paradox yet one which in no way threatened unity. Indeed it was only because of the oneness of God that the two aspects of the divine with the human could be understood. Reflection seemed to bring one close to a place or a point – like the cross of Christ – where 'mercy and truth,' i.e. pardon and 'righteousness' had 'met together', but only because God was that sort of God.

25 *The Event of the Qur'an*, London, 1971 and *The Mind of the Qur'an*, London, 1973, the offshoot of my study time in Cambridge England, as Bye-Fellow of Gonville and Caius College.

26 William Wordsworth: *The Excursion*, Book iv, lines 960–68.

27 For long years the Bible Society's Agent in Istanbul, a fine scholar and an enthusiast for all things Turkish. See: C.E. Padwick; *Call to Istanbul*, London, 1958.

28 Ed. Richard N. Frye: *Islam and the West*, S. Gravenhage, 1957. It was there that I met the Ahmadi scholar, Muhammad Zafrullah Khan, with whom I had much converse in later years both in Lahore, London and West Yorkshire which he frequently visited.

29 See his *Memories and Meanings*, privately printed, U.S.A., 1985. and his major work: *God of Justice: Ethical Doctrine in the Qur'an*, Leiden, 1960, in which he developed 'contextual exegesis,' studying pivotal terms in the light of their actual usage in the text. 'That which is eminently worthy to be worshipped' was his criterion of a true theism, the reason why faith in the Incarnation could not be excluded from any doctrine of the divine and of divine 'unity,' if one were to be loyal to the Islamic repudiation of *shirk*. i.e. forbearing to worship what did not deserve to be.

30 The loyal Egyptian verger at All Saints' Cathedral, 'Aziz Wasif', later ordained and becoming 'Canon Wasif,' had been imprisoned and roughly handled in anti-British resentment. Everything was at a nadir. I was able to report to the absent Bishop and try to hearten my brethren. It was all in all a parlous time.

31 My Bishop in Jerusalem, Weston Henry Stewart, who was in U.K. throughout that time, later reproved me, insisting that if any 'statements' were to be made they should come from him. I explained the acute local tension at the time. He contented himself with a double negative, namely that 'he was not sure that the invasion was not correct.' Alack. A long letter from Canon Max Warren about the fine stand of Hugh Gaitskell and others at that time as well as the resignation of Anthony Nutting (whom Conservatives, in character, never forgave) helped greatly at that woeful juncture.

32 'A theology of attention' was an apt concept, coined – I think – at that time by Max Warren.

33 See an example in *The Muslim World Quarterly*, Vol. xlviii, No. 3, 1958, pp.237–47. 'A West African Catechism.'

34 Surah 12.21: *Allaha ghalibun 'ala amrihi*. The phrase comes in the story of Joseph after he was safely established in the house of his Egyptian master. 'God prevails in the purpose He intends' might take the graphic sense of the Arabic.

35 French, after ten years as Bishop and Cathedral builder in Lahore, had repaired to Muscat as a lone emissary of Christ. A septuagenarian, he soon succumbed to heat and exhaustion. His grave lay, with sundry lost mariners, on a tiny cove between the cliffs, only accessible by row-boat.

36 The great Maidan, flanked by the city's two most superb mosques, Masjid al-Shah, and Lutfallah, and by the Ali Gapu, where the Safavids had assembled court to watch the games. Bishop Dehqani-Tafti used the words for the title of his eloquent autobiographical study: *Design of My World*, London, 1959.

37 The former in 1952 to a summer Parish in Baddeck, on Cape Breton Island, Nova Scotia, the latter in 1955 to Green Mountain Falls, among the hills west of Colorado Springs where I had month-long care of the local Church. Christopher was much interested in overnight motels.

Chapter 5: Forfeit in Canterbury

1 Christopher Marlowe: *The Jew of Malta*, Act 5, Sc, 5, lines 36–38.

2 The Grace Cup belonged to John Foche (alias Essex) who was the last Abbot (1522–

38). It is in the form of a coconut raised on a round pedestal with, originally, a silver gilt foot, on the rim of which is the inscription: 'Velcome ye be, dryng for charitie.' It would seem to have been made in 1505.

3 Bede: *Ecclesiastical History of the English People*, Chap. 30. See note 15 below.

4 See R.J.E. Boggis: *A History of St Augustine's College*, Canterbury, 1907, and G.F. Maclear: *St Augustine's, Canterbury, Its Rise, Ruin and Restoration*, London, 1888 and: Henry Bailey: *Twenty-Five Years at St Augustine's College: Letter to Late Students*, Canterbury, 1873. Also C.R. Peers and A.W. Clapham in *Archaeologia*, Vol, lxxvii, 1926, pp.201–18, 'St Augustine's Abbey Church, Canterbury.' Also Margaret Sparks: *Archaeologia Cantiana*, Vol. c, 1984; pp.325–44: 'The Recovery and Excavation of the St Augustine's Abbey Site, 1844–1947.'

5 See Chapter 6. Newman recorded what he called 'the Jerusalem scheme' of which he had first heard in Rome in 1833, in *Apologia Pro Vita Sua*, as having been enacted by Parliament on October 5, 1841, 'enabling the consecration as Bishops of British, or foreign, citizens . . . in any foreign country' without the usual oaths of allegiance and supremacy. (Everyman ed. p.142). For the first time this made British soil not necessary to Anglican episcopacy, except for what American Episcopalians had already done.

6 *The Cambridge Review*, Vol. lxii, No. 1530, June 6th, 1941, pp.486–88 printed the sermon. See also W.F. France: *The Oversea Episcopate, Centenary History of the Colonial Bishoprics Fund, 1842–1941*, London, 1941 (a pamphlet)

7 *The East and West Review*, London, Vol. ii, No.1, January, 1936, pp.5–12. France returned to the theme on the eve of the opening of the Central College in the same Journal, Vol. xviii, No. 4, October, 1952, pp.123–27.

8 G.V. Bennett in *Preface to Crockford*, 1988, pp.61–66 wrote pointedly about what he saw as the English 'frame of reference' of Anglicanism and implied a dismay about aberrations from it. The Central College had been wrestling with this issue but in a far more trusting and hospitable mind about the role – and the authenticity – of the dispersion. The faith could only well be in the care, thought Bennett, of those who could *theologize* and, preferably English *churchmen*.

9 Stephen Paget: *Henry Scott Holland; Memoirs and Letters*, London, 1921, 2nd ed. p.86.

10 *Lambeth Conference, 1948*, London, 1948, p.48.

11 *Lambeth Conference, 1958*, London, 1958, pp.114–15. It did so approve. (Italics mine)

12 Dickens used a nice ambiguity in order to allow his readers a happy assumption, while hinting that it might not be so. We was both yielding, and not yielding, to the popular demand that stories should end well without fail. The savour is obvious here.

13 D.H.S. Cranage: *The Home of the Monk*, Cambridge, 1926, p.23. Intriguing is the provision in the Rule that all should share in 'counsel,' since 'often it is to a younger person that God reveals what is best.' p.14.

14 *Ibid.* p.18.

15 See note 3 above. Gregory added the thoroughly Anglican proviso about retention of the temples, namely: 'if they are well built.' He was less so in proposing 'holy relics' as somehow assisting the relegation of the past. Would they not rather serve a lingering superstition? He foresaw the newly converted English (to whose 'affairs he had been giving careful thought') as 'flocking more readily to their accustomed resorts,' while coming 'to know and adore the true God.' A festival to Holy Martyrs, he suggested, would displace 'Oxen to demons'

16 Edward Carpenter: *Archbishop Fisher: His Life and Times*, London, 1991, p.461.

17 See Stephen F. Bayne: *An Anglican Turning-Point, Documents and Interpretations*, Austin, Texas, 1964, pp.23, 42–43, 54, 62 (where Bayne notes 'in 1961 we finally met the minimum needs in full *three years* after the Bishops at Lambeth had agreed what the minimum need was.') 79 ('that remarkable institution').

18 Note 16, p.462.

19 Namely Alden Kelley, first Sub-Warden, Edward Hughes, of Caribbean experience, Owen Brandon in Pastoral Psychology and myself, Stuart Snell had wide experience as a colonial officer in Africa (later Bishop of Croydon)

20 Owen Chadwick: *Michael Ramsey: A Life*, Oxford, 1991, p.278 He writes, tersely. 'It was valued . . . expense had to be justified.' 'The large deficit' to which Chadwick

refers arose from the reneging on pledges constitutionally made. He makes the valid point about western post-graduate study requiring different handling but ignores the whole concept of the Central College (to which he does not refer by its name) as aiming at community in spirituality and not only in scholarship. The churches in Asia and Africa and the Caribbean were not going to be enriched by an accumulation of western Ph.D's. He adds: 'To this day there is disagreement as to whether this (i.e. closure) was a disaster.' The foregoing tries to supply the evidence.

21 William Shakespeare: *Timon of Athens*, Act 4, Sc.2, lines 17–22.

22 Robert Frost: *Complete Poems*, New York, 1962, 'Reluctance,' p.43.

23 The story-study of this Chapter has some parallel in *Anglican and Episcopal History*, Vol. lix, No. 2, June 1990, pp.224–42.

24 Perhaps the University of Kent at Canterbury, but primarily the King's School, Canterbury, which some few years later added the whole to its domain within the Cathedral precincts, after a brief period of occupancy by fourth year ordinands from King's College, London, under the Wardenship of Canon Anthony Harvey, now of Westminster Abbey.

25 A.N. Whitehead: *Religion in the Making*, Cambridge, 1930, p.9.

26 Theodore Roethke of Northern Michigan, a latter day American Wordsworth nourished horticulture, with a keen sense of landscape and the rural scene. See *The Lost Son and Other Poems*, 1948.

27 Dorothy Sayers: *The Zeal of Thy House*, New York, 1937, quoted from *Religious Drama 1*, New York, 1957, pp.333–34.

Chapter 6: Unease in Zion

1 Robert Browning: *Poetical Works*, Oxford, 1940, p.422.

2 The versions, in sequence, after Coverdale, are: Moffatt, R.S.V., American Bible, Jerusalem Bible. See also: *The Psalms*, trans. H. Hartwell, London, 1959, 5th ed., p.749.

3 They were complicated further by the role of the missionary societies with their structures of decision, parallel to, or independent of, the Bishopric. These are carefully studied in the perversely titled work of A.L. Tibawi: *British Interests in Palestine, 1800–1901: A Study of Religious and Educational Enterprise*, London, 1961. A.J. Arberry, ed.: *Religion in the Middle East*, Vol.1, Cambridge, 1969, pp.570–95, summarizes the Anglican story. See also *The Arab Christian: A History in the Middle East*, London, 1992, pp.131–36.

4 See: George Appleton: *Unfinished, Remembers and Reflects*, London, 1990, pp.170–73, where he tells, not of the 'agenda' but of the circumstances of his own acceptance of the task. It was his standing in Perth and his age which, in the context, made him the proper appointee, though he was older on taking up the task than his predecessor, Campbell MacInnes had been when he laid it down.

5 Three consecrating bishops were the legal minimum, but they sufficed! – George Appleton, Najib Qub'ain and Hasan Dehqani-Tafti. My *The Mind of the Qur'an* was affectionately inscribed to them in 1973.

6 The Teggart buildings, named after their originator, were designed as local bastions to help ensure the security of the Palestine Police in their increasingly perilous operations up to 1939 and after 1945.

7 Borrowing the title of Elizabeth Monroe's book, London, 1963, an excellent study of the Mandatory's policies, dilemmas and growing impotence between 1914 and 1956.

8 See the reproduction of the document in Harold Wilson: *The Chariot of Israel, Britain, America and the State of Israel*, London, 1981, opposite p.188. Balfour was to write almost two years later to Curzon: 'Zionism . . . is . . . of far profounder import than the desires and prejudices of the seven hundred thousand Arabs who now inhabit that ancient land.' Ten years later, Weizmann wrote that 'the Balfour Declaration was built on on air.' (*American Bar Assn. Journal*, xliii, 1957, p.522.) He saw nothing 'airy' about what would be built on it.

9 In the Shakespearean sense of 'enlargements' (*Henry V*, Act iv, Sc, 3, line 50), but also in the familiar sense of 'increments' which were always with Israel.
10 Elie Wiesel: *Legends of Our Time*, New York, 1968, p.233.
11 *London*, 1982. Sadly, delay between writing and publishing meant that the invasion of Lebanon by Israeli forces in the summer of 1982 had no mention when it was so conspicuously relevant. However, the over-all analysis was tragically confirmed.
12 Quoted from Flavius Josephus: *The Jewish War* in Yigael Yadin: *Masada*, London, 1966, p.232. See note 11 above, p.127 f. for a fuller discussion of the implications of the retreat of the Zealots under Eleazar. Having begun the War, first the city, then the Temple, then the wilderness, then the fortress, proved not to allow the inviolability they sought and which they assumed God meant them to enjoy. When the wind turned around the fire, they had to conclude that they had misread divine intent. God's final verdict on their action disconcerted their entire belief in it.
13 As noted in Chapter 4 this was the hope of his educational projects.
14 See Chap. 4 above. If he had not stopped the car to pick up a Jewish stranger the level-crossings might have timed no danger.
15 The name was long debated and was a careful solution to a nest of problems. 'The Jewish State' would have alienated diaspora Jews, as would 'Judea.' 'Israel' satisfied the secularists but left room for the Orthodox to think a theocracy. Non-Jews inside could be called 'Israelis' in a secular sense. The Declaration of Independence was free to talk of 'the Rock of Israel' as its mention of God. But the name 'Israel' evaded the question: 'Who is the Jew?' Would the 'ordinary' Jew still be so only spiritually as in the ghetto? The relation between 'state' and 'Rabbinate' would be ambiguous. See Chap. 7. The naming of 'Israel' made for acute difficulty among Arab Christians by compounding its Biblical connotation. See *The Arab Christian*, note 3 above, Chap. 10.
16 July, 1947. One of them, Clifford Martin, had a Jewish mother which, by Rabbinic law made him a Jew. Had it been known it would not have saved him.
17 See the translation of his Russian text: 'On the Iron Wall' in Wric Silver: *Begin: A Biography*, London, 1984, p.12.
18 To be 'de-nativized' in this theocratic way was radical disavowal of any 'Palestinianism' that could relate to any 'Palestine.' In varying ways, Zionist theory and polity have reduced to 'non-entity' what they also combated and perceived therein no contradiction.
19 The logic of political Zionism stemmed bitterly from diaspora experience among the nations as proving that these left no dignified or viable occasion for Jews to be themselves. 'Cheerful prognostications of world brotherhood' had perished. 'Zionism faced this reality, explained it, and offered a solution that worked.' (See note 20 following, p.164.) It is true that Theodor Herzl, at one point, allowed that 'the land' could be anywhere but the pull of Palestine was irresistible. There could be no other place for 'home' and 'state.'
20 See Arthur Hertzberg: *The Zionist Idea, A Historical Analysis and Reader*, New York, 1973, p.319.
21 *Ibid*. p.319.
22 Jacob Neusner: *Torah through the Ages*, Philadelphia, 1990, pp.153–65. It was odd to see the *sole* condition of survival in the will to Zionism, given that Neusner's entire scholarship was pursued with the security of American academia.

Chapter 7: A Christian Judaica

1 Christopher Dawson: *The Formation of Christendom*, New York, 1967, p.17. How blandly the inferiorization of Judaism by displacement can be assumed may be cited even in sensitive writers like Ninian Smart and S. Konstantine in: *Christian Systematic Theology in World Context*, London, 1991, pp.388–89. 'The Christian vision centers in Christ, of course, and there are special meanings in the Jewish life as it flowed from the dim past towards the foundation of the Church.'

2 See *Troubled by Truth*, Durham, 1992, Chap. 6, pp.108–26 for my perception of Rabbi Abraham Heschel.

3 Ignatius of Antioch to the Magnesians, in ed. J.B. Lightfoot, *The Apostolic Fathers, Ignatius and Polycarp*, 2nd Book, Vol. 2, London, 1889, Chap. x, p.133

4 Note 2 above, for a discussion of James Parkes, one of the main advocates of the two covenant theme, Chap. 5, pp.91–107.

5 See, for example, Hyam Maccoby: *Paul and Hellenism*, London, 199 , where Paul – so far 'Hellenized' – seems hardly to be a Jew at all. It also prompts heavy accent on 'Jesus the Jew' – an identity which was never in doubt.

6 Yeshayahu Leibowitz: *Judaism, Human Values and the Jewish State*, ed. Eliezer Goldman, Cambridge, Mass, 1992. pp.256–62. See also the dismissal of 'Messianism,' p.9, and how 'Judaism avoids pathos.' p.13.

7 David Hartman: *Conflicting Visions, Spiritual Possibilities of Modern Israel*, New York, 1990, pp.4 and 264.

8 Jacob Neusner: *The Religious Study of Judaism, Description, Analysis and Interpretation*, Vol. 1, New York, 1986, pp.141–42 and 152.

9 Arthur A. Cohen: *The Myth of the Judeo-Christian Tradition*, New York, 1970, pp.30, 33, 211. Cohen regards it as basic to the Jewish faith that the Messianic question remains for ever unanswered. He sees Jesus as 'being pleased to be confused with God' while denying that he is God. (p.206) Happily, he says that the enmity of contra-theological understanding is not absolute before God (p.216): let there be no common tradition! For Eliezer Berkowitz see *Disputation and Dialogue: Readings in Jewish-Christian Encounter*, ed. F.E. Talmage, New York, 1975, pp.284–95 on 'Judaism in the Post-Christian Era.'

10 This was a frequent emphasis in the thought of Martin Buber. Thus, for example, in *Mamre: Essays in Religion*, trans. Greta Hort, Oxford, 1946, p. 18f. 'For us at no definite point in history has a saviour appeared, so that a new redeemed history began with him. Because we have not been stilled by anything which has happened, we are wholly oriented towards the coming of that which shall come.' Cf. also Arthur Cohen: p.xxi. 'Christians must learn to speak . . . to that in the world which is untransformed and unredeemed.' Note 9

11 Gershom Scholem: *The Messianic Idea in Judaism and Other Essays in Jewish Spirituality*, New York., 1971, p.35.

12 See note 10 above, and quoting Robert Browning's question (with 'unredeemed' inserted) from: Poetical Works. Note 1. intro. p.486
It is this concern which probably underlies the degree to which the Messianic theme is now often discounted or marginalized in Jewish thinking, in spite of its obvious relation to basic doctrines of creation, history and divine fidelity to both. Cf. Eliezer Goldman on Rabbi Leibowitz, note 6 above, p.xix. 'Messianic expectations have no genuinely religious significance. At best, the Messianic idea represents an ever receding goal. At worst, as an anticipation of nearby redemption, it disrupts the religious life of the community.' also Jacob Neusner: *Messiah in Context*, Philadelphia, 1984, p.ix. 'Does Judaism present a messianism and may we, therefore, speak of the messianic idea or doctrine of Judaism? The answer . . . is a qualified negative, yielding a flat no!'

13 Howard Kee in Jacob Neusner, ed. *Judaisms and their Messiahs*, Cambridge, 1987, pp.192–93.

14 Echoing a frequent note of Elie Wiesel in his numerous works in post-Holocaust study. Cf. the Christian poet, Ernesto Cardenal said the same in *Love in Practice: The Gospel in Solentiname*, tr. D.D. Walsh, London, 1977, p.35, adding: 'That is why he is called "Emmanuel."'

15 J. Leslie Houlden: *Jesus, A Question of Identity*, London, 1992, p.60.

16 Martin Hengel: *Between Jesus and Paul*, tr. J. Bowden, London, p.95. See also the same author's *The Hellenization of Judea in the 1st Century after Christ*, tr. J. Bowden, London, 1989.

17 I made some effort to study the Messianic motif in the ministry of Jesus and its origins in his 'mind' in *What Decided Christianity*, Worthing, 1989. Note also how the precedent of Numbers 27.17 about 'sheep without a shepherd' aligns with Jesus in

Matthew 9.36 and that same verse with 2 Esdras 8.15: 'The people for whom I am in pain . . . About Israel I agonize, about the seed of Israel I am troubled.' Above all, there the Servant Songs of Deutero-Isaiah.

18 See note 17, Chap.2, pp. 51-68.

19 The issue here is one we meet again in Islam where the instinct to 'isolate' God in sheer sovereignty and thus preserve worship from any taint of 'idolatry' is at odds with the relational significance without which transcendence could have no meaning and would, therefore, never require to be 'immune.' In that sense a non-incarnational theism is a contradiction in terms, meaning by 'incarnational' 'world-related,' 'having ways and means of human concern,' and 'undertaking what fulfills being.'

20 As in Jacob Neusner (note 8 above) when, p.142 he writes of 'Matthew's Pharisees as hypocrites and John's Jews as murderers' 'poisoning Christian conscience.' This kind of hyperbole distorts a situation that needs more careful exploration.

21 The term has come to be used in study of the matrix of the Fourth Gospel and the factors in its composition. See, *inter alia*, most recently, John Ashton: *Understanding the Fourth Gospel*, Oxford, 1991.

22 Always so named to demonstrate that Zionism knows nothing of 'aggression.' The pioneers envisaged a state without an army.

23 John Donne: *Sermons*, ed. E.M. Simpson and G.R. Potter, London, 1953, Vol. vi, p.344, where he insists 'It was so to the Jews and it was so to the Gentiles too . . . Christ hath excommunicated no nation, no shire, no house, no man. He gave none of his ministers leave to say to anyone: "Thou art not redeemed."'

24 The truth of these common denominators was argued more fully in *The Privilege of Man*, London, 1968, and in a contribution in ed. A.J. Arberry: *Religion in the Middle East*, Vol. 2, Cambridge, 1969, pp.365–76.

25 A point further explored in note 2 above, with Heschel references.

26 The passage Zechariah 8.22–23, has a rich quality. The 'seizing' is very urgent, like David clutching his lion's beard. The 'skirt' symbolism indicates a plea for admission into fellowship, as in Ruth. It also knows that there is a reluctance to be overcome.

27 Quoted from Jacob Neusner: *Between Time and Eternity: The Essence of Judaism*, Belmont, California, 1975, p.98.

28 Peter Conn: *Literature in America*, Cambridge, 1989, p.95.

29 William Shakespeare: *Richard II*. Act 3, Sc. 2, lines 170–72.

30 Arnold Zweig: in *Caravan*, trans. John Manifold, London, 1962, p.278. Sadly, it rarely happens that way. Shakespeare's Shylock was too tragically broken – and bankrupted – to be brother to all others likewise wronged.

31 One has to phrase it this way as one may wonder whether the invasion of Palestine under Joshua was really as bloody as the Book of Joshua makes it. But that the writers wrote it that way tells what they thought it should have been. Could it be said that Jewry set the conceptual framework in which enmity itself was nourished?

32 Note 2, above, pp.74–90.

33 Vine De Loria: *Custer Died for Your Sins*. 1969, p.175. He knew well the point he was making for he wrote a book 'God is Red,' (Indian).

Chapter 8: The Tribunal of Islam

1 Though some of the meanings at stake were latent in the first Christian centuries, they only come into the form we are here concerned with, when Islam emerges. It is necessarily to have 'historically' here to safeguard the point that Islam believes it to be 'from patriarchal times' as *islam*, or 'human submission to God.' This, however, is only institutionalized with the Qur'an, Ramadan, the *Shari'ah*, as 'Islam,' with the time of Muhammad.

2 Frithjof Schuon: *The Transcendent Unity of Religions*, London, 1953, p.131.

3 See: Issam al-Said and Ayse Parman: *Geometric Concepts in Islamic Art*, London, 1976, and Titus Burckhardt: *Art of Islam, Language and Meaning*, London, 1976.

4 *Iltizam* is the action of 'pressing the self against the stone,' *multazam* is the name of the place on the Ka'bah, between the door and the eastern corner. The action of

'embrace' belongs with the hope of *barakah*, the 'blessing' that associates in points of great sanctity and has to be gained by necessary physical contact. The verse in Surah 17.13 has to do with the omen of destiny 'necessarily attaching' to the individual.

5 The second is in fact found as a definition of 'theology,' in W. Schmithals: *An Introduction to the Theology of Rudolf Bultmann*, London, trans. John Bowden, 1967, p.46.

6 This being the Qur'an's reiterated phrase by which to refer to the Creator. The plural in respect of 'the heavens' has rich significance for the exegetes as for the mystics.

7 The verse is exactly in line with the Qur'an's criterion of 'gratitude' as the due form of human recognition of divine grace and with its wry comment on the human scene: 'Most of them give no thanks.' (10.60 *et al.*)

8 Some effort to study how Quranic content might have been fitted to different context was made in my *Returning to Mount Hira'*, London, 1994 – Muhammad, there and then in Mecca/Medina and Muhammad here and now.

9 Quoted from Najmeh Najafi: *Persia is My Heart*, New York, 1953, p.113.

10 Shams al-Din Hafiz, (d. 1389), most justly renowned of Persian poets, from Shiraz. *Hifz* means the 'preserving' (lit.) of the Qur'an by committing it to heart in its entirety: hence *hafiz*, one who does so. On the poet see A.J. Arberry: *Hafiz*, Cambridge, 1947.

11 Verses on the theme of 'adoption' are 17.111, 19.35, 25.2, 39.4. The word is often used of pagans 'adopting' lords and 'gods' at their deluded whim. Where 'adopting' is used of Allah, as being always reprobated, the singular, 'a son,' is the object of the verb, differentiating it from '*the* Sonship' the Christian faith understands, where 'Son' and 'servant' are interchangeable terms and denote, not random 'taking up' into divine status, but an essential outgoing of divine grace which, for eternal ends, employs the human means.

12 That this oft-quoted clause, 'underiving, underived,' is denying, as impossible with God, the contingency of human generations in their sequence, seems clear if – as is the consensus of the Surah – it is taken as enlarging, or elucidating, the meaning of the previous clause, that 'God is *Al-Samad*' (used only here). For *Al-Samad* means 'One who has all resources self-sufficiently.' It is of the completeness of those divine resources, not some lack or loss of them, that the Incarnation tells.

13 When Surah 112 concludes with 'and there is none like to Him,' we all agree. For it is precisely what that single 'likeness' is that Christians believe they are given to understand in the human terms that any human understanding needs and can only be had by divine granting.

14 This point seems clear from the Qur'an's words about those (pagans) who 'did not esteem God an esteeming that was true,' or who, more freely translated, 'did not have the right measure of God.' There is implicit idolatry in a false theology no less than in a crude superstition, when things are wrongly 'associated' with God. (Cf Surahs 6.91, 22.74 and 39.67.)

15 See Browning's poem 'Easter Day' where it is suggested that the Christian doctrine of the Incarnation has in it 'too much love.'

16 Surah 2.2. The term *raibah* here may mean that the Book has nothing to arouse distrust, or nothing that requires question. Surah 3.7, however, notes that there are passages, *mutashabihat*, in the Qur'an – 'allegorical' or 'non-categorical', about which readers might have doubtful ideas.

17 Isma'il al-Faruqi in his *Christian Ethics*, Montreal, 1967, did equip himself with careful reading in the field but brought little scholarly sympathy to all that the New Testament requires of the reader and the exegete. Much writing on the Gospels and Christology from within the Ahmadiyyah Movement is harshly polemical. Shabbir Akhtar in: *A Faith for All Seasons*, London, 1990, expounding Islam, demonstrates a sense of what Christology is and means to Christians yet pronounces it 'incoherent' and devoid of 'intelligible . . . true metaphysical foundation.' (p.156)

18 S. Petrement in: *A Separate God: The Christian Origins of Gnosticism*, trans. C. Harrison, London, 1991, sees only Gnostic factors in New Testament faith. She writes, in double negative: 'It is not true that Gnosticism cannot be explained on the basis of Christianity.' p.211. It is wise to add: 'Christianity cannot be explained on the basis of Gnosticism.'

19 Could it be that that account was affected by the actual context of Muhammad's Qur'an which, unlike that of the major Biblical prophets and of the ministry of Jesus, had to do with a people being newly addressed in their pagan 'ignorance,' not with a people accused of infidelity to what they had long known. The Qur'an saw all else in its own perspectives, assumed that Jesus' ministry was like Muhammad's and had no occasion to reckon with its real dimensions, its actual content or its dark climax – or of the last only as something calling for the vindication of heavenly rapture since it did not attain, by no fault of Jesus, the 'manifest victory' achieved by Muhammad.

20 It was this lack which made so welcome to me the insights of Muhammad Kamil Husain's *Qaryah Zalimah* noted in the Introduction. While Christology in the Jewish context has had notice in Chap. 7, its more personal expression in my confession will come in Chap. 9.

21 The reference here is to Surah 2.20f where, in heavenly conclave, God announces the appointment of the human 'deputy' in earth. Alone among the angels, Satan refuses to acknowledge the divine purpose or to 'worship' Adam, the creature. Instead he vows to trip and beguile man into sin and thus demonstrate to God the folly of His scheme. It thus becomes our human duty in resistance to Satan's blandishments to 'deny the denier,' And so vindicate God. Far from 'approving Satan's scepticism' a realism about evil only registers how critical are the issues attending on our human dignity.

22 Shabbir Akhtar: *A Faith for all Seasons*, London, 1990, p.169.

23 Surah 90.4 describes man as 'created *fi kabad*,' i.e. 'in trouble.' Exegesis varies as to how this 'unease' should be understood.

24 See note 8 above, the Introduction to *Readings in the Qur'an*, London, 1988, and *The Christ and the Faiths*, London, 1986, Chaps. 2, 3 and 4. See also, note 3 in the Introduction above.

25 Shabbir Akhtar, *Op. cit.* pp.180 and 241, with several verbal echoes of phrases I had myself earlier used. I was grateful indeed that there should be debate: I was only anxious that it should be fully joined.

26 In bold capitals, too! on the tomb of a certain Lord Arran. Perhaps there was some prior 'small print,' but the sentiment is one most mortals have felt, meant, and perhaps perversely made habitual. *Dalal* is the Qur'an's own term for a wilful waywardness, a deviance from divine law.

27 Notably Muhammad Kamil Husain in *City of Wrong*, note 3 above in Introduction, but also deeply self-examining Sufis like Al-Muhasibi, the medieval 'accountant' of his own soul.

28 The *Ummah* is the single 'nation' of Islam, not – as purists insist – properly sundered into separate nation states, especially if these incorporate non-Muslims on roughly equal terms of citizenship. The Caliphate is the institution of 'rule,' in abeyance since 1924, that carried on the political authority of Muhammad after his demise. In the Qur'an, the term *'khalifah'* – apart from a reference to David – has to do only with 'man' as 'deputy' for God in the earth. The political 'deputyship' for Muhammad as ruler has no textual source in the Qur'an.

29 The term has become familiar in contemporary Muslim politics. Its use in the Qur'an denotes the Muslim 'side' in the tensions and conflicts of Islam after the Hijrah to Medina. (Surahs 5.56, 58.22).

30 The Qur'an's view of divine obligation here and elsewhere was fully studied in Chap. 5: 'A Theology Worthy of God,' in *Returning to Mount Hira*', (see note 8 above) pp. and need not be further expounded here.

31 The possibility was closely studied in *Truth and Dialogue*, ed. John Hick, London, 1974, pp.126–139, and also in *The Christ and the Faiths*, London, 1986, in 'Capacities in Revelation,' pp.51–73.

32 I found Christians, for their part, distrustful of my relating prophethood and Incarnation through the theme of divine 'sending,' but they did so only by failing to see the urgent difference between *Shirk* (with which they knew Islam – and we – could have no truck) and some inconceivable dissociation between Creator and creaturehood. Thus, for example, Bishop Michael Nazir Ali, reviewing the relevant

chapter in Hick: *Truth and Dialogue* (note 31 above), wrote: 'This is a very dangerous idea to propound to the Muslim since "association" with God – *shirk* – is the worst possible sin. To the Muslim the Prophet is a mere tool of the transcendent God as an axe is the tool of the carpenter.' However that may be as to 'tooling,' Muhammad is emphatically 'sent.' I was not saying, as the reviewer charged, that Muhammad 'possessed any divinity.' I was saying that by any kind of sending God was 'involved' with mankind. I was hoping it may come to be seen that 'sending' on God's part might include, or need to include, personality as well as speech and that, either way, the divine was employing the human and 'signifying' (the Qur'an's own word) by doing so.

33 As in the poem by W.H. Vanstone, in his *Love's Endeavour, Love's Expense: The Response of Being to the Love of God*, London, 1977, p.120.
'Thou art God: no monarch Thou
Thron'd in easy state to reign.
Thou art God, whose arms of love,
Aching, spent, the world sustain.'

34 As noted by Shabbir Akhtar, *op. cit*, notes 17 and 22, p.157.

35 The pain of the other concept of a divine spectator of human history to whose absolute power its claims are irrelevant. Also the weariness of suspicion and ill-will fortified against all fair meeting and pre-occupied with a spirit of rejection and enmity. See, for example, Ed. A. Hussain, R. Olson and J. Qureshi: *Orientalism, Islam and Islamists*, London, 1984, pp.203–58, where I am accused of 'an obese certainty fed by the prolonged military supremacy of the West' and lacking in 'radical caring in (my) intentions towards Muslims.' (Re 'obese' my weight is a mere 60 kilos.)

37 As Robert Browning has it throughout his poems and his philosophy in the conviction that
'This world's no . . . blank:
It means intensely, and means good:
To find its meaning is my meat and drink.'
'Fra Lippo Lippi,' in *Poetical Works*, Oxford, 1940, p.431.

Chapter 9: Life's Faith - Conclusion

1 On Muslim understanding of the crucifixion as 'only apparent' see, for example, my *Jesus and the Muslim, An Exploration*, London, 1985, Chapter 6, 'Gethsemane and Beyond,' pp.166–88.

2 See Khalid A. Sulaiman: *Palestine and Modern Arab Poetry*, London, 1984, and Chapter 4 above.

3 *Op. cit*, note 9, Chap. 7, pp.206–07.

4 E.C. Hoskyns in ed. K.K.A. Bell and A. Deismann: *Mysterium Christi*, London, 1930, on 'Jesus the Messiah,' pp.70–71 was perhaps over-stating when he used 'wholly' in 'There is no event or utterance recorded of Jesus which does not wholly proceed from a conception of Messiahship smelted . . . from the ore of the Old Testament.' Otherwise, the point is well taken.

5 Gerhard Kittel in *op. cit.* note 4, pp.34, 41 and 49.

6 Denis E. Nineham in ed. John Hick: *The Myth of God Incarnate*, London, 1977, p.202.

7 Ludwig Wittgenstein: *Culture and Value*, Oxford, 1970, p.32.

8 Samuel Beckett: *Disjecta: Miscellaneous Writings and a Dramatic Fragment*, ed. Ruby Cohn, New York, 1984, p.26.

9 See following Chapter. This is not to suspect or decry the miraculous, to accept which may be part of an authentic faith. It is to say that the real credential lies in *who* Jesus proved to be, not in *how* He was born. There are, of course, serious problems about the translation 'virgin' for *almah* in Isaiah 7.14, where motherhood in virginity was not the point the prophet was making. See below on 'Christ and Scriptures.'

10 N. Pittenger, ed.: *Christ for Us Today*, London, 1968, p.162. The wording here is not entirely satisfactory but the intention is right. Cf. John V. Taylor: *The Christlike God*, London, 1992. Or, as Robert Browning has it more tersely: 'The Christ in God.'

11 My own effort to explore this issue was *What Decided Christianity*, Worthing, 1989. See also below.
12 Stanley Hauerwas: *The Peacable Kingdom*, London, 1982, p.15.
13 As, for example, Psalm 10.4. where 'God is not in all his thoughts' does not mean mere forgetting but a will to deny divine reality. Cf. Jerusalem Bible: 'There is no God! . . . is the way his mind works.' This theme of 'nullifying' God is uncannily close to the very frequent Quranic phrase: '. . . to the exclusion of God' as a comment on the ungodly.
14 In contradiction to Albert Camus who went on to write that faith also means 'resignation to injustice.' *The Rebel*, note 13, Chap. 1, p.56.
15 Edgar Allen Poe: *Collected Works*, ed. T.O. Mabbott, Cambridge, Mass., 1978, Vol. iii, p.852, story entitled: 'The Black Cat.' Poe may seem a strange witness but the point here is sound enough. It is odd that a mind so perceptive as William Temple's could have thought that 'any man ever chose evil knowing it be evil *for him* is to me quite impossible.' *Nature, Man and God*, London, 1934, p.362.
16 William Shakespeare: *Hamlet*, Act 3, sc.3, lines 146–47.
17 The exhortation in 2 Timothy 1.8 where 'sharing' and 'suffering' are made into a single verb. In Colossians 1.24 Paul links the sufferings he undergoes with those already borne by Christ as being one in the same tally.
18 Martin Hengel: *The Charismatic Leader and His Followers*, trans. J.C.G. Grieg, Edinburgh, 1981, p.86.
19 Retaliation and revenge in effect 'justify' the doer of the wrong, since the 'tit' for 'tat' confirms the state of enmity the originator had assumed, though – from the side of the injured – it may not have been there in the first place.
20 Habakkuk 2.4. Wait in faith for what God's faithfulness will do and, meanwhile, do not consent to evil out of impatience or despair. This principle is more active in the fidelity by which 'suffering servants' hold to righteousness and trust at the cost of tragic loss or travail. In Romans 3.20–24 and 5.1 etc. Paul sees 'being suffered for' in Christ, and trusting that truth, as a receiving of pardon which leads us on to 'good works' – not as a ploy to gain merit but as self-offering in gratitude.
21 Cf. the remarkable passage in Wisdom of Solomon, Chap. 2.10–22 about 'the mysteries of God' in 'blameless souls.'
22 Assuming that the story concerns a Jewish family. It need not since it begins: 'A certain man . . .' and is universal not ethnic.
23 Cf. the warning of Herman Melville in *Moby Dick*, Chap. xlv. 'For God's sake, be economical with your lamps and candles! not a gallon you burn, but at least one drop of man's blood was spilled for it.'
24 Emil Auerbach: *Mimesis*, Princeton, 1973, p.158.

Chapter 10: Faith's Life-Ministry

1 The passage is clearly pivotal. Peter's being reproached as 'not having the mind of God' can only mean that Jesus is caught up in what being 'with that mind' must mean in the Messianic situation which is increasingly presenting itself to him out of the gathering evidence of hostility and rejection attending on his ministry. Withdrawing, for the time being, to a remote place to reflect on that ministry and its logic thus far, Jesus communes with his disciples about his identity and what it must spell. This Messianic repute in the popular mind ('who are they saying I am?') – how does it seem to these intimates of mine? ('Whom say you . . .?') Such is the import of the whole exchange, with Jesus converging on the 'messianic thoughts' of God.
2 Matthew 5.44–45. Divine and human perfection, conjoined here, seems to reproduce Leviticus 19.2: 'Be ye holy, for I am holy.' The basic word *teleios* does not mean, Greek-wise, abstract 'virtue' but rather the Hebraic sense of that which is 'entire.' Entirety proceeds from unreserved fidelity to the command and a total reception of the whole yoke of duty. It implies a task thoroughly undertaken and discharged. Hence the suggestion of 'inclusive' here – in line with the whole case we are making.

The 'You' is plural and emphatic. There is to be no limit to the reach of 'neighbourhood.'

3 See D.M. Kay: *Ante-Nicene Christian Library*, new vol. ix. pp.263–79, The Apology, now longer extant, survived in Syriac and Armenian translations. See also: F. Millar: *Emperor in Roman World*, London, 1977, p.561.

4 *Kerugma* is the Greek New Testament word for affirming and announcing the Gospel – the sequence that moves from event to meaning and from meaning to witness.

5 A term used by Bishop Phillips Brooks, of Massachusetts (1835–1893) See below.

6 Was there a suspicion of divine 'negligence' behind the altar-inscription on which Paul commented in Acts 17.23 about 'the god whom it may concern'? Only in that context, it was thought necessary to placate (with an altar) that disinterested deity in case he/she *was* interested in acknowledgement, if in nothing else. The issue in Graeco-Roman paganism was not whether the gods 'existed' but how far, existing, they 'bothered' about humans. Now belief in God necessarily involves belief in divine concern for the world. Agnosticism is at least consistent in reversing that. To allege 'unconcern' is to mean 'non-entity.'

7 *Letters* [*Selected*] *of Bertrand Russell*: Vol. 1, 'The Private Years, 1884–1914,' ed. Nicholas Griffen, London, 1992, pp.406–11. Personal love can do much to soften atheist rigour and give new dimensions to honesty.

8 Characteristic of his playfully wistful mind and poetry.

9 *The Works of John Ruskin*, ed. E.T. Cook and A. Wedderburn, London, 1903–12, Vol. 35, p.628.

10 Since the parallel from art must not be pressed too far. Theology has to be more objective and responsible about where technology is taking us than Ruskin or other romantics like William Morris contrived to be. See A.E. Housman on Ruskin on 'pollution' in G.L. Watson: *A.E. Housman: A Divided Life*, London, 1957, pp.73–4.

11 Sidney and Beatrice Webb, (1859–1947 and 1858–1943), like H.G. Wells, but more professionally, applied all their tireless energies, and their unusual partnership, to the socialist reform of all things human.

12 *Loc. cit.* note 9, Vol. 10, pp. 141f.

13 See: Thomas Hardy: *Collected Poems*, London, 1932, 'The Impercipient,' p.59. At a Cathedral Service, he writes: 'With this bright believing band, I have no claim to be. Faiths by which my comrades stand, Are fantasies to me.' At least he called them 'comrades.'

14 Ed. M. Bradbury and J. Cooke: *New Writing*, London, 1992, pp.169–84 Interview by Chris Bigsby. Somerset Maugham: *Summing Up*, London, 1938, pp.185–86. He writes of himself as writer: 'Everything is grist to his mill. Nothing befalls that he cannot transmute into . . . a story, and, having done this, to be rid of it.'

15 Daniel Berrigan: *The Face of Christ*, London, 1958.

16 Note 1, Chap. 4, Poem 53, p.87. The poem continues: 'My tongue had taught thee comfort, touch had quenched thy tears, Thy tears that touched my heart.'

17 The point is more fully argued in my *To Meet and to Greet*, London, 1992, pp.14–24.

18 Alice Meynell: *Complete Poems*, London, 1940, 'In Portugal, 1912,' p.115.

19 Richard Crashaw: *Poetical Works*, Edinburgh, 1857, p.38.

20 It is true, of course, according to 1 Corinthians 11, 26, that we 'declare,' 'publish,' (*katayyellete*) 'the Lord's death.' We still have to ask how that intimate meaning attains to minds outside.

21 Some assessment of Arnold Toynbee in this context will be found in *Troubled by Truth*, Durham, 1992, Chap. 12. On the great cross in the Abbey at Ampleforth, see: *A Study of History*, Vol. ix, Oxford, 1954, pp.634–35. Also Vol. vi. 1939, pp.276–78.

22 A.M. Ramsey: *The Gospel and the Catholic Church*, London, 2nd ed. 1957, pp. 10f and 68f. Ramsey's central clue was that of Jesus' Passion and 'the dying to self and rising to new life' as the very being of the Church. This would seem to argue that no 'Orders' should read themselves as indispensable to the reality of the Gospel (however sincere their conviction) For how, in that 'self-importance' would those dignities be 'dying to themselves'? If 'valid Orders' and, thereby, authentic sacraments, were exclusively vital to 'being in Christ' would not the 'sufficiency' of personal faith in

Christ (for which Ramsey stood, and pleaded) be at risk? It cannot be said that he succeeded in making a case for the Gospel/Church fusion in the terms for which he opted.

23 See the discussion in Owen Chadwick: *Michael Ramsey: A Life*, Oxford, 1990, pp.333–43.

24 *Soundings: Essays concerning Christian Understanding*, ed. A.R. Vidler, Cambridge, 1962. Eleven wide-ranging essays by nine Cambridge scholars.

25 Note 22, p.219, where Ramsey referred to those he alleged were 'indifferent to questions of Order' and who 'harped upon the distinction between the *esse* and the *bene esse* of the Church.' Many such were in no way 'indifferent' and 'harp' was a strange way to relate to a profound issue.

26 R.C. Moberly: *Ministerial Priesthood*, 2nd ed. 1907, p.285.

27 Quoted in Lawrence Hyde: *The Prospects of Humanism*, London, 1931, p.81.

28 Note 18 above, p.115.

29 It is odd that the psalm (8) is so often read as if it were dismissive of the human against the vastness of the universe, whereas the meaning is quite the contrary.

30 John Milton: *Paradise Lost*, Book 1, ll.287–91. Galileo was blind when they met in 1638. One might compare – for consideration – Wilfred Owen's line about 'the thoughts that hung the stars.'

31 William Shakespeare: *King Lear*, Act 4, Scene 5, line 172. Gloucester had been blinded.

32 F. Dostoevsky in *The Brothers Karamazov*, on his central theme of vicarious suffering and redemption.

33 Ezra Pound: *Selected Poems*, 1908–1959, London, 1975, p.180, Canto lxxxi.

Chapter 11: 'Some Strange Divine Complicity'

1 *Homilies of St Bernard*, No. 4.9.

2 Quoted in S.H. Uphaus: *John Updike*, New York, 1980, p.7. The poet in the sentence following is R.S. Thomas.

3 Robert Browning: *Poetical Works*, Oxford, 1940, in 'Johannes Agricola in Meditation,' p.426.

4 The two words of greeting, in Semitic usage, the one for Jews, the other for Muslims, not to be inter-changed but drawn from the same root. As for apprehensions about impending war one has merely to recall that in September, 1939, it was estimated officially that 120,000 would be killed or injured in air attack. Mass evacuations from London numbered ten times the expeditionary force sent to France that month. Blackouts were enforced and theatres and cinemas closed. All this came through via news bulletins to anxious listeners in Baghdad. Perhaps there was point for me in Churchill's reputed *bon mot*: 'Do not ask yourself questions as you ride at a fence.'

5 Note 3 above.

6 So named for Judas' tragic suicide. It was on that same hill that the British High Commissioner for Palestine had his Residence.

7 'Home' and 'overseas' was, at that time, the handy distinction, perhaps in the manner of that sorry misnomer 'the British and Foreign Bible Society.' The Bible was never 'British' or 'Foreign' but 'Hebrew/Aramaic/Greek' and 'universal.' No doubt the coiners meant the adjectives to go through to 'Society,' but that was not what they said in making a compound noun.

8 Cited in *The Call of the Minaret*, 2nd ed., New York, 1985, p.242, from Edwyn Hoskyns: *Cambridge Sermons*, cited by A.M. Ramsey in *The Glory of God and the Transfiguration of Christ*, London, 1949, p.6 without reference.

9 Psalm 55.14 where the psalmist deplores a treacherous friendship. In marriage, 'working together with God' is working it out together.

10 The phrase is Robin Day's in *Grand Inquisitor: Memoirs*, London, 1989, p.285.

11 W.H. Auden: 'For the Time Being,' *Collected Poems*, ed. Edward Mendelson, London, 1976, p.360.

12 Connected, it would seem, with the rabbinic argument which he develops. Our redemption into 'sonship' is through Him who partakes fully of our humanity where 'being of woman-born' is our universal condition.

13 'You acknowledge us as Yours' is the Jerusalem Bible's translation of Wisdom 15.3. The Browning quotation that concludes is from *Pippa Passes*, Scene 3, lines 305–6, See note 3, p.181. 'Love of loving' occurs in *Fifine at the Fair*, lines 685–7, for which see *Poetical Works*, Vol. 2, London, 1897, pp.335–36.

Index

(Since people's titles vary during life none are used here)